ONE + ONE IS ONE

Making Oneness A Way of Life

By Howard Caesar

Table of Contents

Author's Note: Bible quotations are from the RSV, NRSV, or the King James Version with those of the latter containing KJV after the chapter and verse.

DEDICATION AND ACKNOWLEDGMENTS

To the Spirit of oneness in all.
To my loving parents, Robert and Fern, for bringing me into this world.
To my dear wife, Diane, for a lifetime of love and support.
To my amazing children, Dawn, Troy, and Star who have so blessed my life.
To my grandchildren, Brady, Dylan, and Ellie Grace, who make my heart sing.

Heartfelt gratitude to Mary Morrissey, my sacred friend, mentor and prayer partner for her unconditional love, and generous support and to Roger Teel, friend, colleague, prayer partner, and spiritual brother.

To Madeline Westbrook and her husband Bill for their blessings as an extended family.

For the love, support and encouragement which helped make the writing of this book a reality, I extend sincere gratitude to Carolyn Lebanowski, Cindy Cline, Dee Quin, Leatha Tukes, Tom Bird and David Willms.

In Love and Gratitude,
Howard Caesar

FOREWORD

As Howard Caesar wisely reminds us in *One + One Is One*, "The One True God by any name lives within every person. To find and evolve into a conscious oneness with God is to find and progress into oneness with your internal Higher Sacred Self." Based on research conducted by the World-English Newsletter, I learned that "one" is the 23rd most commonly used word in the English language, with "all" following just behind. In the New Thought-Ageless Wisdom tradition of spirituality, we refer to the "One"— meaning Source — to be the "All" of existence, so this statistic caught my immediate attention. Further curiosity led me to the Hindu Upanishads, where we find the Sanskrit statement, *tat tavam asi*, which translates as "thou art that," pointing to the universal truth that our primordial Self is one with Source.

Oneness is our natural state of being. "If this is so," you might ask, "then why is it so difficult to consciously experience this truth?" That is the self-reflective question we ask ourselves when our soul is on fire with the desire to discover the Reality of our existence, one that also reveals the answer to, "Who am I, and why am I here?"

Lao-Tzu instructs us to "Use the light that dwells within you to regain your natural clarity of insight." It is time-tested, universal teachings such as those offered in this book that will illuminate for you the insight that we are not isolated individuals, that we are intricately, intimately interconnected to Source and one another. Through the stories and examples described in each chapter's pages, you will come to realize how the events occurring in your everyday life serve to connect you to the oneness of being.

Each of our life structures is an inlet to a realization of our Essential Self, into becoming an agent of restoring the collective memory of our oneness with all creation. As Carl Sagan reminds us, "The nitrogen in our DNA, the calcium in our teeth, the iron in our blood, the carbon in our apple pies were made in the interiors of collapsing stars. We are made of starstuff." In exploring the cosmic dimensions of oneness, there is tremendous down-to-earth value in the examples Caesar shares about how our everyday activities—whether it's working at the kitchen sink, driving the kids to school, posting on Face Book, during times of deep affirmative prayer or meditation—reveal the potential to expand the limits of our boundaries and increasingly touch our boundless oneness of being. What could be richer than tasting a realization of oneness within one's own self in the ordinariness of each day's activities?

The book you hold in your hands is an invitation to accept, welcome, and embody your spiritual inheritance and that of every human being: oneness, wholeness, unconditional love, joy, contentment, creativity, abundance, and generosity of heart. In *One + One Is One*, Howard Caesar generously shares skillful transformative practices, fruits of his many years as a spiritual teacher. Because he has immersed himself in practicing the principles he teaches, they are offered by one who knows from direct experience the essential steps of the journey into a conscious realization of oneness. I encourage you to read these pages slowly and mindfully, to take their practices to heart, letting them guide and bless your own unique path to oneness.

Michael Bernard Beckwith
Founder, Agape International Spiritual Center
and author of *Spiritual Liberation* and *Life Visioning*
February 2017

INTRODUCTION

Why oneness? For some it can sound too vague, idealistic, unrealistic, pie-in-the-sky. However, don't be fooled, for it is a word that represents your spiritual heritage, what you've come from, where you've been, and more than anything, where you're headed back to in consciousness as an eternal soul.

Oneness is a word that summarizes all the spiritual principles ever written, spoken, taught, and sought to be lived. It is at the root of every world religion and contained in the ancient texts dating back to the beginning of recorded history. Spiritual masters, avatars, and teachers down through time have conveyed it is essential and that the principle is of paramount importance in any soul's progress. Our goal is to evolve spiritually into an awakened oneness with God. Even to use the word "with" makes it sound as if we are separate, when in fact we are not. The illusion is separation. So oneness is something to awaken to and evolve toward as a consistent experience of being conscious of God's presence, energy, and life being around and in us at all times.

The universal principle is that One + One is One. Any combination of life forms or creations of God adds up to one. If you can get your heart around this, it is energetically very powerful.

Oneness is your true reality.
Oneness is the spiritual ideal the Divine would have you live.
Oneness is what every soul has come into this life to learn.

The universal spiritual principle of One + One is One exists in all space and time, and is the answer to every human problem. The writing of this book has involved a process of my stepping back, pausing, and looking at the steps I've taken backward and forward in my life and how they relate to my spiritual progress toward oneness.

When I reflect on the various phases of my life, beginning with my youth and through my adulthood, there seems to be a continuing theme having to do with oneness. It's as though it was what I'm in this life to learn as well as teach. I still have much to learn and grow into, of course, for we are all evolving in spiritual consciousness. I have come to believe all progress in regard to one's spiritual evolution and awakening is directly related to oneness and eventually realizing that the main universal spiritual principle is One + One is One.

In this book I share experiences and stories that I hope you can relate to from your own life experiences. I recognize we all have had life lessons revealing how best to direct our life energies. At times we have felt the vibrations of love and oneness in our hearts, along with times we felt fear, and the energies of separation brought on by the mind. Whereas the intelligence of the heart knows the way, it is the mind that is to be mastered and transcended with the knowing that One + One is One.

Oneness has seemingly been the thread that has woven itself throughout my life. This is not to say I've always been the model of it, but that the intent and desire has been there from the beginning to learn and evolve into it. I've experienced the void of its absence and the bliss of its presence. It's as if my whole life has somehow prepared me to write this message and explore this topic with you, the reader. Life has shown me through a progression of experiences the significance of oneness. I feel the Divine has been at work in me, steering me, revealing to me the validity of the universal principle of One + One Is One. Where and when I've been able to demonstrate a consciousness of oneness with Source, the principle of One + One is One has prevailed with its rewards and benefits. It can and will for you, too.

Oneness is our natural state as spiritual beings, just as love is who we are as children of God. The journey of life is a return to love, peace, and joy through oneness with Source. It's an internal walk. For it's not that we are separate from God, we just have allowed our minds to believe we are. We are all meant to return to our true natural state of being one with our Creator. This process is for here and now. The experience of oneness is not to be waited on, until we pass from this world, but is most importantly to be learned and lived here in this life on earth.

Whether you accept the biblical story of The Garden of Eden to be an actual place or a metaphor, it represents our original state of oneness. Oneness with God and all life was humankind's reality. The Tree of Life represents the tree of oneness that is always life giving. It is where One + One is always One.

What is referred to as the Fall of Man was brought about by humans eating of the tree of duality, something we all do every day. The fall was into states of separation in which was born the illusion that we are separate from God, separate from each other and from God's creations. As a result, One + One became two in the mind of separation consciousness. As one of my teachers in India says, "We then had a 'me' and a 'not me.'"

We look out through our physical eyes and say, "There is a tree, a dog, a person, an apple," or whatever it is. That tree, dog, or person is over there and I am over here. From an objective world perspective, we can say, "one tree + one tree is two. One apple + another apple is two. One person + another person is two." But if we accept what the Greek philosopher Empedocles stated, that "God is a circle whose center is everywhere and whose circumference is nowhere," we begin to see the bigger picture. In other words, nothing is outside the circle of God's Presence. It's ALL GOD. From the spiritual perspective, the reality is that we can draw a circle around it all, all of creation, and see it as One Life, One Love, One Presence, One Intelligence, One Power, that moves through it all and makes it ALL ONE.

Although most of the world would say you and I make two, and one + one is two, from the spiritual perspective, the reality is that you and I are ONE... and One + One is One, whatever the life form inside the Circle of Divine Life. We are all part of the Whole, of the One Life. I am in God and of God, as you are in God and of God. So the Truth is, we are one. Throughout eternity, you will never leave the Circle of Life, which includes all realms seen and unseen.

Whatever your chosen religion, denomination or spiritual path, our common destiny is to learn to live from a consciousness of oneness with God (whatever your name for God), oneness with others, and to experience the interconnectedness of all life. The One True God by any name lives within every person. To find and evolve into a conscious oneness with God is to find and progress into oneness with your internal Higher Sacred Self. It is to break away from the separate self that we each have created in our minds and to become free.

It seems this was part of Jesus' teachings and that of other avatars as well. Jesus said, "In the world you will have tribulation. But be of good cheer, I have overcome the world." There exists varying degrees of misery and distress that we and others go through in this world. We can do it to ourselves and to each other. The "world" Jesus refers to here represents the domain of separateness, the temporal conditions of an "us and them" world that are inconsistent with love, peace and joy.

How did he do it? How did he overcome the world, we ask? In one very powerful declaration, he made that clear when he said, "I and the Father are One."(John 10:30 RSV) Inside that statement and the living of it rests the foundation of Jesus' entire ministry, what he taught and demonstrated. Our deepest desire should be to evolve spiritually to where we live from this consciousness as our true experience in life as well. For if you recall, he also said "Follow me."

Inside a consciousness of oneness, you will find all the gifts of the Spirit, which include love, peace, happiness, prosperity and wholeness. Its opposite is a separation consciousness in which a person will experience pain and suffering. The world is hungry for oneness. The way that every person can contribute is by giving themselves to the pursuit of awakening into oneness in their life. We know the world needs it.

Inside CHAPTER ONE you will learn my story of how Spirit has steered me in the direction of oneness throughout my life. I take you back with me through aspects and incidents in my life where the principle of One + One is One took on meaning and revealed itself to me. It can be as if you and I have just met and are becoming friends. You might consider we are sitting down over a cup of coffee, getting to know each other as I share some of the ways my life unfolded to heighten in me the ideal of oneness and the eventual writing of this book. I share where it led me in terms of career, travel, and a continual deepening into oneness.

It's my hope that what I share in this chapter will help you get to know me and provoke memories of incidents from within the story of your life, things that also may have had the taste of oneness in them. I encourage you to pause along the way as you turn the pages of chapter one and reflect on those events, incidents, exchanges and happenings that come to mind as possible reminders that you too, received signs along the way and were being given opportunities to see and learn the value of oneness. I know you have your own story, and although the details may differ, I know there are similarities. Perhaps you will discover through the reading of this book that my story and yours blend together into our story, and some elements of everyone's story. For, as this book seeks to make clear, we are one.

In CHAPTER TWO, you and I explore the most important relationship we will ever have throughout eternity. You already know I'm referring to the one Source that has given us life. Our concept of God can vary and I respect whatever yours may be. Nevertheless, it's important to continually deepen and grow in your understanding of God. It actually should not become stagnant or remain the same, but continue to expand. God isn't changing, but you are.

God can only be experienced in accordance with the borders of your beliefs, many of which have been molded by voices from outside yourself. There is much we can learn in reflecting on our concept of God, where we received it, who and what helped shape it, and whether or not we allow room in us to expand with it. Oneness is rooted in the oneness we have currently grown to experience with the Divine. In this chapter I hope you reflect on what you believe about God and that it helps you open to an ever-deepening experience and partnership with the Presence through love and oneness.

CHAPTER THREE is a continuation of our understanding of God. However, in this chapter, the focus is on an aspect of God in you. It is coming to know the Divine Presence as a dimension of you... that resides in you. This very thought and truth leads us down the path of learning more accurately our true identity as a spiritual being and learning to live from it.

We look at ways in which the real you may have gone into hiding and what may have caused it. Some of what I share will possibly dislodge some buried wounds you have. Understand that sometimes we are meant to review them only to see where we may have made a decision about ourselves causing us to take a turn away from loving ourselves fully and being our Authentic Self. This chapter is designed to at least begin the process of returning the real you back to you, with renewed peace and joy, through a deepening oneness with your Higher Sacred Self.

CHAPTER FOUR is an extension of our understanding that all of life is relationships. Chapter two was about our relationship with God and chapter three explored our relationship with ourselves, and more specifically with our Higher Self, or God within us. These are part of the mix when it comes to our relationship with others. However, in chapter four, among other things, you have the opportunity to go deeper into the realization that I am you, and you are me… that we are all one family inside the Circle of God's infinite love and oneness. You are given insights that can help restore and expand love and harmony in all your relationships.

CHAPTER FIVE helps to expand the realization in you that God is in all Its creation. It is the life and intelligence in everything around you, including all of nature. This chapter reminds you to stop and smell the roses, because while you are doing so, God may speak to you through the experience. In other words, as you heighten your sensitivity and awareness of God being present everywhere, in all things, you open yourself to new avenues through which help, guidance, and gifts of the Spirit can flow.

This chapter is one in which nature lovers and pet owners will likely resonate. Wherever you are in your relationship with nature and all life forms, this chapter will either awaken new energies or expand what you've known, through the awareness that it's All God.

CHAPTER SIX addresses the role the principle of One + One is One can play in the world. It looks at ways it has worked its seeming magic in people's lives and gives examples of the results oneness promises when applied on any scale of any challenge.

CHAPTER SEVEN is our closing chapter and in it you are given the opportunity to assess where you are in relation to oneness and the steps you can take to implement much of the content and ideas offered in earlier chapters. It invites you to ask yourself what steps you intend to take and what ways you can help bring change through living the principle of One + One is One.

Much more than an intellectual concept, oneness is a feeling that comes from a direct inner experience with the Presence of all life. Although brief at times, it is a feeling beyond mind that touches the heart like a wave of energy passing through. Perhaps you can relate to one of my favorite writings from the great Sufi poet, Rumi:

"There is a candle in your heart, ready to be kindled.
There is a void in your soul, ready to be filled.
You feel it, don't you?"

The void is not new. It's been spoken of by spiritual masters, mystics, and teachers through the ages all saying the cause is in our minds, our consciousness, or more specifically in a belief in separation. Separation and division create the void. The ego mind has its tactics, mainly driven by fear, which sets us apart and at odds with ourselves, others and the world. At times you feel it, don't you? The answer has always been oneness. Oneness is our heaven. Separation is our hell.

The awakening into oneness is a gradual kind of inner development as you set the desire for its energies to grow in you and put in place the practices that support it. The consciousness of oneness promises to deliver in so many ways: greater inner peace, heart-filled love, a new perspective on life, and much more. My hope is that this book will open you to its energies and heighten your awareness of One + One being One.

Oneness is our essential spiritual curriculum and the answer to humanity's problems. It is the key to anyone's soul growth. It is what will heal the planet and your life. It is your purpose and mine in this life... to Be One!

CHAPTER ONE
The Journey Into Oneness

Life is a precious gift. It is to be honored and treasured as an opportunity to bring into expression that which we have come here to be. Although our paths and pasts may differ, what we all have in common are certain universal truths that are ancient, reliable and powerfully freeing. A large part of every soul's divine plan is to discover the true from the false, the eternal from the temporal, the light from the dark. Paraphrasing Jesus, he said that to KNOW and live universal TRUTH would set us free and help us to be a light in the world.

I have always been one to question many aspects of life, not in a rebellious tone, but mostly in a rather quiet, internal manner. It's as though I have always intuitively known and accepted that this life calls for progress, inner growth and advancement as a soul. I do not believe this is uncommon. It is an inherent knowing. Everyone has a place inside them where they sense they are part of something grander than the mind can conceive, a life force that refuses to be static and unchanging, but is dynamic, transforming and expanding, like the acorn becoming the oak.

This loving Life Force so wants to pour Itself into open and willing vessels like you and me. It wants to reveal Its character and likeness so that it might be expressed through us into the world. Creating an openness and willingness is part of the process of life and living, with its many choices and decisions, as well as its many distractions. You and I are in a continual process of learning to live life, finding out what works and giving ourselves to that. Along the way we err, adjust, and hopefully choose higher ideals.

Through all the various ages and phases of my life, its ups and downs, successes and failures, wins and losses, I have come to the conclusion that the single most important life lesson for me or anyone to learn hinges on the principle of oneness. This school called Life has consistently sought to provide evidence designed to teach you and me

1

that we live in a unified field ruled by the universal spiritual principle of One + One is One. When we fail to cultivate this field within our consciousness, there is suffering. I'm convinced that you, too, have had moments when you have experienced the unifying energies that carry the fulfilling feelings of a connectedness and wholeness, in contrast to those times you've felt separation and fragmentation. My story may not exactly match your story, but I believe there are similarities that bind us together on a corresponding path meant to awaken us to our higher purpose. That purpose includes having our lives be about learning oneness and living from the spiritual principle of One + One is One.

Jesus said, "God is Spirit..." (John 4:24) Jesus also said, "...the Spirit of truth... dwells with you and shall be in you." (John 14:17) Because we all share the same inner Spirit, whether aware of it or not, this Spirit has been leading you to some of the same realizations. For instance, you may agree that if we are to travel the spiritual highway, it must be fueled by the energies of love and oneness. You may also agree with the belief that there are no accidents and therefore you have been led to having this book in your hands at this time for a reason. The intention of this book is to fan the flames of a heightened awareness that Oneness is the one principle, law, motive, and foundation of the universe in which we live. It is to have this very precept become the lens of your livingness. It is to amplify the experience of oneness through the unifying energies of love. It is to deepen your bond with the All That Is.

As I have mentioned, looking back upon my whole life, I can see it has been taking me in the direction of learning, living and serving oneness. I'm sure you will agree that in some ways, so has yours. The One Spirit of all life has been guiding you, just as it has me, although through different situations and circumstances. We are in the classroom of life being given the opportunities to pass seeming tests in which we get to choose whether oneness wins over separation, whether love prevails over fear, and whether we awaken to the principle of One + One is One.

In this chapter, I present a brief history of my life path related to oneness. The Spirit of Oneness has taken me from an inquiring observer of its properties while in my youth, to believing in its vital importance through the years, and finally to being led to go deeper into these energies and impart its message to others. In sharing my journey, I hope to trigger in you possible sacred memories of past insights and similar realizations.

As a young boy I had not put Bible verses into my memory. I didn't really need to know it was in 1 John 4:8 that it states, "God is love" to somehow realize this was true. Surely I'd heard this in Sunday School and it was not much more than an intellectual teaching at that point. Later, in adulthood, I came to dearly value this passage at a deeper level. It actually states, "He who does not love, does not know God, for God is love." Said another way, "He who DOES LOVE, KNOWS GOD." So all who set the intention to learn and live love more fully, set themselves on a path of a deepening intimacy with God, the one Spirit and Source of love itself.

For most, love requires a reason to be activated in them. However, there are deeper levels of love we can grow into which do not require a reason. It is known as causeless love. It becomes one's state of being. The person is so at one with the Divine that they can't help but be love. I do not claim to be there yet, and I assume you're not either, but it gives us something to strive for.

The energies of fear are rampant in this world. One cannot be in the energies of love when fear has us in its grasp. Much of the current human experience involves fear overcoming love. In fact, the spiritual journey of every soul is one of letting love cast out all fear.

I was eight years old and sitting on the front steps outside my Midwest, small-town church waiting for my mother to pull up and take me home in our red Oldsmobile. Although she attended church only periodically, she made sure we kids went regularly to Sunday school followed by church service. It was what would be described today as a very conservative Christian church of the "hellfire and brimstone" variety. It had the typical Midwest small-town appearance with a white steeple and bell tower. It was located near the end of one of the two main streets in town. You had to walk up ten or twelve steps to enter the front door. The sanctuary seated about three hundred people and had two elevated pulpits on each side of center. In the middle front wall was a huge painting of Jesus praying in the garden of Gethsemane. It also had a large pipe organ that I still recall as a boy, vibrating through my body.

We have poignant moments in our lives that we can recall vividly no matter what the age, and this is one of them. After listening to that day's sermon, replete with frightening statements and images of the devil, hell, and damnation, I sat on the steps outside the church and reflected on the message I'd just heard. Is this God's message or the minister's interpretation and understanding?

Although it was a sunny day, a dark cloud hovered within my mind. I was very young and hadn't learned all the things a person can come to fear in life. I was at an age that I could still be easily influenced. Nevertheless, in this instance I was led to these questions: "What am I to do with this fear? What is God? Where is God? What is his role regarding these ideas of fear I've just heard?" Who can claim to know and have an understanding of God at age eight? I sure didn't. And I hadn't yet been privy to what scholars had written about the origination of such concepts as the devil and hell. These ideas and images containing fear were unsettling. I knew I preferred not to experience them.

I recall having received an epiphany in that moment. It was less about me making a life decision and more like a life decision overtaking me. Something inside me said not to be swept away by fear and the fear of God, but to remember that God is love, God is good, and to hold onto that, and be one with that as I went forward in my life. It was one of the earliest times I can remember feeling like God had spoken within me, as if a Presence inside, conveying a feeling of being one.

I believe it was there and then that I began to learn not to always allow the voice of authority to reside outside of me in others, but to listen for the voice of Spirit within. With a kind of childhood simplicity, I simply let go of the fear of any opposing power and instead chose to trust in a God of love.

This message that God is love and goodness became a theme for me, although at times, it was somewhat wavering. At times a battle raged inside as to the validity of this truth and what the ego mind of separation tried to convince me of otherwise. As many others have questioned, I was asking myself how it is that God allows wars, illness, disease and many hardships. In my heart I knew not to pin this on God even though I didn't yet have an answer. All I knew at the time was that God had been portrayed to me as a loving Father. I reasoned that my earthly father was one I loved, trusted and knew I could depend on to protect and guide me. So surely, I reasoned, God, the Father, was the same – and more.

As the years went on I learned about the laws of consciousness and how through free will humankind is always creating its own experience. In or out of harmony with one's Higher Self and universal laws and principles, good or ill issues forth from within us and others. Like a household lamp, we either are plugged into the Source and give light, or we are disconnected and darkness, the absence of light, is evidenced. Over time, through my own progress spiritually, the result of study, prayer and meditation, I learned the mind cannot be trusted with its worldly conditionings, but instead one must learn to follow the heart, for it knows the way. We do not always know to look to the heart, because the mind is so dominant with its incessant chattering.

All the mind knows is the past. The amount of information the mind has stored over time is enormous. It draws on the subconscious mind where a storehouse of data from the past surfaces to judge, analyze, interpret, evaluate, assess, and often conclude things based on information already received. Most minds have an ongoing commentary about whatever is before them. Wisdom cannot be found in the mind, only in the heart. The mind can only regurgitate the past. But the heart draws on a deeper knowing that comes from within as a result of being fully present to what is. There is a compassionate oneness built into the heart. Where the mind may judge and cause us to react in a polarizing manner based on what a parent, teacher, or the world has conditioned in us from the past, the heart will be present to a fresh, in-the-moment, healthier approach that is more in keeping with our higher nature.

Brief moments occur when we see and feel that which vibrates with energetic ripples of oneness. There on the steps of my church, although I had not yet formulated any depth of understanding of oneness or articulated it into the principle of "One + One is One" — and did not for a number of years — it had begun to emerge in many areas of my life.

My father had an affection for nature. He loved to hunt and fish, but more than landing fish or game for the table was his sheer joy of being in the outdoors. My father owned and operated, with his brother, a plumbing and heating business that had been in the family for generations. It had begun as a Blacksmith Shop back when our hometown had dirt streets and horses that required shoeing.

He worked hard during the week and I can recall several times while we were hunting together in the woods on a beautiful weekend autumn day, seeing him sit down at the base of a big tree and with his gun laid to the side, take a thirty-minute snooze in the lap of nature. I would sit down at a nearby tree, not to sleep, but where I could observe the peace that seemed to blanket him in that pure setting. I could see it come over him, bringing a peaceful rest and renewal to his soul. The energies of oneness can be noticed even when they seem to be occurring in someone else. I could clearly see that peace is found inside oneness.

We can have moments when it seems like we are carrying a wheelbarrow full of cares, concerns, and responsibilities with many decisions to make. Yet, we are able to find a precious internal pause button, a prolonged sort of sigh, a personal time-out from the busy outer game of life. We lay it aside, internally let go and allow ourselves a respite for what lies ahead. Letting go is a kind of emptying out, putting the mind on hold and just allowing ourselves to be. There, in that internal space, we are plugged in to a flow that can charge, refresh, and bless us. My Dad seemed to be there.

When the threat of death looms large, there arises a greater sensitivity to the preciousness of life and into our relationship with it in its many forms. Although I personally have not faced a situation of my own mortality, as a minister I have witnessed it in others. Upon being told of some prognosis of limiting days or having had a near-death experience, a person is almost always thrust into a period of reflection and contemplation. Typically, we motor along through life, rarely slowing down to see and experience what surrounds us.

Suddenly we see with new eyes and begin to engage with life having a greater reverence. Things that once were important no longer are and others that were secondary now take their place. A new and deeper sensitivity to elements of life that weren't important, now are. We become more in touch with the relationship we all have with the broader circle of life. Suddenly, our love for life can expand.

My father was a man highly regarded for his honesty and integrity. Growing up I had people in our town share what a fine man he was, how he had helped them out in some way. He was a handsome man, with wavy dark hair and a strong, sturdy build. Only five foot ten inches tall, it was said that he was quite a good athlete in baseball and basketball while in high school, though he never talked about it due to his modest ways. He was not inclined to share much about himself, or even sit and rap with us kids. It hadn't been that way in his family, I was told, and he had little time to himself during the years he was running the business. Even at the dinner table, many times he seemed to be far off somewhere in his mind, dealing with the ongoing stresses of the business. Sometimes our dinners and his evenings were interrupted with after-hour phone calls related to work. There were times he would get a call on a bitter cold Wisconsin winter night after he had gone to bed. Usually it was someone whose furnace wasn't working and they were out of heat. My father would get dressed, drive to their home, fix the problem and return home to bed. He was a quietly caring man. Although my father didn't open up a lot, and had an awkwardness in sharing his feelings, he still managed to convey that he loved you.

When I was twelve years old my father fell asleep at the wheel of his auto. He was alone, making a long late-night drive home from out of town. He crashed into a massive old oak tree on the side of a country road. Hours later, at daybreak, a farmer heard him groaning, found him, and called an ambulance. He almost died at the scene due to a loss of blood and other injuries. After weeks in the hospital, I remember the very day he came home. He had lost weight and his jaw was still wired shut. I watched him make a slow walk around our one-acre large backyard, stopping for several moments at each tree, be it a Maple, an Oak, an Evergreen or Willow. He was pensive, silent, staring, as if in reverence of the one unifying life energy living in each unique tree. Although my Dad was not one to talk about God and was not inclined to attend church except on an occasional Easter or Christmas, he found his God in the fields and forests of nature and appeared to be deeply engaged in God while on that backyard walk. There was some kind of an exchange that went on between him and those trees, and I could feel it. The Source of their life was also the Source of his life.

Looking back, I can see this was a moment for him in his life where the principle of One + One is One was a reality within his soul. Although the connection appeared to be going on with those trees, he was plugged into the bigger picture involving all life being one. You could see he felt it. Oneness with The One Source can occur anywhere and anytime and is not limited to inside a Temple, church or religious facility. In fact, I believe, as many do, that the Divine Presence plays no favorites and loves us all equally. We are all one despite all the ways and reasons humanity finds to divide and separate.

From the time I was in the lower grades, I wondered why there were so many different Christian denominations. I asked myself, "Is there not one God of all?" As I entered my teens, I had already embraced the idea that whether Hindu, Buddhist, Christian, Jew, or whatever the religion, we were all one. This may have been a unique intuitive conclusion to draw in my late teens, but I find it somewhat more common in many of our youth and young adults today. I don't know with certainty what is their path of reasoning, but mine was simply that I believe the same God created all people, whatever the part of the world they live in, and whatever their history.

Each era in time had its awakened ones that impacted people spiritually, be it Krishna, Lao Tzu, Buddha, Jesus Christ, Muhammad, or others. People recorded what they could of the teachings and other information, handed it down through the years, interpreted some of it correctly, but lost some of its true intent. Divisions formed even within Christianity; we now call them denominations. I reasoned that humanity had complicated things by implying one path's dogma and god-concept was superior to the path and dogma of another. In reality, no path or dogma calling itself spiritual should ever contribute in any way to creating division and separation. The letter divides and the Spirit unites. Concepts are of the letter and tend to derive from the mind, absent of the heart. People have waged wars over concepts that they have never experienced. If they had experienced the true teachings in their heart, they could not bring themselves to wage war. A spiritual teaching may start out in the mind but eventually must find its way into the heart because that is where it gets experienced. It's true that we are all on a journey from the head to the heart.

Simplistically, as a teenager, I felt that all human beings had been given the spirit of life by the same Creator. Therefore, we must all be one in some way, regardless of all the variations. Though the outer garment may vary, inwardly we are of the same one Spirit. I could not believe, as some do, in a God that could punish or have disregard for those born into other countries of other religions or were not Christian. I agonized over those families I came to know whose members would become divided or even outcasts if not willing to continue to follow in their family's chosen church and its doctrine.

Ego is the voice of separation and can be found in us all. It is the voice of smallness, the "want to be" of us that is always measuring ourselves, comparing everything, often labeling what and who is right, what is best, and hoping we fall into that category ourselves. It is a product of the mind driven into fear, and walls us off, separate from the voice of Spirit and our Higher Sacred Self. Always arguing for separation, the ego sends us into judgment that is divisive. It is both inferior and superior thinking of the mind. Ego often chooses the way of the herd because there is seeming safety in numbers and the person doesn't want to risk being wrong, though their heart may be pulling them to a higher way.

Additionally, ego lives in religion when a sense of superiority exists or a message of being the only way is espoused. That never made sense to me even as a youngster, especially if the teaching was that we are not to judge, but to love unconditionally. I learned to believe along with many others that we are meant to respect each other's chosen religion or spiritual path. The exception is, of course, the extremists that twist and distort the teaching and do harm. It is the ego mind in separation from the Spirit that finds most anything on which to pass judgment, including religious or spiritual concepts, teachings and paths. Although everyone must be true to themselves and go to that which feeds their soul, there should remain an openness to the virtues that exist in other paths and teachings.

William James, the famous 19th Century American philosopher, wrote, "This overcoming of all the usual barriers between the individual and the Absolute (God) is the great mystic achievement. In mystic states we both become one with the Absolute and we become aware of our oneness. This is the everlasting and triumphant mystical tradition, hardly altered by differences of clime (region) or creed."

The mystical tradition of oneness is indeed everlasting, lives in you and me, and is destined to be triumphant over any and all barriers and differences that would set us apart. Every soul has buried at different depths beneath their past, their pain and their polar perspectives, the deep noble knowing that we are spiritually One with it All. Each individual as a growing, evolving soul is called upon to peel away the layers of sedentary separateness, shake off the dust of division and accept that they are a contributing member of humanity, belonging to one family.

Our chosen religious path should be seen as just one serving among many at the spiritual table to which all are welcome and can dine in peace and love. As Jesus stated, "My food is to do the will of Him who sent me and to complete His work." (John 4:34) He never established a loyalty to one religion or one existing path. He challenged the religious establishment of the day and Christianity did not even exist at the time. His loyalty was always, first and foremost, to oneness, love and the One God of all. His teachings, like that of other spiritually enlightened teachers, were universal. While continuing to be fed and nourished by the spiritual food of Christianity, it can be helpful for us to feel free to reach across the spiritual table and taste elements of others. For the path should not command loyalty over the Power Itself... and can one really suggest that there is not spiritual nourishment to be gained in Hinduism, for example, one of the most ancient of all spiritual teachings?

Our paths can be different from others just as some people have a favorite restaurant where they find the food is most satisfying and fulfilling. If God is the Source of even the food we eat grown on mother earth, should my eating of it from inside a different restaurant than yours be reason to deny our oneness? We are eating the food of the same Source. When we seek to be fed by the One Spirit of all, be it inside a church, temple, mosque or synagogue, should that be cause to think we are not one, when it is in reality the same Spirit that feeds our souls. Beyond time and space, the spiritual principle remains; one + one is one.

We gravitate to that which we believe and is in alignment with our basic system of thought and belief. We are drawn to what feeds us in Spirit and soul. Personally, I define myself as one who is in relationship with Jesus Christ and is an avid follower of the teachings of Christ, but choose not to give myself the label of Christian. For who in this day and age sets the standard, determines the qualifiers, gets to define and decide what is and isn't a Christian? There is so much that is subject to interpretation. It can be both a sad and dangerous thing. It's another dividing wall that mind gravitates toward to establish exclusivity.

Mahatma Gandhi had evidently wrestled with this issue and concluded, "I consider myself a Hindu, Christian, Muslim, Jew, Buddhist and Confucian." In other words, rather than being exclusively just one, or choosing none, he implied he was one with all, that one + one is one... a Hindu + a Christian is One... a Muslim + a Christian is One... a Jew + a Christian is One... not two... and this is true of any combination of paths you wish to add together. The sum and total of universal Truth is always "ONE," in God, because the universal spiritual principle is One + One is One.

I had an aunt and uncle, Edith and Roland, who were special to me. Edith, who was my mother's sister, was twenty years younger than her first and only husband, Roland. Edith is still with us and Roland passed on at the age of 98. They had a wonderful marriage, and were parents to three of my cousins, all delightful in their own right. Edith and Roland were very knowledgeable and successful in running several businesses in the field of health and nutrition. As a result, they lived what they preached, used the products they sold and were always slim, trim, vibrant and healthy. They were great to be around because they were always so radiantly alive, loving, and positive of nature.

Both were quite open minded and progressive in their thinking. After discovering they had been driving an hour from where they lived to attend a church only ten minutes from me, I decided to check it out. I was twenty years old at the time. It was a non-denominational church called "Unity." It had me at "hello." By that I mean, that first day, when the minister welcomed visitors, he added, that if this did not become our chosen spiritual home, he prayed that we would find the one that best met our spiritual needs. Wow! That was my first introduction to what felt like a mature approach of recognizing that there are many paths, that we are all at different levels of spiritual unfoldment, and that our needs may vary. It was clear no one was made to feel wrong or bad for choosing another path. To promote anything of the sort would go against its name, "Unity." I was drawn to its teachings emphasizing unity with God, unity with the Spirit of God in you, and unity with others. For me it was all about oneness. But most importantly to me there was a freedom given to think for yourself, adhere to what made sense to the inner you, and the encouragement to remain open to progressive ideas and ancient teachings of others. Unity has served me as a sort of vehicle for being of spiritual service in the world.

The Unity Movement was begun in 1889 by its co-founders, Charles and Myrtle Fillmore. Charles had explored and studied all religions, meditated many hours per day, with his focus and enthusiasm landing on the Jesus Christ teachings with a slight blend of Eastern thought. One of his favorite Bible verses was from the apostle Paul; "Christ in you, the hope of glory." The power of prayer, that thought was creative, and the kingdom of God resides within you were among its tenets. Because Unity was so positive, diverse, open to progressive thought, honoring of other paths, and attuned to oneness, I was very drawn to it.

Unity became my non-denominational spiritual restaurant where I would go over the next several years to be fed. Later on I will tell you about my even becoming a spiritual Chef... so to speak. I loved the name "Unity" and that it stood for oneness in the world. Not that it was about bringing the world inside its doors; its mission from the beginning was never to become another religion, but to offer teachings that everyone in or out of religion could use to promote a way of life on the foundation of oneness. I honestly hesitate to offer a name to my path, whatever it might have been. Because as soon as I do, it is quite likely to cause division. If it's not your chosen path, the temptation for some is to turn away, make some assumption or judgment.

So hang on long enough to hear me say that my loyalty is not with a name, denomination, or frankly a particular religion. These are all elements that historically have shown they have the potential to separate us. I am an advocate of the God of Oneness beyond all division and separation. To this one Spirit I am loyal. Rather than get caught up in the name of a church, denomination or world religion... or even a race, color, lifestyle or political affiliation for that matter, I'm asking you to lay aside any potential differences, to transcend all that would separate and divide, just long enough to find the place in you, in your heart, where a universal oneness exists and wants to be lived. If you give it a chance, it is here that a person begins to realize and experience that One + One is One... not two.

All religions and spiritual paths that have the integrity of the Spirit and the Absolute Truth of God, will have somewhere in its teaching, if not at the forefront, that there is One God, inside a Universal Unity and that we are One with the All That Is. When doing even a light amount of study into the various religions through the ages and the sayings of the saints, sages, spiritual messengers and enlightened teachers, it is hard to miss the importance and emphasis that across the board is placed on Oneness.

Kabir, an Indian poet and mystic from the 15th century, made a similar observation when stating, "Unity is the essence of the teachings of all the saints."

Our Christian Bible states, "...for us there is One God, the Father, from whom are all things and for whom we exist..." (I Cor. 8:6)

The Torah of Judaism states, "Hear O Israel, the Lord our God, the Lord is One." (Deuteronomy 6:4)

In Islam, from the Quran, "Say, He is God, the One! God the eternally besought of all!"

From the Buddha, "He who experiences the unity of life sees his own self in all beings."

From Bahá'u'lláh of the Bahá'i faith, "You are all leaves of one tree and the fruits of one branch."

From Chuang Tzu, co-founder of Taoism, "He perceives the oneness of everything, does not know about duality in it."

From the many quotes available on oneness found in Hinduism, Ramakrishna states, "Nothing exists except the One."

From Nicholas of Cusa, cardinal of the Catholic Church, "He is God the Father whom we might also call 'One' or 'Unity.'"

And Gandhi says it in a most concise way, "I believe in the absolute oneness of God and, therefore, also of humanity."

I could go on and on with more clear, pure, powerful messages on oneness that have come from thousands of inspired teachers, writers, poets, singers, songwriters, known and unknown, from various time periods. All were inspired by something they had merged with at the core of their own being that knew oneness was the True Reality and their divine heritage.

At times humanity has used religion and other thought structures to build a fence around themselves, thinking it will bring a sense of security when in fact it only fences them in, often to the exclusion of other segments of society and progressive thinking. Let whatever path you choose be less about protecting your freedom apart from others and more about setting you free to be one with all others.

Although we live in a world of groupings, clusters, and labels, it becomes important to free our identities to transcend this limitation and free our minds from any domination of differences. It can often be rooted in fear, which can lead the weak to far-away lands distant from the heart of oneness and in extreme cases into harmful behavior.

In the teachings of a perhaps somewhat little known 20th century writer and philosopher, Jiddu Krishnamurti, who taught the importance of freedom, he once stated how labeling can even qualify as a form of violence. He writes, "When you call yourself an Indian or a Muslim or a Christian or a European, or anything else, you are being violent. Do you see why it is violent? Because you are separating yourself from the rest of humankind. When you separate yourself by belief, by

14

nationality, by tradition, it breeds violence. So one who is seeking to understand violence does not belong to any country, to any religion, to any political party or partial system; this person is concerned with the total understanding of mankind."

Could it be that these thought systems of separation that get conditioned into the framework of people's minds play a role in the over-reactive nature of violence being played out on the streets of our communities? They may only appear to be race, and "other" related, but may originate with the labels by which we identify each other and thereby fuel fear and a sense of separation from the whole of the human family.

At age twenty, I learned to meditate. My first experience of it was in five-minute guided meditations that were built into the Unity worship services I attended on Sundays. I wondered why I hadn't learned of this sooner. It was different from praying, which was all I had ever known. This was so calming, relaxing and created an experience of feeling connected, and plugged into the Divine Presence. For a while I attended a group in the church that met one evening each week to meditate together. I made meditation a daily practice and even took a course in TM (Transcendental Meditation) which had come on the scene.

Meditation is a powerful tool for letting go and has continued to be an important part of my life. Oneness is found in the silence of stillness. It always has been. It is in quieting the mind that a person enters a unique space that might be described as "Beingness" in which the Spirit is able to be heard and felt. We are all meant to learn to "go ye apart a while."

When first learning to meditate it can be difficult to disengage from thoughts, sounds, body sensations and the like. In the beginning stages, my mind was accustomed to having its way, often active, full of chatter, commentary, and numerous topics of intrusion. The mind, however, can be taught and conditioned to slow down, give way to the moment, thereby opening to the Spirit Within where peace and wisdom reside.

Over time, meditation offers a portal into non-attachment from it all and an inner beingness that is undergirded with a feeling tone of oneness with it all. It sounds like a paradox… attached to nothing, free of it all, yet one with it all. However, for me, it is a kind of power zone of consciousness in which the energies of oneness can be found. The practice of it can be as simple as focusing on your breath with an overriding sense of being in the Presence. Like all experiences, the description of it never equates to the real thing. Nevertheless, meditation has been and continues to be a practice that contributes to a growing awareness of oneness.

If you have not as yet taken up this practice, I strongly urge you to take steps to learn. Entering the Silence on a regular basis, if only fifteen minutes a day, devoted to your spiritual awakening, opens you to new fields of energy and insight the Divine has waiting for you. And inside those fields there emerges the growing awareness that one + one is one.

Around this time, I began to read voraciously. I had stepped into a new frontier as though my soul had been secretly hungering for it and now I'd been led to a spiritual buffet. People I met at Unity, knowing I was new, gave me books to read and told me about others. These new more progressive ideas and teachings which seemed so inspiring, heart opening, and empowering were feeding my soul as if I had a spiritual stomach without a bottom. It was as though the school bell of the universe had rung and class was in session. It was my time to enter the next higher grade of spiritual understanding. Where I had never been enamored with attending school growing up, I was loving this. I would sit in bed reading into the wee hours of the night.

My awareness was expanding. I was getting much more than intellectual knowledge. I was integrating information at an experiential level that was taking me to new places in my relationship with God, myself, Jesus, others, and life. Jesus began to represent more to me than ever before as I came to understand him as a Master Teacher of love for all and of oneness with all.

There was a shift in how I perceived and understood Jesus. He had always been presented to me as a Super Being, with abilities unique to Him and unattainable to others. I was taught He was God in human form and that He was the exception. No one could ever duplicate any of the things he achieved and demonstrated. For me this understanding was not conducive to a budding, intimate relationship. But now I'd been given a new view of Jesus that allowed a door in me to open to Him. I learned He was not the Great Exception, but the Great Example. That He was our Elder Brother, and Way-Shower, leading the way to love and oneness while being a model and example of what we are in truth and what we are capable of as children of God.

I was introduced to often-forgotten or overlooked statements and passages in the scriptures that brought new clarity to me about Jesus, His message, and our relationship. Examples include his statement: "Truly, truly, I say to you, he who believes in me will also do the works that I do; and greater works than these will he do,..." (John 14:12 RSV)

Growing up in the Midwest, if one were to think or say it was possible to do the things Jesus did, it would be considered blasphemy. It is implied within Jesus' statement that there is significant inner growth and spiritual advancement in consciousness required. Nevertheless, He is pointing out that it's all about one's relationship to the Source, God, the Father.

Jesus states, "I can do nothing on my own authority;" (John 5:30) It is followed by, "If I bear witness to myself, my testimony is not true." (John 5:31) What that says is Jesus realized that on His own, apart from the Source, He could do nothing. He had learned how to connect and access the Divine and that we can, too.

He wanted us to awaken to our true spiritual nature and Authentic Self when he said things like, "You are the salt of the earth," (Matt. 5:13) and "You are the light of the world... let your light shine..." (Matt. 5:14-16). The teaching that we all are divine and have the divinity of God in us, though not yet fully awakened and expressing it, had a huge impact on me.

This idea was made ever more clear after the Apostle Paul had his mystical conversion experience on the road to Damascus, giving him the awakened clarity to state, "When we cry, 'Abba! Father!' it is that very Spirit bearing witness with our spirit that we are children of God, and if children, then heirs, heirs of God and joint heirs with Christ..." (Romans 8:15-17) He wanted us to realize that as "joint-heirs with Christ" we have the divinity of God, the Higher Sacred Self called

"Christ" in us all, waiting to be awakened and have its light shine. Paul even implies that this sacred truth has been somewhat kept from us down through time. He shares, "The mystery that has been hidden throughout the ages and generations but has now been revealed... which is Christ in you the hope of glory." (Col. 1:26-27) The implication is that as joint heirs with Christ, we have that part of us as well, the part that is Divine, the Christ, the Higher Sacred, although buried beneath layers of false, limiting ideas and illusions generated by a separate self of our own making.

It should be pointed out that "Christ" is not Jesus' name. It refers to a state of spiritual consciousness. "Christ" comes from the Greek word Christos, meaning "anointed one." Everyone has within them an "anointed one," a Higher Self that is the Divine Self which is called by Jesus to be a light in the world. We all have that One Spirit, anointed one, Christ, thus causing Paul to declare, "Christ in you, the hope of glory."

Among my favorite and most powerful statements made by Jesus was in the 17th chapter of the Gospel of John. Actually, Jesus is praying a prayer for you, me and everyone, that is steeped in the principle of oneness. He prayed, "The glory that you have given me I have given them, so that they may BE ONE, as WE ARE ONE, I in them and you in me, that they may BECOME COMPLETELY ONE..." (John 17:22-23) I capitalize certain words in this passage so as to emphasize their magnitude.

Is there anything more clear and powerful than that in regard to our quest to rise into the consciousness of oneness? His prayer is that we come to realize and experience the truth that just as God is in him and he is in God... the reality is that we, too, are in God and God is in us. There is only oneness. We are all inside the Circle of God's Living, Loving Presence, but we are lost in the illusion of separation. That is what spiritual awakening is! It is moving further and deeper into the awareness that it is ALL ONE!

From this passage, the words, we are "made perfect in one" (or oneness) became embedded in me. That passage has continued to convey most powerfully to me the universal principle of One + One is One. Ministers talk about getting the calling. Something inside of me knew this would be my path. I was in my early twenties when I acknowledged an inner desire to enter ministry. The God I had now been introduced to brought a new intimacy, clarity and expansiveness.

I had found the vehicle for me and a message that I felt was positive, uplifting, inspiring and about oneness. Its foundation was about unity with God and all life. It began as a kind of secret between myself and Spirit. Somewhat of an introvert and not being a person who was at all drawn to public speaking, I looked for reasons to delay. At this point I had told no one. Although I knew this was what I was guided to do, in my mind, I decided to wait until age forty so as to have more life experience to draw from. It was just my fears causing me to procrastinate on the calling. Nevertheless, one evening in prayer, I received clear and undeniable guidance from Spirit that I was not to wait. I rarely if ever pray on my knees, but that evening I found myself kneeling at the end of my bed, mostly due to feeling the frustration of being unfulfilled in my job. I actually heard a voice in my mind so distinct that I knew it had come from beyond me. It said, "I told you what to do, you are the one putting it off." So I applied to the ministerial program at Unity World Headquarters, requesting acceptance a year in advance of actually beginning. I had married my wonderful wife, Diane, only months earlier and felt it best to wait a year. They agreed and my application was accepted. It was a good feeling to think that my life could be about serving God and promoting oneness. I thought to myself that along with my other duties as a minister it would afford me the opportunity to study spiritual traditions, teachings, teachers, philosophies and philosophers having to do with the principle of oneness.

During the year leading up to enrollment, while working my 8 to 5 job weekdays, I purchased a half-acre home lot and in my spare time became the general contractor in constructing a new home on the site. I wanted to make some extra money as savings for the time I'd be in ministerial school. This was a valuable learning experience. I learned the role that cooperation, coordination and communication plays in the realm of relationships with workers, contractors and subcontractors in creating a fairly large project.

Building a new life, or building an organization, a business or a better world carries some of the same principles as building a new home. Many factors and decisions come into play, must be dealt with, and can't be ignored. There are skills of various types that must be applied, including those of cement masons, carpenters, plumbers, electricians, brick layers and more. Inside and out, the creation of a house, just like a life, will reflect the quality and discipline of certain skills put into it. Building that house involved elements of the principle of oneness that served me later in projects I would undertake. Again, it reinforced that all of life is relationships and the important role human relationship skills can play in all areas of one's life.

I consciously had Divine Spirit as my partner through the entire project. Many had advised against my taking on the project. I had constructed the new home through the heart of four Wisconsin winter months and when it came time to sell, our country was in a serious recession in which home sales were almost nonexistent. Family all around me were nervous it would not sell before I was to leave, but seven days before moving to Missouri to begin school we received a deposit for purchase. I gave my father power of attorney to do the closing in my absence.

I used the construction project as a sort of incubator process for oneness to grow within myself. Through all the challenges of building, I tried to maintain a sense that I was connected to the Presence of divine intelligence and that it would see me through to its success. It was a time I look to in my life where I had to totally trust that my partner, Spirit, would help make it happen, and it did. It was another instance of a growing body of evidence in my life where I got to see the results of an internal commitment to align with the one Source of all life that was continuing to reveal one + one is one.

I was not very comfortable speaking in front of groups, so while in ministerial school, to develop my skills I worked about 30 hours a week in the PR Department of World Headquarters as a tour guide. In the hub of 1,500 acres were a number of buildings and points of interest including the historic tower building, the printing department, 24-hour prayer ministry, rose garden, fountains and more. It was a valuable experience for me to meet local people as well as those from all over the United States and even other countries who came to attend retreats and enroll in one- and two-week class sessions offered there. I'd show these groups of people around, tell them some of the history and make many wonderful acquaintances. It was in many ways a confidence builder.

It was one of my classmates already employed in the PR Department for several months, and who had become a good friend, that suggested I apply, and helped get me the job. Thanks Phil, you were another instrument of God at work in my life bringing me exactly what the next step was for my growth, development, and exposure to the energies of oneness.

Ordained in 1976 and heading into field ministry was a sort of scary proposition. One never feels fully prepared for any new experience even if you have gone through the schooling and mental preparation that precedes it. By now Diane and I had a one-year old daughter with another child soon to be on its way. Once again I was called upon to trust Spirit. The scripture verse "Greater is He that is within you than he that is in the world" became my friend.

I was one of three candidates for the Senior Minister position of a small church in Olympia, Washington. I was selected and began with an attendance of about seventy-five on a Sunday. The ministry's outstanding expenses when I arrived required the Treasurer and me to meet each Monday morning to decide what bills had highest priority to be paid. That went on for only several months, for the church attendance grew steadily through the years to more than 500 people.

It grew due to a number of factors. I was youthful, energetic, with a lovely wife and family that many enjoyed adopting as theirs. I was intent on providing an inspiring and uplifting experience through the Sunday lesson, creating quality music, getting involved in the community and going on the radio with a daily 60-second positive message. More than anything, I got others to join me in creating an energy field that was loving and accepting of all. Word got around about the energy of love and oneness we created. People who visited, stepped into it, felt it and stayed. Oneness and the principle of One + One is One was a winner.

In the seven years there, we completed three building expansion projects. It involved lots of wonderful people coming together to get it accomplished. As they say, "It takes a village." I saw how the project of building a new home earlier in my life had prepared me for the application of the same principles for the success of these building projects in the church. The principles of oneness entered into every success. At the forefront of my approach to ministry was an effort to be all inclusive and convey basic positive, practical teachings that spoke to the heart of anyone. People resonated with teachings on love, the power of affirmative prayer, oneness with God and each other, the creative power of thought, internal transformation through application of universal spiritual laws and principles that bring prosperity, health and happiness.

I found that it did not matter to people what church they were affiliated with when it came to a basic message that was uplifting. This was shown to me when I was guided to purchase time on the radio and deliver one minute inspirational messages that were spiritually universal and everyone could relate to regardless of religion. It was known as "The Unity Thought for the Day" and would begin with those words followed by "is on love" or peace, joy, oneness, perseverance, etc. It aired every week day morning at 7 a.m.

Many people set their clock radios to go off as my voice came on. I'd actually run into people in town who were not of my ministry, who would tell me they woke up with me every morning. I'd respond in good humor by saying they should be careful how they say that and to whom. These radio messages were my attempt to say we are all one. They became very popular to a segment of the community. I would always end with the tag line, "This is Howard Caesar, minister of the Unity Church of Olympia, reminding you 'Life Is Meant To Be Good.'" I became the "Life Is Meant To Be Good" minister in town. It caught on. (This was before the now commercialized trademark saying "Life Is Good" came about.) I honestly did not care if these spots brought people to our church or not. I loved that it was a way to reach any and all people with messages that inspired love and oneness.

In that same desire of wanting to bring people together with a generically spiritual and positive message, I got the idea for our ministry to sponsor a large community event called "The Winner's Circle Evening." We rented the local college auditorium and featured three main speakers: Dr. Norman Vincent Peale of Marble Collegiate Church in New York and Guideposts Magazine, Olympic Gold medal winner Wilma Rudolph, and popular motivational speaker Dr. Denis Waitley. It was a big undertaking for our ministry and was a big success. We had over 2000 people attend in what was at the time a relatively small community in Olympia and it brought people of all walks of life together to hear inspirational messages that crossed all barriers. It was another example of One + One is One.

What I loved about it was that although it was being sponsored by a church, people of all denominations and no denominations came out for it. It seemed to me that people realized it was not about recruiting people to a church, and that the message of the evening was to be universal, for young and old alike. Oneness prevailed over separation, at least on that night. One + One is One.

I was a person that wanted to fit in and be accepted as a regular guy. It was more important to be categorized as a spiritual friend rather than a minister. I wanted other people to let down their guard, be themselves, be real and authentic and to treat me as one of them. This often is not the case, for people often stereotype clergy, project that they are a certain way, and tend to be guarded around them. I felt this would result in some degree of feeling separate.

Although not the leader of a mainline Christian church, I tried to connect with others in various ways just to let them know I was a regular person who was like them. I became an active member of Rotary, helped to start the first Optimist Club in the community and attended the ministerial association. People everywhere can learn and live One + One is One. There are always steps we can take, places we can get involved, serve with others in a good cause. That way we further an awareness of a kind of oneness, realizing we have many of the same needs and desires, and have more similarities than differences.

I recall being present at an event with His Holiness the Dalai Lama. I remember him stating that it would be very beneficial if the leaders of two nations who were at odds, would take the time to bring their families together for at least one week of vacationing. That way they could see each other in the presence of each other's children, grandchildren, etc. and the importance each puts on love and happiness of family. In the softness of the commonalities of the heart, a oneness and cooperativeness can emerge. Again we find that One + One is One.

We never know if, when, or how the Divine is going to move us into our next zone of growth and development. But trust we must because growth is one of the laws of life and trust is usually required. It is often our resistance to growing that is the cause of much of our suffering. And open we must also be to the Divine plan for our life. Because we all have one. We all signed on to a plan before we arrived, but just don't remember the details. Along the way we get signs, signals, and inner promptings we can either ignore, delay, or act on. It is natural to resist change and I was no different. Change was coming for me and my family.

By 1983, after seven years in my first ministry, Diane and I had three children, lots of friends, a thriving ministry and loved our lives in the Northwest. I'd received offers and invitations to serve at other ministries, including Hawaii, which was oh so enticing. However, I always declined after seeking inner guidance.

Guidance is not a head thing. It comes as an inner feeling that is hard to argue with. It is being sensitive to the energies that accompany a choice, option, alternative or offering of change. A person may say he or she doesn't have any energy around moving to Baltimore or taking that job. Also, over time, as a result of meditation and a prayer life that has sought guidance many times, one develops an inner knowing. Whether you call it intuition, a holy hunch or that "still small voice within," after becoming quiet inside, you have a knowing deep down if something is right for you or not.

In 1983, the Unity Church in Houston, Texas, began to pursue me. I communicated to them I was not interested. I did not want to be interested and even avoided checking my inner guidance. But they were persistent in asking me to visit and speak on a Sunday, which I finally did. This was a benchmark moment in my life pertaining to the dynamic of following one's guidance. Humanly, I did not want to leave Olympia. Life there was happy and gloriously successful. But when I finally checked inside, spiritually, I got that feeling from Spirit I was being led to go. Every time I got quiet and listened inside for the guidance of Spirit, there was a strong inner impulse that I was to go to Houston. In my humanness, over a six-week period, I delayed returning an answer to their invitation to come serve there. It was because I didn't want to go, didn't want to face my fears and preferred to stay in my comfort zone with what was familiar. So I continued to pray in the hopes that I'd receive a change in guidance, be led to stay in Olympia. But it never came.

So in May of 1983, I began serving in the ministry in Houston, Texas. It was a difficult adjustment in the early going. There were several reasons. My body literally went into a kind of withdrawal due to the absence of the energies of nature. In the Northwest, there were forests all around. The church itself sat in the middle of a forest of trees. There were mountains, including the Olympics you could view from our backyard, and Mt. Rainier in full view from several points out the front of our home. At a favorite local restaurant located alongside a stream, you could look out the windows and see salmon jumping. The life and beauty of nature all around was intoxicating. Houston had its own beauty, but it took my body two years to get over its craving for the vibrations of nature while adjusting to concrete as its replacement. There were also many natural adjustments in moving, learning new responsibilities, new ways of doing things, getting to know staff. Immediately, I was given a great deal to oversee and found it taxing.

But it opened me up to a whole host of new experiences that expanded me and led to my next greater good. I found again that listening, trusting, and being one with my inner guidance had enormous blessings. It was another monumental example to me of how oneness with Source and following its guidance works toward the revealing of a divine order in life. This time it guided me to Houston, just as a similar divine impulse had sent me into ministry, overriding my mind's fearful rational to delay until age forty. In both cases it was fear that had to be overcome with an internal movement toward trusting in Spirit. Looking back, it was oneness that moved me forward.

One soul, me... plus the One Source and Its guidance, equaled becoming One with my next highest good in life. I'm convinced that we are being guided all the time. Spirit is not static, but dynamic, and takes any soul who surrenders to it deeper and higher into the experience of peace, love and joy through oneness. It requires that we maintain a more consistent conscious connection to the Presence of divine intelligence and wisdom. Life can pull us in many directions and we sometimes fail or forget to check inside or even believe that these inner promptings exist. Or our human resistance to change enters in, as it did for me, almost causing me to wait until age forty to enter ministry and almost blocking a move to Houston. The more one begins to build a consciousness of oneness with Source, and realize that it is not something outside you, but within you at all times, the more easily it becomes to recognize Its inner stirrings.

Through the years I served on a number of Boards of Trustees in which I was honored to be part; all of them had as their cause the helping of others and expanding spiritual consciousness. I personally learned, grew and expanded my own consciousness from the experiences it brought me. In most every instance I was learning about people, groups, organizations, their effectiveness or ineffectiveness, the ego of separation and the Spirit of oneness,

For a number of years, I served on the Board of an organization known as the International New Thought Alliance (INTA), which is a 100-year-old alliance of members that included ministers, spiritual teachers, leaders, and lay people from around the U.S. and the world. It was made up of progressive-minded people interested in raising spiritual consciousness and oneness in individuals and the world.

In the mid-1980s I began attending its annual conferences and after a couple years was asked to serve on its board. Through my involvement I was introduced to a group of people from South Africa who were active in New Thought there; we became good friends.

In 1991, the President of INTA, myself, and one other minister friend were invited to be the keynote speakers at a conference they were hosting in Johannesburg, South Africa. After the conference they took us around their beautiful country for three weeks, meeting and speaking with various groups. This was during apartheid and much change was occurring in the country.

Apartheid was the name given a system of legislation used by the government of South Africa to enforce policies of racial segregation. Nonwhites were forced to live outside the cities in residential areas known as townships and shanty-towns. This caused poverty and hardship for them. In 1985 the United Kingdom and the U.S imposed economic sanctions on the country to pressure the government to end apartheid. This brought additional hardships.

During my time there, I went to many places including cities, outlying areas, and townships like Soweto, where I met many people, whites and nonwhites, from the poorest to the more affluent. Although demonstrations had taken place in previous years, during my visit there I witnessed a coming together of the people to find solutions to ending apartheid. It was very much in the conversation of the people and was being worked on. Although it may not have been going on everywhere, I experienced a friendly, peaceful, cooperativeness between blacks and whites. I sensed the South African people were hungry for solutions to their problems. Most importantly, I found they were communicating with one another. And because communication leads to creation, progress was under way.

In 1991, the year of my visit, the government began to repeal old legislation that provided for apartheid. Concessions were made and an agreement was reached in 1993. A new constitution that enfranchised blacks took effect in 1994. Although it didn't result in an immediate perfect world for all their people, South Africa showed that by taking steps in the direction of oneness, progress can be made.

When dealing with the consciousness of masses of people, seldom will you hit a home run in your first at bat. And yet, if we want to move toward a world that works, we must call for progress toward taming the energies of division and separation while opening to and expanding the energies of a united cooperativeness. Humanity must work on taking steps toward demonstrating the One in the many that brings the many into being One. Application of the principle of One + One is One wherever and whenever possible is essential.

The current state of our world indicates humanity is in a tug-of-war between separation and oneness. It's a battle of polarities between energies of peace and violence, harmony and disharmony. Those souls devoted to higher consciousness and uniting their life forces for good are being tugged at by opposing forces made up of those souls in lower consciousness and dominated by a separate self.

Our outer world is a reflection of our collective inner world. Therefore, if all living souls on the planet contribute to an ocean of consciousness, then to move the world forward we must expand the efforts and numbers of individuals adding the purity of oneness through thought and action, so as to dilute the polluting nature of separation. The quality, character and frequency of every person's life energy becomes a tributary for good or ill, streaming into this ocean of the collective. Therefore, how every person lives his or her life matters and contributes in some degree to the whole.

I felt my heart open to the people of South Africa. The warmth, kindness and hospitality received everywhere from everyone, including both whites and nonwhites, made for a memorable, meaningful experience. Despite the problems they were facing, a loving acceptance was extended to me and my visiting companions. It was encouraging to meet people who would not give up hope, who remained positive, upbeat, and devoted to their faith in God for brighter days. It helped me see once again that everywhere people are faced with many of the same challenges related to separation and that the spirit of oneness is a main ingredient for its cure. The principle of One + One is One applies to all people, everywhere.

Everyone faces challenges in this life which can take them into separation consciousness. It can be a relationship breakup, loss of job, loss of a loved one, health related, or any number of things. How we learn to deal with them is crucial. Various addictions can come into play in people lives, often as an attempt to escape the feelings associated with suffering separation symptoms. We most likely all have a family member, relative or friend, if not ourselves, who has faced some kind of addiction or need of recovery.

Through AA (Alcoholics Anonymous) millions have risen from serious states of separation and conditions caused by addiction.

Recovery through the Twelve Step Program includes the establishment of oneness through relationship to a Higher Power. Here again I feel it is the principle of oneness that is at the core of restoration and a return to any kind of wholeness of life.

In the 1990s, I served for seven years on the Board of Trustees of a Recovery Center called The Pavilion, located in North Carolina. The Directors were good friends of mine and in my first year on the Board, I was given a scholarship to be an attendee of their thirty-day recovery program. I really did not know what I was getting myself into, but it was actually a very enriching experience that has stayed with me.

I joined 35 other men and women of all ages, dealing with addictions of every kind; alcohol, cocaine, heroin, relationships, sex, work, and some dealing with more than one. It was very spiritually based in the Twelve Step Program. Although I had no substance abuse addiction, I did learn a great deal about myself and also discovered I had symptoms of being a workaholic. What was most amazing to me over those thirty days was the transformation that took place through the restoration of love and the establishment of oneness with a Higher Power. That came after each person faced themselves and their issues. They then returned to living inside the principle of One + One is One.

I will be forever grateful and indebted to the experience gained from this program. I witnessed people with horribly broken lives, some having been abused or beaten in childhood or beyond, many trying to escape the pain of their past and present through substance abuse. For the most part, these people hated their lives, hated themselves and had distanced themselves from any form of love, coming in or going out. These people found the courage to face their fears, tell their painful stories, and discover a way back. Many times I found myself crying through the stories and process of these dear souls. It was so moving to watch people emerge from their dark caves of separation and in the last week or two get put back together and become loving souls again. During the process that unfolded over the thirty days, a beautiful, emerging, supportive energy developed that had the group became as one. They understood each other, had become authentic, bared their souls, and come clean. I got to see first-hand as a board member that it was a very effective program in which virtually everyone opened again to love and life. I witnessed again that the principle of One + One is One holds true in every kind of situation.

In the years since, recovery programs have evolved in their treatment and more often than not require ninety days or more, depending on the situation. But whatever the time involved, the essence of every individual's return to health and wholeness is a return to who they really are, and the recovery, at least to some degree, of states of love and oneness.

Consciousness is creative and systems of thought within individuals and the masses shape our world. Endless studies and experiments have proven that thought is creative and whether on a small or large scale the scripture from Proverbs 23:7 KJV, "...for as he thinketh in his heart, so is he..." is a powerful truth. It can be accurately expanded to say "...as he, she, the world, thinks in their heart, so is he/she/it." Therefore, it becomes important to motivate people toward the spiritual and constructive, and away from separation and ego driven ways that are destructive.

In 1996 I was fortunate to join a small group of spiritual leaders in co-founding The Association for Global New Thought. Our vision was to bring about positive change and contribute to an awakened world. It was based on the conviction that there are universal spiritual truths that reflect the core teachings of the world's great spiritual traditions of both east and west. That the community of all life is sacred and that a new vision of society governed by love and oneness is necessary to bring about global healing.

Conferences attended by thousands along with various projects and programs were set in motion to help create a world of greater togetherness and cooperation. One project named "The Gandhi-King Season For Non-Violence" was instituted annually as a series of events taken up in scores of cities. The focus was on the principles of non-violence espoused by Mahatma Gandhi and Dr. Martin Luther King.

Our leadership council coordinated and facilitated three "Synthesis Dialogues," which were a coming together of thirty-plus leaders from around the world to meet with His Holiness the Dalai Lama to discuss solutions for a better world. They were usually a week long and the first one was in Dharamsala, India, where the Dalai Lama resides. The two others were held in Italy.

Having attended all three, I had the privilege of sitting down to an informal lunch with the Dalai Lama himself, joined by a few others. Naturally, everyone's attention was focused on him and most of the conversation was directed to him. He was appropriately serious and reflective at times when answering questions regarding problems of the world when appearing before larger groups. However, in this small group setting he seemed more freed up and was most delightful. He would comment on something and then add a bit of humor, throwing his head back as he went into a deep hearty laugh. I remember him being asked if he had met with then President George W. Bush. Laughing, he said he had and that they had eaten chocolate chip cookies together. I'm sure there were deeper matters dealt with which he kept in confidence.

In the larger group meetings with him he had a way of addressing problems in the world without pointing a finger, but speaking more generally about the kind and character of leadership necessary to make a difference. He was a peaceful man who was and is dedicated to peace in the individual and the world. As a spiritually centered soul, for decades throughout the globe, he has represented and stood for true compassion. Compassion, of course, comes from love and the deep knowing we are one. He lives a philosophy of peace and has a reverence for all living things. He teaches that our own happiness is bound up with the happiness of others, and that we have a universal responsibility to embrace all mankind through truth and justice.

In the opening session of the Synthesis Dialogues held in Italy at Castel Gandolfo, the Papal Palace, I remember the Dalai Lama beginning our time together by saying, "We are here to explore ways of serving the whole human family. When no concern but your own life – is very foolish. The great teachers, (pause) did not think only about their own, (people) but for all humanity. No discrimination. The teachings were for all people, all humanity, (pause) not this culture, not this color, not this nation. (pause) If we use religion for division, I think that not right." I understood him to mean that he was not against religion, but opposed to religion being used to divide people. We are to honor and respect each other's path and not use it to divide or do harm. You see, it was very clear that the Dalai Lama was an advocate of oneness and, although stated differently, he understood that the universal spiritual principle is that One + One is One. I have been very blessed to meet many wonderful leaders, authors and speakers who have devoted their lives to articulating a message that is intended to better people's lives and at least transform a piece of this world.

During my thirty-plus years as Senior Minister of our spiritual community in Houston, the ideal of oneness has continued to be one of my main passions. For a number of years, I continued the one-minute radio messages with the tag at the end, "Life Is Meant To Be Good." It became a slogan for many inside and outside our ministry. Eventually, we replaced radio with a TV broadcast airing Sunday lessons for more than a decade. We established "The Dynamic Speaker Series" in which we scheduled nationally and internationally recognized authors and speakers. You may know some of them: Deepak Chopra, the late Dr. Wayne Dyer, Marianne Williamson, Og Mandino, Iyanla Vanzant, and many others. They were people with positive, expansive, inspiring messages that would be described as all-inclusive, more spiritual than religious, and all of whom believed in the ideal of oneness.

This inner passion to go deeper into the consciousness of oneness in my personal spiritual growth took me to India. Early in 2007, a friend from Rhode Island said she was coming to Houston and wanted to have an appointment to talk with me. When she arrived, this very professional, down-to-earth person told me she had received very strong guidance directing her to come tell me about a recent experience she had attending the Oneness University in southeast India. I had not heard of it. She had taken a course there designed to clear one's consciousness and become more of an open channel or conduit for Divine energy to flow.

We all have the potential to access Divine energy, but are often clogged up as a vessel and block its flow due to a chattering mind, life's distractions, and unresolved issues from our past. She proceeded to tell me about her experience and then gave me what was called a "Oneness Blessing." She offered no suggestions as to what the results might be. However, for a period of four days, I experienced an undeniably quieted mind that noticeably had me stress-free and in a more present state. That visit took place in January and by August I was in India, enrolled in the process for myself.

With my passion for oneness I had to check out this place that was actively helping hundreds of thousands of people from all around the world move into deeper states of oneness. I learned they were not interested in becoming another religion, which they said the world did not need. But they were about what I describe as the science and experience of oneness, offering sacred teachings, ancient processes and mystical initiations that cannot be adequately described, all of which helped to advance an individual toward a deepening consciousness of oneness.

Since 2007, I have been to the Oneness University eight times, taking courses that have ranged from nine days up to thirty. I was amazed to see large groups of people coming from Europe, Russia, China, Asia, Africa, and scores of other countries from all around the world. Some classes had more than a thousand people with translators for the various languages speaking into the headsets of attendees. Although I recognize that this rather intense experience was not for everyone, I have found great value integrating what has been gained there into my life and ministry.

I have had profound experiences and been taken into deep states of oneness through my times at the Oneness University in India, adding to my personal growth and convincing me further that one + one really is one. We cannot argue with a direct experience that is given or comes to us from Spirit. Skeptics there will always be, because the mind judges what it does not know and has not experienced. No one will ever take away from me the experiences I have had, and the same is true for you or anyone.

Awakening into oneness involves a neurobiological shift in the brain. By changing mental focus patterns, we begin to create new neural pathways. Brain science has shown us that we are able to create a new neural network by blazing new trails of higher thought. Actually, oneness is about becoming free of the mind or at the very least quieting it. We all have thoughts, but instead of identifying with them, we become the observer of them. Our freedom begins by no longer identifying with the mind. We all have a mind, but we are not our mind. Also, we have thoughts, but are not our thoughts if we choose not to identify with them. We are spiritual beings given a mind to use, not to be used by the mind. It is possible to learn to see your thoughts come and go. Herein, more freedom lies. Oneness involves learning not to identify with the ego, or separate self, but instead with our Sacred Authentic Self, the unchanging spiritual essence of who we are.

We live in a rapidly changing world. We see it in science, medicine, technology and every field. Our bodies are changing, our thoughts are changing, our perceptions are changing. The old is dying and the new is being born. Part of life is learning to cope. Learning to cope is learning not to identify with mind, but to become the observer of the mind and learn to be master of the mind rather than allowing it to be master over you. Developing this facet of awareness translates into being more present, in the moment, of the heart, and into the energies of oneness. Back in the year 1905, Albert Einstein proved that we can break matter down into smaller components and particles, and that when we do, we move beyond the material realm, and into a realm in which everything is energy.

The late Buckminster Fuller, recognized by many as a genius, reminded us, "In 1928, humans first discovered the existence of a galaxy other than our own Milky Way. Since then, we have discovered 100 billion more galaxies, each averaging over 100 billion stars. Each star is an all-out chain-reacting atomic energy plant." He made this statement back in 1983 and you can be sure it's inaccurate today, only in the sense that a vastly greater expanse has been uncovered. The point is that energy is moving, flowing, and vibrating in and around us all the time. Nothing rests. Let us not get caught in smallness; instead, let us begin to step into the big picture. There are forces working in our favor and for our behalf of which we are unaware. It does not deny their existence.

We take for granted that a cell phone in our hand, through invisible forces, can connect to a friend across the planet and have us carry on a conversation. We take for granted that we can open on our lap an independent thin compartment called a computer and on its screen, again through invisible forces, receive visual images of actual happenings of events across the world, as they happen. Most of us don't fully understand how it works and yet messages travel through the invisible and we easily accept it.

How is it, I ask, that it is so difficult for some to accept that we could receive messages and help from angels, light beings, entities or whatever name you wish to give to discarnate souls or beings who are in service to humanity and bring good, though from beyond the veil of this physical world? Inside the universal principle of one + one is one comes the realization that this principle puts us in touch with and at one with any other and all dimensions and realms. If we can nonchalantly accept the workings of cell phones invisibly connecting us to receive messages, there should be some opening to the idea we can receive messages and help from higher realms. This truth was to become my next phase of discovery on the path of oneness.

Jesus said, "In my Father's house there are many dwelling places." (John 14:2) I take that to mean many realms and one of those is the realm beyond the veil of this physical life. At times the physical and non-physical worlds merge and we can receive a thought from the other side or feel the presence of a loved one who has passed on, or receive guidance and healing. All things that work together for good are of God.

In 2008 a dear friend shared that she had been to Brazil to experience the healing work of John of God. He is a Brazilian healer who for more than fifty years has healed and helped a multitude of people. Although a rather common man, he is also a gifted medium. Three days a week he allows spirits from beyond the physical to take over his body and treat thousands who come in need of healing. My friend had met and stayed with Heather Cummings, a friend and translator to Medium Jao, as he is called. Heather is the co-author of the most popular book about his life and work, titled "John of God."

Some years prior I had heard about John of God, his healing gift, and the amazing work he was doing. At the time I remember telling myself I'd like to look into this sometime in the future. After listening to my friend's personal experience, and then reading the book, I was feeling led that this was the time. In my quest to explore oneness, I was guided to go alone to Abadiania, Brazil for two weeks to experience for myself what went on there. I went with a mixture of skepticism and openness, mainly wanting to understand how the many thousands of people had been healed by God through the more than fifty years of his work.

What I experienced is difficult to put into words. It is what most everyone who visits there says. I witnessed people being helped and healed by God, but in ways that were new and unfamiliar to me and most people. Even in their approach, as in all manifestations of healing, the openness, faith and inner work within spiritual consciousness on the part of the individual is a necessary ingredient. What was new and unfamiliar was the understanding that the process of healing was being assisted and administered on an unseen level by loving, light beings, who were spiritually advanced and in service to God.

As amazing as it may sound, I learned that just as there are doctors, nurses, and surgeons in this world, there are those of the same or greater knowledge and abilities beyond the veil who can be accessed to do their healing work on a level invisible to the human eye... just as is the cell phone. Actually, it is fairly common and accepted by the people of Brazil that this goes on. People from all over the world have come there to be helped and have received healings. It is clear to me that although our understanding is limited regarding the invisible side of life, there are other dimensions from which we receive help. In other words, we really are one with all life... both physical and non-physical. In God's great house of eternal life there exist other rooms and realms beyond the veil of this three-dimensional, physical world in which we currently live. There is life going on beyond the borders of what our physical eyes can see and help is being offered on unseen levels.

Should the advanced skills that advanced souls have learned in this world and the next go dormant and unused simply because they are now beyond the boundaries of our familiarity and what is conventionally accepted by yesterday's religion? In the same way man would never have taken to the airways if someone hadn't been open to once undiscovered principles of aviation, humanity must grow beyond its skepticism and closed rigidness of thought so as to evolve and advance into the next wave of spiritual understanding whose time has come.

Just as a time came for man to discover, accept and put to use the principles for flight, so it is also true that in the vast spiritual world there are laws, principles, insights and understandings that can seem new but have always been there and are now surfacing for the awareness of a larger body of people to benefit. If you see yourself as one with the God of ALL THAT IS, then you must come to understand this means you are one with ALL THAT IS in this world and the next, this realm and all others, the seen and the unseen, that which is known, familiar and understood by man, and what currently is not. One + One is One is a principle that exists everywhere in all of space and time. Therefore, it makes us one with angels, entities of light and goodness, beings of love, pure intent and the abilities to help and guide, though they may be invisible to the human eye.

I was so impressed and convinced by what I experienced in Brazil that I have taken groups there annually. John of God's work has shown me another avenue in which the Divine can bring a soul into the oneness of healing and wholeness. I simply cannot argue with what I have continually seen, witnessed and experienced each time I take a group there. In many more ways than we can see or fully understand, One + One is One. Oneness with God is the main door to it all. I'm not suggesting everyone must go to visit John of God in Brazil, but am simply attempting to pry open those minds seemingly sealed shut by old, rigid, limiting, outdated dogma, beliefs, and fear that robs them of experiencing the transcending dimensions of life and living born of the universal principle that One + One is One.

I have gained a deepening feeling of connection to all people of the world through my visits to other lands and cultures, learning of their history, religion and way of life. In recent years, in addition to my personal-growth trips to India, and group-led trips to Brazil, once a year I have teamed up with my close friend, Mary Morrissey, to take groups of people numbering up to 65, on spiritual pilgrimages. We have taken groups to Egypt, Greece, Bali, the Holy Land, Italy and other places, visiting sacred sites and temples, seeking to learn and honor all people and all paths.

These have been extremely rewarding experiences as we discover over and over that people everywhere look to find love and happiness through the God of their understanding. We really are one people, though our pasts, our traditions, and our ways of life may vary.

My life, and I believe yours as well, has seemingly been an unfolding series of events, experiences and explorations intended to reveal the path toward oneness.

Perhaps this book is a book of seeds. The stories here are intended to break open those seeds in you that may have been long dormant inside, imprisoned in false and limiting concepts and the conditionings of this world. Like you, I am a child of God looking to learn, grow and do the best I can to live from love and happiness while making a contribution to life and this world.

I invite you to join me in further exploring our oneness with God, ourselves, others, and all of life. The following chapters include stories and vignettes of my own and others related to oneness. It is my sincere desire that you find yourself in them, and will relate them to your own personal life path, its various examples and evidences revealing the universal spiritual truth of one + one is one.

CHAPTER TWO
The Heart of It All

All of life is relationships. One has no life without them. The most important relationship a person can have is with their God. Ideally, all others branch off from this. Actually, it's all God. As explained earlier, everything is inside the Circle of God. However, through the pages of this chapter, join me in exploring and addressing first our relationship with the Divine. In the chapters that follow we will address the relationship of oneness we are meant to have with ourselves, others, nature, and all life.

God is found and experienced in the heart, not the head. Have you noticed that you can't feel or experience anything with your mind? The scriptures state, "God is love, and those that abide in love, abide in God and God abides in them." (I John 4:16) Sounds like "One + One is One" to me. Love and oneness are two sides of the same coin. Can you imagine what it would be like to live in the energies of love consistently? That is called unconditional love… to be true to love no matter what. Those are big shoes to fill and for now we just want to talk about making small strides in the process of evolving into love and oneness.

What do we mean when we talk about "evolving spiritually?" Growing up in the Midwest, my father loved to hunt and fish. Most of the things he went after required dogs. Foxhounds for hunting fox, beagles for hunting rabbits, Springer spaniels to flush out pheasant and quail, and Black Labs to retrieve fallen ducks. Through the years growing up we had anywhere from ten to twenty dogs and once even had twenty-eight after one of the Beagles had a litter of puppies.

My mother, although soft, gentle and kind, was very firm that there would be no dogs in the house. And there never were. They stayed in pens or chained to a hut. I know, it sounds a bit cruel or cold to all pet lovers, but those were the rules. These dogs were for hunting and not to be coddled or domesticated into household pets.

Consequently, when married and with children, I had been conditioned to institute the same rules when it came to having dogs in our house. There were to be no dogs in our house and everyone knew it. We have all been conditioned to many things and ways of being from the time we were very young up through the present time. Many can be unconscious.

One day my daughter, Dawn, eight years old at the time, came home crying because she'd been to a neighbor friend's house that had a litter of puppies. One of the little puppies had won her heart and she so wanted to have it as a pet. She was crying because she knew I was against having a pet dog. Well, I caved in and we got our first dog. That meant allowing it to be in the house. I set a rule that it could be in only certain rooms, but never in anyone's bedroom.

When our youngest daughter, Star, went off to college and was living off campus, she bought herself a miniature Dachshund and named her Abby. It was the cutest thing. She allowed it to go anywhere. A time came in which she was traveling for a week and my wife, Diane, and I were asked to dog-sit for her. I was okay with that as long as the rules remained the same as always at our house. Well, this dear little dog was accustomed to sleeping not only in Star's bedroom, but in the bed! This breed of dog has a natural desire to burrow, so it loved to crawl down near her feet to sleep at night. Well, of course, I would have nothing to do with that. It could be in the house, but that's all.

In short order the will of this little pooch defeated mine. She barked until we opened the door and let her into our bedroom. But that was as far as I would go. We made a makeshift bed with a blanket on the floor for her to burrow under. The dog was so cute, snugly, and loving that it only took a couple days to win my heart. I made another concession and allowed it to snuggle next to me on the sofa while I was watching TV. It had a way of looking into my eyes with a sweetness that I couldn't resist. So, after the fourth day, when she leaped onto the bed as we were turning in for the night, I said to Diane, "Okay... just this once."

Well... it wasn't just once. She slept with us in our bed the rest of her stay. Most of the time she would sleep under the covers at our feet.

However, there was a night or two when half asleep I became aware of something next to my face, breathing on me… and it wasn't my wife. By now this miniature wiener dog had won my heart and far from pitching a hissy fit, I was overtaken by affectionate feelings I'd come to have for it. I went from, no dog in the house, to a dog in the house, then in the bedroom, then in the bed, and then on my pillow!

I had evolved! If we step back from this transformation of sorts that took place in me, we can see that old conditioning I'd learned about dogs as a kid growing up had given way to a new way of being. What I had learned in my head was overtaken by my heart. One would say I evolved in the sense that I transcended the intellect by opening to an experience of the heart.

The process of evolving spiritually and into the heart is of great significance to everyone's soul path. Within our spiritual consciousness, we are not to shift into static mode and cling to old limiting concepts that we have been conditioned to about God, life, and ourselves. Many a person has been brought up and conditioned to a concept of separation. They were introduced to the concept of a Divine Being that was separate from them. This concept, although now fading somewhat among the younger generations, was often depicted as a Being off in the sky, or somewhere separate and apart from us standing in judgment and issuing punishments according to errors committed. Actually, when it comes to the idea of evolving spiritually, separation is the concept where many start out, having been introduced to it from their youth. But it's just not the truth. It's not what any of the great Master Spiritual teachers have conveyed down through the centuries, including those recognized as awakened beings like Jesus, Buddha, Krishna and others who have spoken and written a very different message and concept. They have all taught that there is absolutely no distance or separation between the Creator and its creation. The Creator has put Itself into Its creation, including you. Actually, we have taken on and inherited the same likeness as our Creator. When connected in the heart, something from within us creatively finds its way onto the canvas of life from a place of spiritual connection. Something within us manifests into the physical dimension and world scene, having emerged from some inner creative zone of inspiration. Everything new, creative and innovative is from the inside out.

If we accept what the scriptures tell us; that God is Spirit, and that we are made in Its image and likeness, then we are Spirit. And that Spirit in us has as Its Divine heritage, the creative capacity to partner with its Source and thereby make all things new and better. To evolve is to progress onward, upward and deeper into an intimate and dynamic relationship with the Source, a Source that "lives, moves and has its being within you." It is "closer than breathing and nearer than hands and feet." Many people have no idea how to approach the Divine, to connect with, bond with, and make as one's Supreme Friend.

Consider how it is with the best friend you've ever had or the best relationship you could ever imagine with a person. There is a level of trust. There isn't anything you would withhold or not tell that friend. You know you would not be judged. There would be only unconditional love and the desire to support, help and assist you toward greater happiness, success and fulfillment.

Realize that the Divine Presence wants to be that friend to you. It wants nothing more than to bond with you, be able to communicate with you daily, and be engaged in your life. As spiritual masters have made it clear, this Presence wants to have you connect consciously, communicate continually and collaborate consistently on a daily basis. Although the Divine is Spirit, a Presence, the relationship is meant to be very personal, intimate and like the best relationship you could imagine with a human. And the Spiritual Presence now is and always has been part of you, dwelling within. So as we realize this Presence is with us at all times, our awareness of It grows. It takes on a life and power in you to the extent that you sincerely acknowledge that It is there ready, willing and able to guide, empower and love you into your next highest good.

Love is the most powerful force in the universe? Why? Because it has the Spirit of The One, The All, in it. Actually it IS The One, The All, in expression. Its nature is to unite, bind together, and counter all sense of division and separation. As stated earlier, it cannot be experienced in the intellect, only through the heart. It isn't easy to consistently love unconditionally.

I recall watching the Montel Williams Show on TV back when it was airing some years ago. He had a family on the show whose lives had been flooded with adversity. The family was made up of a mother and two sons. The oldest boy was 17 years old. He had been through a lot. His mother was a drug addict. The father was no longer present in the family. Child services had split the family up because she wasn't fit to be a mother in her condition or able to provide for them. This boy and his younger brother had been taken away from their mother. The brothers had also been split up and went to different places to be cared for. There had been problems upon problems for these boys and this family... a seeming deluge.

Finally, the mother had gotten help with her addiction, pulled herself together, gotten a job, got the boys together, and became a family again. They were so happy and relieved to be together. Then, the mother met a guy; they started to have a serious relationship and he moved in. One day, not long after, they came home and he had moved out and taken everything. The place was empty. Not a piece of furniture left. Nothing. Everything they owned was gone.

It so devastated the mother, that she started using drugs again. And again, the boys were faced with a drug addict mom and a dim future. But the older son had nothing but love in his heart. He was not bitter toward his mother. He said he understood that his mom had a big problem with drugs; that she had an addiction, a disease and he forgave her. He just wanted to get his mother help and the family back together again. In his voice there was such sweet sincerity. This young seventeen-year old, with an aura of love, acceptance and understanding beyond his years, met a policeman who started to get involved by supporting him in getting his mother help, into rehab, and working to eventually get the family back together. The plight of this boy and family had touched this policeman.

The boy's love for his mom and brother, along with his desire that they be one again, was so strong that it was seemingly working miracles. Amidst a sea of problems and complications, this boy had not gone under... he had not lost hope... he had not become angry and bitter… but kept his heart strings vibrating with the strength of love for his mom and brother.

As this story was being told, the manner in which it was related and the aura of love being shown by this boy captured the emotions of the studio audience. The TV cameras scanned everyone. Everybody was crying. The TV audience was crying. Montel Williams was crying. The mom was crying. I was crying. It was so very moving. The energy was palpable. This boy was demonstrating that love could win and help them rise up out of their deluge of adversities. This young boy was spiritually mature beyond his years. It was like he was a light shining through a dark situation. And because of it they were rising out of it.

I had to ask myself why was I crying? Why was the audience crying? Not that it was out of place to do so. Not that I was wanting to avoid the onslaught of this emotion. In fact, I like to cry happy tears at movies and such. In the process of relating their story and having them share it with such deep emotion, twoness became oneness. I felt like I became that boy. I was him and he was me. I felt what he felt. It was a feeling as though we had all jumped inside of him, as if in the one same energy pool. I became one with him, his mother, his brother, the policeman, Montel Williams, the studio audience… we were all in that same pool of loving energy. All who went to their heart and opened it, got to splash around in it. There was something very beautiful about it. I was deeply touched. What took place on that TV show stayed with me for several days; actually, longer than that if I'm sharing it now, years later.

It took me deep because it resonated with my soul's curriculum. The boy refused to accept separation, in this case of family, his mom and brother. He kept his heart pure. He didn't let conditions get the best of him…didn't resent his mother for her mistakes, weaknesses, and their consequences. He held to the image of her wholeness and goodness. It occurred to me that because he stayed in the purity of his heart, the energies of love drew solutions to assist in the reestablishment of their coming together again as one. His love even caused the universe to send an open-hearted policeman into their lives to join in the goal of their being reunited.

Something inside me recognized what I had witnessed that day on TV. That's who we really are. That is the love we came to be. It is a microcosm of the macrocosm to which we are here to contribute. I thought about that statement Jesus made in beginning what is known as the Sermon on the Mount, "Blessed are the pure in heart, for they shall see God." In the purity of that boy's heart, I saw the Divine expressed that day and not only saw it, but felt it and wept in it, with all who were in the studio audience along with however many hundreds of thousands who may have been tuned in on their TVs.

I'm willing to bet you are somewhat like me. You want to feel that kind of love with some consistency. I believe you and I can. I believe it helps to remember to live from the universal principle that says "one + one is one!" Love + love is love.

How far can its energies go? If others along with me were brought to feel this way about this boy and his family, what is to stop us from feeling this way about virtually anyone… that they are us and we are them? We are one. Perhaps this is a small taste of what masters and mystics have related about us all being one? This realization needs to be expanded upon by greater numbers of people in our world.

For me, God is a feeling. It is the feeling or inner sense of a Presence. I even recall moments from my childhood of having this kind of feeling.

During my childhood we had big snow storms in Wisconsin. One might blow in and drop an eighteen- to twenty-four-inch blanket of white over the landscape. It was a nightmare for most adults, but a dream for us kids. It meant sledding and tobogganing was in the works.

At times strong winds would create drifts in some places that were five and six feet deep. With a slight thaw followed by a freeze, it would create a crusty top layer that a small kid could walk on. I liked to locate a deep drift and to shovel out a snow cave. The roof of it wasn't inclined to cave in because of the crusty top layer that had formed by the changing temperatures. Upon completing my cavern in the snow, I loved to sit in my semi-dark snow temple. There, out of the wind, away from all sounds, I felt nurtured by the quiet, a sense of the sacred in that stillness. I would sense that I was not alone… that a

Presence was there with me. I'd sit in that kind of holy atmosphere which one would think was frigid and cold, yet I was actually filled with an inner warmth that transcended any potential chill. There was something there with me that was beyond the physical touch. It emanated from within me but extended all around me. I guess it was the beginnings of what I later learned was a form of meditation… being in the Silence. I would lie there in my snow cave for thirty minutes or more and soak up the feeling. That Presence has been with me all my life. And it has been with you your whole life, too. Spirit is everywhere present and dwells within us all. It takes getting quiet and still to sense it is there.

Oneness is like a stream of divine current and every soul is in the process of moving into its flow bit by bit… first as if dipping in only a toe, and in time learning to wade in farther and farther to where there are more wonderful moments of love, peace and joy as a result of having become saturated in these energies.

I assume most every person has had times in their childhood when they laid on their back looking up at the blue sky of day, or the twinkling stars of night and contemplated what it was all about. I did. And I recall having a few of these times when I was all alone. They were the best. Without interruption or distraction, my thoughts were allowed to be swept upward until the thoughts actually quieted. Then with a mind now void of questions, I was able to let myself give way to the moment and what was in it to be experienced. What I would be left with was a feeling of oneness. In that space, I didn't need to know how the moon and stars got there, or when, or how long they had been there. I simply was soaked up in the realization that they existed, that they somehow got there and most importantly they were there for me… there for me in that moment. And by being fully in the moment, and allowing it to own all of me, I could, on occasion, be swept into its expansiveness. Inside the expansiveness there was also a feeling of oneness. It was more than a sense of being one with the moon and stars in view, but one with the ALL of It, the Whole of It, the Source of It, and the Great Beyond of It. For the truth is, it hardly seems possible to gaze into a starry night and imagine a finite space, a place where it all stops, as if the universe were some enclosure. It is infinite.

And it is alive. All of It… even when you cannot fathom what the "ALL" might include. As a child, it is possible to sense the infinite expanse of it, though you haven't the words to articulate the feeling.

It is a glorious and sacred tenderness that you can carry with you all the way from childhood. I was in the process of learning that One + One is One.

Over time I have continued to learn that the feeling of oneness is beyond words. Trying to put words around it takes you out of the experience. If we get caught up mentally in words, we have left the state of oneness behind and been captured by the mind. The experience of oneness, which is our purest spiritual vibration, our truest frequency channel, and an energy to which we can become attuned, is beyond mind. It is a feeling that originates in the heart, and actually takes you even beyond that to the essence of your core beingness. Sages of old and master teachers tell us there is a place of beingness at the core of every person, plant, planet, animal or living creation. And when people find their way to that kingdom of beingness in them, they sense they are part of and at one with the Whole of It, the All of It. That it's all one living Being… you, others, nature, nations, the earth, the sky, the stars, the cosmos… the infinite and the All of It.

I know, that sounds like some pretty far-out stuff, but there are very deep states of consciousness that some have been able to enter and experience. Varying levels of oneness exist because there are varying levels of awareness that people have attained, opened to, and attempted to tell us about.

What is important is to realize that an amazing kind of life is waiting for us once we take the steps to expand our perspective and gain a more awakened awareness of our oneness.

Diane and I were visiting our grandchildren in the State of Washington on the Fourth of July. Brady, our then five-year-old grandson, had been highly impressed by fireworks the previous year as seen through the windows of their home situated on the side of a hill. He was wound up with enthusiasm as he told us all about what they were like and what to expect. Being on high alert and excited for himself and us, when they began to burst into the sky he pulled us to the window to see. We heard the thunderous booming sounds, but looking out could only see a small spray of color above the neighboring rooftops.

Five-year-old Brady had spoken so emphatically to us prior, about how big, beautiful and amazing these bursts of fire in the sky would be once they began. He had a vivid remembrance of how it had been the previous year. But now, able to view only the top spray of color, he was quiet and pensive.

Suddenly, Brady grabbed the hands of Diane and me, saying, "Come with me." We ran up the stairs to the second floor, up to the large window off the master bedroom. Just as we approached, a magnificent explosion of colors burst into the sky in full view. Now, at the higher level we could see the whole array of color above the neighbor's rooftops. We were all captivated by the impact of its sheer beauty and bright colors. Then, Brady turned to us, threw out his chest, pointed out the window and shouted, "Now THAT'S what I'm talking about!!!" It was an exclamation of confirmation. It was the big "YES!!! That is the reality of what I know!" He had a vision and memory of what was true and what we could expect when the fireworks began. He had to lead us to another level to experience what it was he had been communicating about.

There is a higher level of life and living waiting for us once we take steps to see from a higher perspective and get above the limiting rooftops of our minds. It is where life bursts forth with new power, energy, creativity, beauty and excitement. When we arrive there or get a taste of it, something inside us, our Higher Nature, seems to say, "Now THAT'S what I'm talking about!" "THAT'S how life is to be lived, experienced and expressed!" The "That" contains the vibrations of love and oneness, for One + One is One.

It's been said that life is a dance. I find it to be an effective metaphor. When I was in grade school we were taught ballroom dancing. Sometimes you would find yourself in a class that had more boys than girls. When that happened, a couple of dance pairs were made up of two boys. That tended to cause a problem as to who was going to lead. Both wanted to lead rather than be led.

The point is that an important teaching to learn in this life is that we must make it our desire to have Something Higher and wiser in us, lead. We must want to be led. We aren't trying to wrestle control away. We are all children of the One Spirit and as we spiritually mature we become good followers of the Divine.

But before we can follow, we have to be willing to dance. When I was in high school, Friday nights after a home football or basketball game, they'd often have a dance in the gymnasium. Sometimes they had a live band and sometimes a DJ. Everyone in the high school was invited but not everyone came, of course. And among those who attended, not everyone danced either. There were lots of "wall-flowers." There were different tempos to the songs. Some were slow, but most were fast and of the rock 'n roll variety.

I attended a number of these dances. But I didn't get out on the floor much, if at all, especially during my freshman and sophomore years. I was rather small and short so most of the girls were bigger than I. By my junior and senior years, I'd grown some physically, and also a bit in confidence. I started to dance some and found out it was a lot more fun than sitting. I learned to dance by getting out on the floor and doing it. It wasn't perfect and I wasn't the best, but I did my best. That's life.

Life is a dance. And the music has to be heard and felt from within. We are to learn to release and let go of our grasp of the wall, and get out onto the floor, moving beyond our fears and limitations. There is a spiritual vibration that we must learn to hear and dance to in this life. It is the vibration of love, joy, peace and truth.

There are times in our life when we aren't hearing the music and we aren't willing to be led. There was something the Master Teacher, Jesus, said about this. He said, "To what then will I compare the people of this generation, and what are they like? They are like children sitting in the marketplace and calling to one another, 'We piped to you, and you did not dance;'" (Luke 7:31) I interpret that to mean we brought you a message of life and Truth, as music unto your souls, but you didn't dance to it.

We can have judgments, perceptions, insecurities, beliefs and illusions that have stood in the way of hearing the music or dancing the dance. Sometimes it takes courage to get out on the dance floor of life and be who you are, to match the vibrations of the Something

Higher that lives in us and pipes to us. There is a part of all of us that wants to dance. We all want to love. We all want to laugh. We all want to let go. We all want to forgive. We all want to go for it. And... sometimes we cling.

Author John Izzo wrote about how he went to see his grandmother who was in bed, having recently broken her hip. This was a woman who had endured the Great Depression years, the death of her true love — her husband — the divorces of all three of her daughters, and the death of her parents. John had flown from California to New York to visit her and to inform her that her oldest daughter had taken her life. After telling her, she paused, and in a serious tone said, "John, it takes a great deal of courage to live..."

Later, John wrote, "I have come to realize that it takes a great deal of courage to live one's whole life in the innocence of youth, holding on to our ideals, moving on through the inevitable hardships and disappointments, living one's convictions, to be a person of faith in the world where people become cynical and jaded, to believe that peace is possible when everyone else has given up... all these things take a great deal of courage." (From his book "Second Innocence" P. 46)

Courage is a choice, the choice to go on, to hold to ideals, to affirm life, and to continue to strive to make a difference. There is a way to live our lives that is geared to dancing the dance of life each and every day. What that calls for is a willingness to listen to the music, and dance the dance, to engage with the Presence, to let Spirit lead. It takes courage to stay on the dance floor, to stay open to the movement of the energies of Divine life, to be excited about life.

The late Dr. Norman Vincent Peale and his wife, Ruth, were friends of mine and had come to speak at our church on a couple of occasions. I always loved to hear him speak and to read his writings. He tells the story in "Guideposts" about a woman that he and Ruth met when they were hiking in Switzerland years ago and who made a lasting impression on them. It was on a fairly rugged mountain trail at a high altitude in a German-speaking part of Switzerland. There is a sort of camaraderie among devotees of these trails and the usual greeting was "Gruss Gott," or "Greetings in God's name."

They encountered an elderly lady who was hunched over and walking with the aid of a sturdy cane and a dogged determination. She was accompanied by a man who was thought to be a guide. As they met on the trail, she looked at them with bright eyes from under an old-fashioned hat. Instead of the usual German greeting, she greeted them in French. Dr. Peale and Ruth replied, "Bonjour, madam," which sent this lady into a rapid flurry of French, to which Norman finally said, "No parle Français." So then the lady began to speak Italian, but seeing a confused look started speaking German, and while Norman struggled to converse with what little German he knew, she finally said clearly and without any accent, "You look like an American. Perhaps you can speak English" and laughed. They said, "Yes... we talk English, American style."

She then informed them that she was 89 years old. Norman told her what a wonderful woman she was, speaking four languages fluently, having a mind that was sharp, having to wear no glasses and climbing mountain trails at the age of 89. He asked, 'Just how do you keep going so strongly?" She replied, "Oh, you see, I'm so excited about everything. The world is such a wonderful place. People are so interesting. In fact, I awaken every morning with as much excitement as when I was a young girl." Norman then said, "Well, if you were as excited then as you are now at 89 you must have been a ball of fire when you were young." She said, "But you see, I am still young. Oh yes, this body is a bit warped in the back, but I'm quite strong and healthy. But it is the Spirit that makes the difference. I'm excited because my spirit lives in a perpetual state of excitement."

She moved along up the trail, pushing ahead with her cane. Norman and his wife, Ruth, marveled at her and what is possible when the Spirit is allowed to lead and remains strong. To this lady, life was a dance, and she never stopped hearing the music.

Years ago there was a film made by Public Broadcasting about people who had lived to be 100 or more years old. It was a documentary that tried to answer the question of "why some people make it to 100 while most do not." They did all kinds of research. Was it what they ate? Was it in the beans or in their genes? Their conclusion was that good genes and a healthy lifestyle can get you well into your 80s. But after that there is a subtler prediction for the extra 10 or 20 years and that they said was "perseverance." They described it as a willingness to move on, in spite of disappointment and to re-engage with life, to hear the music again.

In spite of the fact that life is not always easy, and has its difficult moments at any age, we must always learn to dig deep, listen for the music and find the will to go on and dance the dance. One can learn to persevere through life by becoming one with the energies of faith, love, joy and hope. The same God who placed the stars holds you in Its arms. And this same God pipes us the music of the stars and invites us to dance with Its Spirit in the lead. The music of the universe vibrates to the beat of a spiritual principle of One + One is One.

The Presence of God fills the universe and orchestrates a level of support that is both fulfilling and fun to notice and experience. In developing and deepening our relationship and becoming one with this Divine Presence, I've found that you can ask of It most anything in the way of help and guidance and get it. If we come from the place of truly believing this, then there will be signs and signals that come our way. There will be a chance meeting, conversation overheard, song lyrics on the radio and other ways we are being steered. As has been said, "Nothing is an accident."

There are so many ways to experience the love that flows from a universe that wants it known "We are One!" that there is no separation, and that the universal spiritual principle to be lived is "One + One is One."

All through my youth I was crazy with the love of sports. In particular baseball and basketball occupied my time; I played both competitively into my twenties. Apparently, as a result of all the hours and years of running and jumping on pavement and in gymnasiums, those sports took a toll on parts of my knees. I was diagnosed with a need for a knee replacement as a result of chronic pain having set in. I delayed seven years from the time of diagnosis to finally having the surgery. Over the course of those years I had three separate appointments with three different orthopedic doctors. Every time I thought I was ready to do the surgery and met with a surgeon, when they brought out the seemingly huge foreign contraption that was to replace my knee and realized that the procedure was the closest thing to an amputation sown back together, I would crater and delay. Each time I would get a kind of sick feeling in my stomach and leave, telling the doctor I'd get back to him, which I never did. I've met a number of other people who had put off doing the procedure, eventually did it, and were happy they did. Their common comment was they wish they had not waited so long and gotten relief sooner.

In my seventh year of discomfort, when it began to affect my sleep and the pain had worsened, I decided I could wait no longer. I got the names of three recommended surgeons and decided I was going to visit, sort of "interview" each one, and make a decision as to which I was guided to go with. In prayer I asked that I be guided, and receive signs to help me decide which one to choose.

At my appointment with the first doctor, I was sitting in the waiting room with two other patients. One was an eighty-eight year-year old spry, vibrant woman wearing a sweatshirt that said "ASK ME" on the front. She took little time in starting up a conversation. She asked me if this was my first appointment with this doctor. I said it was and that I was in the process of interviewing doctors to decide which one would do my surgery. She proceeded to go on and on about how wonderful this doctor was, about the date he replaced one of her knees and that several years before he'd done the same surgery on her other knee. She was definitely an out-going delightful lady spilling over with a joyful enthusiastic energy that defied her age. Wanting to be all the more convincing, she stood up, danced a bit of a jig right there in the waiting room. She went on to share that she and her daughter had just come back from Italy where they had walked for miles sightseeing. I told her I liked to garden and asked if you are able to kneel down after this kind of surgery. She leaped to her feet, walked over to where I was seated, kneeled down in front of me, placed her hands angelically on my knees and said, "Honey, does this answer your question?" Before getting to her feet, she added, "He is a wonderful surgeon who has helped me stay active and mobile. He is the best!" There was a husband and wife also in the waiting room with us, taking all this in. They were smiling and clearly enjoying the vibrant sell job this dear lady seemed to be putting on.

I could not ignore that this was a sign! Needless to say, without any further searching, I chose this surgeon and have a new knee for which I am grateful. One + One is One. One person, + the guidance of Spirit, is Oneness with your next highest good.

We are one with the Source of all life at all times whether while in this physical dimension with our spirit housed in a body, or in the unseen, non-physical dimension of spirit before birth and after death. You are here in this physical world to learn and grow beyond separation consciousness into a deepening relationship of oneness with your Source and all Its creation. With that comes lessons to be learned through experiences that I believe we may have on some unconscious level agreed to, signed on for, or created for ourselves.

You and I have amazing support from this world of the seen, and from the unseen spiritual dimensions, to assist us through our challenges both large and small. These experiences have the potential for you and those surrounding you to learn the power of love, faith and prayer, all of which can activate and galvanize powerful energies of oneness with the Source. Seeming miracles can occur and do occur at various times to help overcome any challenge amidst seemingly overwhelming odds. You are designed to triumph over tragedy and climb out of crisis.

I was attending several days of meetings in Oregon for an organization of which I was a member of the leadership team. It was late at night when I was awakened in my hotel room by a call from my wife, Diane. She had received word that our youngest daughter, Star, a sophomore attending a Texas university at the time, had been in a serious automobile accident. Diane had limited information but was told Star was being life-flighted to a local hospital nearby.

I got the earliest flight I could, but due to a route of connecting flights, I flew all day and didn't arrive until early evening. All I did during the whole trip was pray. In my prayers I felt I also received a sense that although this was very serious, Star was going to make it. It's just a feeling or message of inner knowing that emerges. So, although very concerned, I somehow had energies of faith and trust quiet whatever thoughts of fear that arose.

Diane had arrived ahead of me and by then had more information to share. Driving in her Honda Civic, our daughter had collided with a Chevy truck. Naturally, she got the worst of it. Her car was totaled and seeing it days later, it appeared as though no one could have survived. She had been life-flighted to the hospital and immediately taken into surgery. The surgeons opened her up to find a host of internal damage, the worst or most serious being that her hepatic artery which connects the liver to the heart had been severed. No one survives this injury, for they bleed to death in a matter of minutes. In this rare case, although severed, the liver had miraculously laid against the heart in a manner so as to keep just enough blood in her to remain alive upon arrival at the hospital. Naturally, they had to immediately give her transfusions of blood. However, the most serious dilemma facing the doctors was how to do the surgery. The connecting tissue between the heart and liver is extremely small and nearly impossible to re-attach. Consequently, the surgeons had no knowledge of how to perform such a procedure and didn't know if any information existed because it was not known if anyone had ever survived this kind of severe injury. They were unaware if anyone had ever attempted to perform this surgery because no one lives from a liver torn from the heart.

They began to quickly research the internet and discovered there were two surgeons in San Francisco who in one rare instance had successfully performed this re-attachment of a liver to the heart, made so difficult by the minimized connective tissue and its location. Miraculously, they were able to contact them at this late hour and via the phone, these two surgeons in California, guided, schooled, and directed the several-hour procedure performed by the two surgeons in a Texas hospital. They also removed her spleen, put a plate in her ankle and several other repairs before placing her in Intensive Care.

She was being monitored closely for there were numerous concerns that they could still lose her from blood clots and other serious factors. We were able to have a short visit with her that evening when we arrived. Her pulse was racing at around 180 beats per minute due to her heart and body still being in shock from the accident and surgery. She was conscious and very frightened. One of the first things she asked us was if she was expected to survive. She had overheard a discussion between two nurses about several of her life-threatening issues due to the seriousness of her surgery. It was clear Star thought there was a good chance she might die before morning. We tried to help her dismiss those concerns. After only a short visit we were asked by the nurses to leave.

My wife and I continued to be concerned with not only our daughter's physical condition but also her emotional state. Upon arriving where we were to stay for the night, I had an overwhelming guidance to return to the hospital and try to see if they would let me back in to talk with her. I dropped Diane off and headed back. It was well after visiting hours. I convinced staff to allow me in to see her. Star was surprised to see me again. I think her first thought was her situation must really be bad. I told her I could not leave her in this frightened state. I did the best I could to shift her fear to faith and the belief that she was going to make it. I said something like, "Star, you were in a serious accident with serious injuries and yet many things have gone right to help you through this. A helicopter arrived in timely fashion to get you to the hospital. Your body kept just enough blood in it to keep you alive. The surgeons found two in California to guide them over the phone through your surgery. I assure you that you've had angels around you from the time of the accident working in your behalf in amazing ways and it is because you are meant to live. You have things you are meant to do and a purpose to serve in this life. God got you through some serious circumstances against amazing odds. You weren't brought through all of that for anything except to live on. So turn your fears to faith. You are going to make it." We said a prayer, I told her I loved her and would see her in the morning. She appeared in a better state when I left.

It was a poignant moment; one in which I felt a deep connection with God and my daughter. As her father I hated to see her there in that condition, yet I recall a strength and inner conviction that she was going to return to wholeness.

Star went on to become a nurse serving in ICU and continues to work at a major hospital in the Med Center of Houston. She and her husband had their first child about a year ago. I know how grateful she is for her life and family. We all are. It was a difficult time for her and all of us who so love her. We recognize the miracles that had to take place for her to go on with her life. Many factors related to circumstance and timing had to come together and were orchestrated, as I believe, by the One, the All, the Source. Again, One + One is One, was proven… making for a happy outcome.

What were the chances of her keeping enough blood in her when others have bled to death in minutes? What are the chances of locating two surgeons thousands of miles away and who were the only ones who had performed this rare procedure successfully? What are the chances of actually contacting them in a timely fashion in the middle of the night so as to guide the surgery via the phone? Looking at the vehicle, one would have wondered what the chances were for anyone to survive. But survive she did and is now happily living her life. Some connection with a Higher Power was made that activated a sequence of events that were miraculous in their timing and creation while necessary to her living on. Some things are a mystery and can't be explained. What we do know is something took over, whether we engaged it through our faith, prayers or love for our daughter. The creative energies of oneness with the One took over. One + One is One rang true once again. One daughter and One Source, made for One happy outcome.

Oneness with God involves the creation of a partnership that runs deep and involves a loyalty on our part. It is to take into every endeavor the feeling that you are being accompanied by the most powerful force for good in the Universe, and that It is assisting you in the fulfillment of your desires which bring good and no harm to anyone.

There is that Bible verse, "We know that all things work together for good for those who love God." (Romans 8:28 NKJV) For me it means that love is oneness, and when we love God we are operating from a consciousness of being in God and God in us. And through this conscious connection the Spirit is leading, guiding and blessing us with the good we seek. It requires an understanding of the creative power of thought linked to feelings of faith, all in relation to what is possible in cooperation with the Divine. It can result in potentially amazing demonstrations and manifestations of good in our lives.

There are many stories of how people have had good things come together for them in seemingly miraculous ways through this partnership. Many have shared just such a story in regard to finding and purchasing their right and perfect home. Allow me to share mine.

Living in a suburb of Houston with a small backyard and neighbors' homes on all sides is a common thing. I had previously lived in Wisconsin on an acre of land. Now I felt closed in. So when we decided to look for a new home, one of the main goals for me was a large lot with a back yard that opened onto a greenbelt. One day we went to visit the offices and showroom of a builder. He had a board map of all the streets in a development where we wanted to live. You could see the size and location of all the lots on the map. Most of them were already sold and had red tacks stuck onto the lot to mean it was sold. Those with a green tack meant it was still for sale. My eyes immediately were drawn to one of the largest lots on the board. It was in a cul de sac and the back yard bordered on a golf course. I told the sales person that it was the one I wanted. He pointed out it had a red tack on it and he tried to steer me to other lots with green tacks. Honestly, something inside me refused to accept that this lot I wanted wasn't available. For whatever reason I felt led to it, red tack or green. Something inside was pushing me past the fact that it was "not available." The two-story track home designated to be built on that lot was exactly the model Diane and I liked. We left the offices and I suggested to my wife we drive to the lot and look it over, just for fun. We discovered that two lots next to each other, the only two with backyards that would border the golf course had not been built on. All other homes on the street were already built and lived in. We walked around on the lot and fell in love with it. It was huge compared to the current backyard we had. It was elevated about six feet above the golf course and looked out across three fairways, one of which was a beautifully designed hole with a body of water surrounding the green. We started visiting the property about once a week in the evenings just to walk around and imagine ourselves there. I can't explain why. Something transcended the part of the mind that would have said, "Give it up, it's sold." We continued to visit the site and I even measured out the dimensions of the house and put rock piles at each corner to visualize how it would sit on the lot. I went back and visited the sales person and said again I wanted to purchase that lot. He of course told me again that another party had money down on it.

A couple months went by and one day Diane was in the grocery store when a lady happened to come up to her and said, "You and your husband are the ones that have been walking that vacant lot a number of times aren't you? I recognize you. I live across the street. The people that have money down on that lot are friends and are going to turn it back in. There is an easement issue being worked out between the developer and the golf course that is delaying the building of that house. Our friends can't wait any longer and are turning it back in so they can build elsewhere." So I went right to the sales person and told him the lot would be turned back in soon and I wanted him to call me so I could be the one to put a deposit down with the rights to build on it. He looked at me like I was delusional. I even made out a check and left it with him.

To his surprise, the lot was turned back in and a few days later it was ours. We ended up waiting two years before the easement issue could be resolved. By that time the price of the home had increased by $30,000 due to improvements the builder made in the home and the prices going up. However, the builder honored the price the home was when we put our deposit down to have that model built on the lot. So, the day we moved in, our home was worth $30,000 more than what we paid.

Diane and I had believed that God was our partner in this whole process. That the One, the All, the Divine, was actively guiding and helping us have the good that we had envisioned and believed was possible. It required the perseverance to stay faithful for two years, never being advised if or when a resolution to the easement issue would finally be resolved. We stayed true to our guidance and realized what became our dream home for thirteen years. Since then we have moved to another dream home which has another amazing story of guidance in it. But one is enough for now. The point is once again that the spiritual principle of One + One is One. You as One spiritual being, + the One Power that stands behind it all, IS what makes you ONE with the good you seek. This is not a new idea. Many have recognized that there are laws and principles at work in our lives if a person learns how to become attuned to and in harmony with them. Amazing things come together in the co-creative process. Life becomes an exciting dance with the Divine.

There is the famous statement about this idea from Henry David Thoreau in his work "Walden", "If one advances confidently in the direction of his dreams, and endeavors to live the life which he had imagined, he will meet with a success unexpected in common hours. He will put things behind, will pass an invisible boundary; new, universal, more liberal laws will begin to establish themselves around and within him; or old laws will be expanded and interpreted in his favor in a more liberal sense, and he will live with license of a higher order of beings."

One might ask how it was that Thoreau arrived at that beautifully articulated communication of the workings of God and universal principles. It was something he had come to witness in his own life, the lives of others, and in the writings of those he had studied. I am convinced it really is possible for us to live the life we have imagined..., to "pass an invisible boundary..." and "to live with the license of a higher order of beings." I have witnessed it many times in the lives of others and tasted it in my own on many occasions. What one has done, another, and potentially all, can do. How about you? Yes, it is true for you too.

All of us live inside the Circle of Life. No one is outside it. It's ALL God. The energies and forces inside that Circle abound. In reality there is no circle because there are no boundaries to Spirit. The One Presence and Power fills all space and time. There is no place where God is not. Therefore, the True Realty Is that you and I are one with the One Life, Intelligence and Power that exists in all the universe. Whether we are aware of it or not, we are all swimming in the energies of God-Life.

Maybe you've seen, as I have, a cartoon picture of a fish inside a fishbowl full of water asking the deep question, "What is water and where is it?" In many ways we are like that fish. You and I exist in what we might describe as God's fishbowl without borders. This borderless fishbowl that we all live and swim in is made up of energy.

The purest form of that energy is love. It's found inside the smallest particles of the atom and in the farthest reaches of the cosmos. Inside this borderless fishbowl, the most important universal spiritual principle you can come to know and live is One + One is One.

Inside that one sacred principle, every other spiritual law lives and branches off from it... starting with love. Think about it, if you are taken internally to the place in consciousness where you know and experience your oneness with another person, or thing... can love be absent? Of course not! Inside the purity of Oneness, love lives... as does forgiveness, peace, joy, kindness, patience, and you can go on and on with every expression of goodness of God. These and all other spiritual qualities and attributes flow naturally from states of oneness. The True Nature of God comes flowing through them.

Any time you establish oneness of consciousness with any of these spiritual attributes of God mentioned above, it equates to oneness. In other words, becoming one with the attribute of forgiveness, or peace, or compassion creates for you the experience of oneness in you and the dispersing of its energies. It becomes more evidence of the Truth that It's All God, and living of the principle that One + One is One.

Hopefully, our analogy of God as a borderless fishbowl of oneness energy, helps you come into the realization for yourself, that anything, and anyone, within it, including all of creation... is one with God the Source. Also realize everything inside the borderless fishbowl of Divine energy... again all of creation... is one with everything else, be it people, plants, animals... everything. Why? Because it's All God. God is the All That Is. That is an expansive thought. It may help you to ponder this for a few moments or days. We may appear to be separate from physical things and each other, but it's only because we believe in and live from our own made-up false realities of one + one being two. It's all the mind's doing. Your heart and spirit know that inside the True Reality of God, we are all one, no matter how many things in the material world appear separate. If you grasp all these ideas... great. If you don't, that's okay. It can take time, and it helps to be with it for a while. To simplify, you are one with the All of God and so is everyone. Everyone and everything inside the great universal expanse is God.

You may ask why it is that there are bad people doing bad things in the world. There are many complex explanations we could delve into. However, a simple answer to consider is that too many fall short of living from these higher spiritual states that reflect the realization of God's Truth and Reality of Oneness. We are all living from varying degrees of separation consciousness. In some ways, our minds have walled us off from the heart of love and the spirit of oneness. Humanity has created its own realities at incrementally lower levels, depending on how true or false, high or low, the spiritual thoughts, ideas, beliefs and overall consciousness. When we look at the various complexities of the physical world, we see evidence of all levels of consciousness being on display, from quite low to very high. You and I are somewhere on that ladder of spiritual consciousness with higher rungs being toward states of oneness and lower rungs being toward states of separation.

The Spirit of God is always present and available. It never sleeps, never retreats, is constant, consistent, unchanging. We are the ones that change, within our consciousness. God is the Light that never goes out. God is the Love that is everlasting. Our experience of the Divine fluctuates because we do. Divine Light comes into our world through love and oneness. Love and Light, which God is, finds its way into expression through our conscious attunement to it. We become energetically like the company we keep. Consequently, entering into a deepening bond with the One, becoming one with the Divine in both mind and heart, puts us into attunement with the energies, frequencies and vibrations of the One Source, which is Light and Love Itself.

As you learn to dance in the consciousness of oneness, get excited about building it into your awareness and partnering with the Divine in all you do. Have the intention to evolve into Its awareness, to be guided by Its inner promptings, and to take time to enter its sanctuary of silence through prayer and meditation. As you do, something wonderful happens inside you and the life you are living. Your life begins to stand for something more than it ever has before. Higher frequencies of life and love will flow through you and you will live with license of a higher order of beings.

CHAPTER THREE
Know Thyself

It is time. It is your time and mine. Yes, it is time for you, me, and more of us on the planet to go deeper and come to know God as an Ocean of Spirit containing all the properties of love and goodness. It is time to realize the truth that you and I live in this Ocean of Spirit and that it lives in us. And yet, it is as though we have gaps or holes in us that still require filling. If we get honest with ourselves, with whatever spiritual maturing and progress we've made, we still feel on some level incomplete, as if there is more – more to discover, more to let go, more to understand, realize, and apply. That is a very good thing to grasp, for life is an upward spiral in consciousness.

I begin this chapter by respectfully inviting you to ask yourself this question: Do I really know myself? Do I really know who and what I am? Surely you have been in and around that kind of question at one time or another. When asking myself the same question, here is my honest answer, "No, I don't really know myself." I say this because getting to really know your True Self is an ongoing process and you and I continue to be in it. It involves soul growth and spiritual awakening of which we have progressed some, yet our journey continues. There is so much more for you and me to awaken to.

All relationships provide the opportunity for learning, loving, and healing, and this includes the one you have with yourself. The Ocean of Spirit that lives in you and me is deep, vast, and expansive. The deep knowing of its life and properties is offered to you and all who sincerely thirst for its living waters. It is important to know that we are not given the "more" until we have applied what we have thus far learned and lived. We can't be taken into the deep until we have mastered the shallows. When the disciples asked Jesus why he spoke to them in parables he answered, "To you it has been given to know the secrets of the kingdom of heaven. For to those who have, more will be given and they will have an abundance…" (Matt. 13:11-12)

In the previous chapter, we focused on our relationship with God. In this chapter we want to focus on our relationship with ourselves and more specifically our Higher Self, God in us. The two may sound different, but are basically much the same and overlap. Perhaps you can relate to a kind of progression, similar to mine, in which through the years you have invested your identity in a number of external things. For example, at times I've thought that who I am is my friends. But they have changed. While some have remained, over time there are those who have come and gone. At times growing up I thought I was my grades on a report card, my athletic ability, or my clothes. In junior high I was my hair, in high school I was who I was dating, then it was my car, and on and on. Can you relate? In a way we are all these things and none of them. And even now, we may notice that we still have our identity invested to a degree in things outside ourselves. However, these things are like ornaments on a Christmas tree. As the seasons come and go the ornaments can change, and they are really not the tree, but a variety of attachments that can be put on and taken off.

Learning to engage and become one with your Higher Sacred Self opens the door to all that your soul has longed for. It is where you begin to throw the switch that turns on the Divine Circuitry of your being, allowing the spiritual energies of love, peace, wisdom, and joy to flow. One of our spiritual assignments is to repair in consciousness any disconnect that has occurred through life's difficult circumstances and painful experiences. It is to build into your consciousness a knowing that goes beyond duality, separation and two-ness, into an awaiting higher reality of the spiritual principle of One + One is One.

Centuries ago in Greece, there was an awareness of a spiritual principle recognized to be so important that the words were inscribed above the Temple doors; "Know Thyself." In this manner, all who entered would be reminded that first and foremost our spiritual growth and awakening hinges on progress made in this regard. To really know yourself is no small undertaking and involves a person's entire life - some would say many lives. The statement "Know Thyself" is not referring to just any ordinary self we have created within our individual consciousness. For it is the "Thy" Self in us, the God part of us. It becomes more than knowing "about" it, but tapping into and magnifying our awareness of an inherent Divine Power that exists in every soul waiting to be awakened. There is so much more to us than meets the eye or even enters our awareness with any consistency. It is the Higher Sacred Self. It is the God seed.

Another important question to ask: "Am I teachable?" That can be a loaded question. It's not asking whether you have the ability to memorize information. It's not asking if you have a strong intellect or can parrot back what a teacher says. The question "Are you teachable" from a spiritual perspective, is a question asking if a person is truly open, pliable, flexible, hungry to learn and progress... or if they are fixed, rigid, unbending, and closed to guidance and insight coming in all ways and from all things. The life of Spirit is all around us at all times communicating to us if we are open and listening.

If you are a lover of nature, as I am, then you may have had experiences in which the energies of nature have lifted you or even communicated to you in some way. I'm one of those people who must surround themselves with nature as much as possible or I go into some kind of withdrawal. Consequently, my backyard is loaded with flowers and tropical plants that bloom most of the year. I have numerous Hibiscus, Plumeria, Bougainvillea, roses, Mandevilla, and a host of other flowers in surrounding beds.

Walking into my backyard becomes for me entering a kind of Temple where every flower seems to shout this universal message to me personally, "Howard, Know Thy Self!" When I slow down long enough to be present, in my heart, listen and truly experience a flower, it's as though it becomes personified and has a message of truth to convey. I have stared into the bloom of a fully opened Hibiscus flower, let it open my heart and on some unknown frequency entered into relationship and a kind of sacred communication. It is as though this beautiful, colorful creation wants to tell me something about myself or reflect a message to me. It seemingly tells me that it's gift of life and beauty emerges from a seed that has broken open to the forces of nature, obsessed with the pursuit of being embraced by the Light, so that the essence of that for which it has been created, may be set free and birthed into glorious, colorful, radiant expression.

Then I may even sense it speaking to me, "So, how about you, Howard? You have the seed of the Divine in you too! The only difference is, I don't have a mind to get in the way and build any resistance to being that which is contained in my seed. My inbred pattern and program is to bloom. Yours is too. But unlike me, through free will your mind is capable of creating patterns and programs that distance you from who you really are. The world in which you live can cause you to lose yourself for a time, to forget the inherent beauty and goodness of your True Self. So, I have a role to play in this world. It is to add beauty and bloom wherever I am planted so as to remind you and all others of the same. That whatever the storms of circumstance, whatever the conditioning of an outer world, your inner work at all times is to KNOW THY SELF. It is to return again and again to the seed of the Divine in you, what has been referred to as 'the image and likeness' in which you were created."

One may ask, can a flower really say all that? Can it exude such wisdom? My answer is yes, and it can and will for you or anyone who opens to it. It can come from the essence of a flower, tree, star or your own essence. Everything is alive and has God-Intelligence in it. It carries a message intended to help us grow and move in the direction of remembering who we are... and having the realization that we are one with all life, that nothing and no one is outside the Circle of Life...that one + one is one... and that in reality the essence of a flower and a person don't add up to two, but are one. So almost every day, in the morning and often again in the evening, I walk into my backyard, engage with the plants and flowers which are like beautiful friends cheering me on with the message to shine some of my inner beauty and goodness into this world in which I've been planted. It is for me an element of support that has positive effects and can lift me up when I let it.

Not everyone has a backyard full of flowers. Maybe you live in an apartment or have limited space. Yet, all one needs is a pot with a plant that ideally has the ability to bloom. Then let it become your friend reminding you daily of your Sacred Self...THY Self, this part you are to know as the Real Self of you. It will help to connect you to higher thought so that when you look into a world of duality, you might know of a reality beyond it where one + one... you and the flower, are not two, but one, reminding you that you are one with the ALL. Like the flower, your true spiritual nature is to bloom. The seed that needs to break open, is that of your heart, where love lives. It is a love for God, yourself, others, all life and takes you into oneness.

To "Know Thy Self" is to learn what you are and what you are not. From that growing awareness, an on-going process unfolds of letting go and releasing all the limiting ideas, beliefs and images of what you have held yourself to be and instead move into a continuing embrace of what you are in truth, your divine design, contained within the spirit of you. It is to know what your true identity is.

In the scriptures we have learned that God is Spirit and God is Love. If we accept that to be true, and I do...and if we also accept that the scriptures tell us we are made in "the image and likeness" of God... then our True Essence and identity as a child of God is that you and I are Spirit and Love. The One True Spirit of God which is love lives within us. We are ONE with the ALL, the Infinite.

We have covered over our True Self or Higher Sacred Self, which is Spirit and Love, with a separate self, sometimes referred to as the ego. The egoic mind argues for separation, sends us into fear, edges God out, and has us identify mainly with externals, rather than our True Self. The ego has us looking outward into the world of form to gain a sense of validation and wholeness.

From the time we are children we are conditioned to depend on our outer senses and the information they provide. What those five senses tell us is not always accurate. My oldest daughter, Dawn, shared a story about something that happened around Halloween with my then 2 ½ year-old granddaughter, Dylan. She loves costumes and had picked out the costume of Super Woman to wear for Halloween night. She was somehow familiar with Super Woman, possibly from animations of super heroes or a TV series that aired around that time. She was all excited and couldn't wait for Halloween night to come. Finally, the time arrived and her mother helped her get into the outfit. When she had it all on... a look of concentration came to her face, she stretched out her arms and gave a jerking motion like she was supposed to fly. After a moment she looked questioningly at her mother, but said nothing. Then, once again, she concentrated even more, looked skyward, poised herself, bent her knees slightly, extended her arms, gave a liftoff kind of jerk… and nothing happened. With a puzzled look, she turned to her mother and said, "No fly, Mama? No fly?"

She had thought that by putting on the costume of "Super Woman" she would be able to fly. Apparently, she had assumed the power was somehow in the garment and that she'd be able to fly once it was on. It was the cutest thing to witness and my daughter did all she could not to laugh and then explained that the costume did not have the power to help her fly. Somehow, somewhere, inside us all, we know we are meant to fly, that our spirit is designed to soar and help us climb to the higher heights of life and living… take us beyond the superficial into the seemingly supernatural, found at higher levels of thinking and being.

If we are to take to flying higher in life, it can only be attained through an inner life that transcends form as one's first "go to" in life. The inner life must eventually take precedence over the outer. As Jesus said, "Seek ye first the kingdom…" And if you recall, he told us it was "within you." Dylan will hopefully learn that it won't be through a change of wardrobe, furniture, location, or roles that she will find freedom and happiness, but through hitching her wagon of consciousness to the Spirit within. We must ask ourselves how many ways we have thought something from the outside world would create an effect on the inside that would propel us to higher states of happiness and fulfillment. In the search we may have pursued or even attached ourselves to persons or things as symbolic garments which may have given us some lift, but proved to be only temporal – and the search continued.

As my granddaughter, Dylan, had to learn, we are not our costumes. We are not the clothes we wear, the car we drive, the house we live in, the roles we play. Our minds would have us believe we are our jobs, career, degrees, that we are a man or woman, a son or daughter, a husband or wife, a father or mother, that we are our appearances… even our religion, nationality or race. These are all roles we play like costumes we wear for a time. Although many of these roles can be important, they are really not "what" we are and do not cause us to fly in higher states of consciousness.

All through life it seems we are attempting to discover "who" we are and "what" we are. Actually, there is a distinction to be made between these two. Surely you will agree that "who" you are being is subject to change daily, hourly or even from moment to moment. We are all likely to be responding and reacting from different levels to what life puts in front of us. Who you are is always subject to change. In addition to whether you are being kind or not, aloof or not, joyous or not, loving or not, "who" you are also has to do with all the various ways you describe yourself from an external perspective - including appearance, personality traits and accomplishments.

"What" you are is a spiritual being along with all its inherent divine qualities. That part of you is changeless, eternal. Whether you identify with this true part of yourself or not, and whether you express the qualities of the Spirit or not, they remain inherently in you. You remain a spiritual being with love as your true nature regardless of how removed and separate you may become from expressing it. This is the True Essence you and I are called to know and take on as our Identity.

You cannot argue with the truth that God created you and put Its Spirit of perfection, wholeness, light and divinity within you. It is the "What" you are that has permanency regardless of where you are in your journey as a soul learning to express it. Whether or not you allow the Light of "What" you are to shine through "who" you are showing up as, the truth remains that "What" you are is the Light of God and the love that lives within it. The soul of you longs to be one with the Light you were created to be.

A 100-watt light bulb is a 100-watt light bulb regardless of how many layers you shade it with and diminish its true capacity of luminosity. Whereas one person can be shining their Light of Spirit by expressing their capacity for contributing love, peace, joy and goodness to humanity, another person can have "who" they are being appear far removed from "What" they are, shading over the "image and likeness" they are designed to be. Our personal history can include negative circumstances, influences, inner and outer suffering, and life limitations that have brought forth one or many elements of anger, frustration, fear, hatred or even violence. Life circumstances can take "who" we are far away from "What" we are. As a result, every soul must find its way back to "What" it is so that the "who" reflects the "what". That is the journey of spiritual awakening.

The parable of the Prodigal Son that Jesus shared reflects this very idea. One son went off on his own into a far country where he became lost, having left the inheritance of the Father. In other words, he left the state of oneness, the inheritance of life lived from the Higher Self in oneness with the Source. He left his true identity and became lost in a separate self of his own making. He left the truth of "What" he was and created a "who" that felt separate, apart, unfulfilled and empty of the energies of connectedness. He then decided to arise and make the journey back home. And there is great inner joy and celebration that comes with this reuniting. As in the parable, we all have a similar journey to make and return home to the Father, and the inner spiritual state of love and oneness. It's "What" we are. And the "What" that we are always reflects the principle of One + One is One.

Through much of life we allow outer conditions and circumstances to define us. I've spent aspects of my life attempting to prove myself worthy of acceptance and love. In our humanness, we tend to identify with the world of form and judge ourselves accordingly. Many have a negative judgment about the form their body takes. Many reject parts or all of themselves as a result of what they may see in the mirror. It can be one's height, weight, shape, facial features or whatever that we can feel dissatisfied or even self-conscious about. It is the work of ego in your mind.

For me, it was my size. I was the short, small, little guy all through the grades, all of high school, until my first year of college when I grew six inches and put on thirty- five pounds. Certainly, others have far more challenging physical limitations to overcome, but I allowed this in many ways to define me. I loved to play sports and one of my favorites was, wouldn't you know, basketball, where height can be a factor. All through the grades I would have my mother measure my height with a pencil mark on the wall in the hallway next to the thermostat in our house. Over a five-year period, there were probably twenty short horizontal pencil lines drawn in a three-inch vertical space. There wasn't much distance between the lines and made for a dirty looking wall in that spot.

I was the smallest kid through my junior high years and desperately wanted to grow. At times I'd cry myself to sleep over it and wondered why God had made me so small. It was my hell. Although I had an eye for and interest in girls, most of them were all taller than I. When I began my freshman year of high school I was four foot, eleven inches tall and weighed eighty-three pounds. I actually remember the precise data on my height and weight through all four years, because I was obsessed with my body size.

Out of fifty or sixty boys trying out for the freshman basketball team in my fairly large school, I miraculously made the team. I could shoot the ball really well and the coaches were banking on me growing. In the yearbook team photo, I appear to be the coach's son in a uniform rather than a member of the team. By appearances, surely no one that small could realistically be on the team. But I was. And I suffered some humiliating experiences along the way.

When we had a scheduled game against another school, after practice the day before, we'd all dash to the doorway of the equipment room where uniforms were being handed out on a first-come basis. It had to do with everyone wanting a uniform that fit or a jersey number they desired. There was really only one uniform on the racks that was anywhere small enough not to be an embarrassing fit for me. I would be in panic mode each day uniforms were handed out worrying whether I'd get the one that fit. Several times someone beat me to it and I had to wear one several sizes too large.

The first time it happened I ended up with trunks so large I could have fit my waist into one of the leg openings. The trunks beveled out, almost looking like a skirt. The tank-top jersey was so large on me that the number on the front and back was not readable. Half of it was not visible because it was tucked inside my trunks and protruding out the legs. That day I was so embarrassed wearing my uniform that I prayed the coach would not put me in the game. But he did. I looked ridiculous and was horrified. After that, whenever I got handed a uniform that was too large, I would pay money to the teammate who had the small uniform. I would pay virtually whatever it took to have him trade with me.

Because I was so small, some of the other players didn't take me seriously. On occasion, some liked to have a few laughs over my size and at my expense. I tried to go along with the horsing around, but at times I was dying inside. One time, after practice, everyone was showering and drying off with their towel. I was doing the same thing when a couple of the guys came over, picked me up and stuffed me inside my locker, naked, and put the lock on it not knowing the combination, of course. They were laughing about it when the varsity coach showed up and scolded them. He told them to get me out. I was inside hearing their conversations. When they finally asked me what the combination of my lock was, with all the emotion, and being in the dark, my mind went dark and blank too. I literally couldn't remember the combination for a minute or two. As a mild panic was setting in, the right, left, right numbers finally came to mind and I communicated them. The locker was opened and with the coach and some of the team present, I came out humiliated, embarrassed and trying to recover my dignity.

It is interesting to note that this occurred about a half-century ago and yet I can still recall the experience vividly and how it felt. There are experiences we go through that can seemingly break us apart and separate us from who we really are. We may hate what happened to us and hate that part of ourselves that contributed to it, in this case my small body size at the time. We may even allow our minds to take us into rejecting not just part, but all of ourselves in total. This becomes the great divide, the separation from "what" you truly are. The mind's assumption is often that you have to compensate for this condition... that you have to become something else or more. In this manner you can lose yourself for a time. You can disconnect from the oneness you are meant to feel with yourself inside... to feel safe and good in your own skin.

I've now shared that one of my issues related to body and physical form was my size. What is your story? The spirit of you is that eternal dimension of yourself beyond form. It is perfect, beautiful and contains the attributes of the One Spirit we call God. This is your True

Identity. When we separate from our True Identify it can lead to all sorts of feelings like anger, jealousy, envy, resentment, or even hate of ourselves. We may project our pain and suffering out toward others and the world. This is mostly all rooted in the fear of not being enough and not being loved. It is the conditioning of our mind that holds the past in place.

The solution lies in doing much as the Prodigal Son did. It is in finding your way back to love, beginning with the fact that you have separated from the love of yourself. You must overrule the mind that holds you in the past and locks you into beliefs that are limiting and untrue. We are not our body, but we have a body. We must return home to identifying with what we are, the spirit of God that dwells within, our True Essence that is our Higher Sacred Self. Love is the energy and spiritual vibration of Oneness. One + One is One is the principle to be lived that will take us there.

Although I graduated from high school at 5'6" tall and 137 pounds, by the end of my first year of college I was six feet tall and approaching 170 pounds. However, it really wasn't a big factor in improving my self-image. Any progress I made away from an inner separation toward an inner oneness was not remedied by an increase in size and weight. It had never been about my physical size. It had been about allowing my mind to go into smallness of thinking. Any progress I've made comes in healing and letting go of the past, getting into the moment, changing the diet of my thought, noticing where I place my identity, and re-engaging with my Higher Sacred Self, the spirit of me that is whole, perfect and beyond form.

The process of growing into states of oneness is not like driving to some destination and taking up residence as if you are done and have arrived and can park yourself. The living from your Higher Self is a life's journey. It is made incrementally, sometimes in very small steps. It can involve a series of strides forward and some backward. I have come to learn that the direction of my focus, and the awareness of what I'm feeling energetically is crucial. I must be checking my spiritual compass, feeling the energies that are pulsating through me. Whenever I feel contracted after something questionable is thought, said, or done, I try to own that feeling, be with it, and realize there is, obviously, a higher and better choice to be made. Next, I ask myself if I have the courage, the strength or whatever it takes to make the correction. When I do, I feel clean, clear and energized inside. The fulfilled, connected, internal feeling tells me I am on some upward trajectory of purposeful living.

My friend, Rick, was sexually abused as a young boy of thirteen by a friend of the family. He said his identity became attached to that event. "Who" he was drifted away from "What" he was as a beautiful child of the Infinite, all because he began to identify himself with the horrific happening that marred his self-image. He went through years of pain and suffering. Looking back, he states it was around this unfortunate circumstance that he remembers separating from himself. The guilt and shame took over as a haunting remembrance that he carried for decades. He said it caused him to stuff his feelings. He tried to run from and escape these buried feelings through alcohol and even drugs for a time. His dominant emotion became one of anger... anger at himself, at the person who did this to him, anger toward life and even God. Then he became numb and stopped feeling at all.

In a conversation with Rick about this experience and the effect it had on his life, he concurs that "who" he was became separated and distant from "What" he was. Inside, he went to a far-away land very distant from any spiritual connection. Rich shared that his mother's belief system didn't help, for she was religiously abusive. She would declare continually, "We have to suffer over and over." "Do you realize how much Jesus suffered for us?" All he recalls hearing was that we must suffer and never heard about the love of God.

Rick had a lot of healing and letting go and forgiveness to do regarding his past. It took time, but he said he discovered that the Spirit in us is resilient. A key to his becoming free of the past and making a comeback to life was learning to no longer stuff his feelings but to get in touch with what he had refused to be with. He sought support in intentionally feeling them through. He did lots of writing and journaling about his feelings. Another key was coming back to his relationship with the Divine which he says was critical to his healing. He found a spiritual path that emphasized a loving God and the belief that God does not punish. He learned that we punish ourselves by holding onto the past in a way that prevents us from living full out in the present. It was only after moving through his buried feelings and discovering spiritual teachings that took him beyond guilt and shame that healing set in. He was introduced to God as a loving Presence and learned to identify with the part of himself, his Higher Self, that is, was, and will forever be loved through oneness to Source. Rick now makes himself available as a speaker on the topic of moving beyond abuse through a journey of healing and love.

Rick had a story. I have a story. You undoubtedly have a story. We all have a story where conditions and circumstances we faced took us to a far-away land. What is your story? I'm sure you have one or more. Most everyone has had to face their own doubts and fears of not being loved or accepted, of being judged and not measuring up. We've all had our mountains to climb or our valleys to climb out of.

It has been said that we are to be in the world but not of it. That is another way of saying to be careful what you identify with in the external world. There is much outwardly that can take you into states of separation. Be in the world but do not tie your identity to it. Instead realize that the inner world is what rules and will keep you whole. In the inner world you will find truth that is lasting and eternal. In the outer world, there is no permanence. Everything is shifting and changing. It is difficult to impossible to maintain states of oneness when all focus is outward toward the physical material realm of form. This is not to suggest you put a negative judgment upon the external world. It is only to emphasize that "what" you are, your true identity, is much more than the temporal world of form, and it is best that you not be attached to the outer as your source.

From the King James Bible Jesus states, "In the world ye shall have tribulation: but be of good cheer; I have overcome the world." (John 16:33) So we live in a world where there is tribulation. The outer world will have its challenges and problems. Jesus was saying that because he had overcome and risen above them, we could too. Therefore, be of good cheer. Because you, too, are a resilient being with the resilience of Spirit sown inside you.

Jesus kept things simple and basic. He really only talked about two emotions, Love and Fear. Numerous times in the scriptures Jesus is quoted as saying, "Fear not…" He knew when we are in fear, we are in separation, and are "in the world." When we are in the energies of love, we are in oneness, and we are overcoming and transcending the world of separation and fear. Love and fear cannot co-exist together. You are either in one or the other. Only your mind can produce fear. Only in the mind can we judge negatively or miscreate. Emotions are a by-product of the mind and its corresponding level of thinking.

Unfortunately, it is true that not only are we all "in the world," but we are also "of the world." I say that because we are all conditioned by the world and its surroundings in which we live. There are many elements and factors. For example, in one culture, when the husband dies, happiness is supposed to die in the wife. It is required that she must not be happy. It is unacceptable for her to show any happiness at any time in any way after the spouse dies. Unhappiness must rule over that wife until she also dies. That is the conditioning of her culture. We all have many ways in which we have been conditioned by life and the world without being fully aware. The challenge is to be aware. The conditioning of one's mind can start when we are very young and becomes planted in the unconscious. From there, we may be at its effect for a long time.

I have a brother who is four years older than I. He was the first-born child in our family, followed by my sister two years later and me two years after that. My mother often said how my brother, being the first-born, had to endure a lot. One reason was the difficult conditions and circumstances we had as a family as my parents struggled economically the first few years of our lives. As a young boy, my brother developed a peculiar habit to offset the feelings of fear that arose in him due to certain challenging circumstances.

The early years of my parents' life were a bit of a struggle to make ends meet. We lived in what was then a small town in Wisconsin. There were five of us living in a three-room flat above a tavern. The entire rest of the second floor consisted of a hallway with single rooms on each side. The rooms were small, containing a single bed for boarders staying there on a nightly, weekly or monthly basis. Sometimes one of the boarders or a patron would become intoxicated downstairs in the tavern and get a room on the second floor to sleep it off. Our family's three-room flat, the only one on the second floor, consisted of a small kitchen, a small living room where my sister slept on a rollaway bed, and a small bedroom where my parents slept. Jammed into their bedroom was a baby crib in which I slept until my sixth birthday, when we moved into a home of our own on the outskirts of town.

Once I was born, that left nowhere for my brother, the oldest of the three, except outside our flat in a room down the hall where he was all alone. We didn't even have our own bathroom and had to share with all other boarders one single full bath, which was also down the hall. So each night my mother would tuck me into bed in my crib, my sister into her rollaway in the living room, and my brother, who was four years older than me, into his bed down the hall before locking him in. It was a dreadful arrangement for any family and one that brought added stress to my mother who felt horrible that one of her children had two locked doors and a hallway separating him from her nightly. The necessity was brought on when I was born and the fact they ran out of space.

There was a long, narrow, noisy, wooden staircase used to get from the first floor tavern to the second floor boarding rooms. It ended very close to my brother's room located near the top of the stairs. Naturally, lots of sounds, including voices, laughter and carrying on made its way to his room from the floor below, often late into the night. At the age of four, all alone in this room, separate from the family, my brother would hear other sounds that frightened him. The effects of excessive alcohol on some of the boarders would at times cause loud sounds as they stumbled up the noisy wooden stairs. Sometimes he'd hear them grunt, cough, or groan while going by his door as they struggled to their own room down the hall. Years later my brother told us that sometimes they would even stagger up against his door as if they were trying to get in. He also shared that one of the most terrifying things was that as a little four-year old boy, he didn't know what snoring was. No one had told him. Consequently, through the paper thin walls he imagined the snoring of a boarder in the next room to be the growling and angry sounds of a wild animal, seemingly there in his own room.

My brother was terribly frightened, not understanding what these noises were. So in order to cope with his fears, he started rolling back and forth, back and forth, over and over again in his bed, attempting to muster up as much sound in the bed springs and blankets to muffle, drown out, and escape the frightening sounds. It was the closest thing to running he knew to do with those energies of fear going through him. He would roll until exhausted, and finally fall asleep.

When my parents had saved enough money to move into a new home, my brother was ten and I was six. We shared a bedroom and each had a twin bed. Many nights I would be awakened to the sound of my brother rolling and rolling unconsciously in his sleep. He was still rolling at age 21 when he left to get his own apartment. Although much less often, he has been known to still occasionally roll in his sleep into his forties, fifties and sixties. I know this because when we were on a fishing trip together in recent years, I heard him rolling. He doesn't realize he does it, of course. It doesn't even wake him up. Perhaps it is provoked by a dream with something unpleasant in its content. Whatever triggers it, he still has this unconscious reflex blended into his sleeping pattern to offset what began as a young boy's run from fear.

What is it that has us rolling in fear in our lives? What was it that we came up with that was either unnatural or unhealthy, but used it to counter or run from our fears? Individuals, family members, employees, CEOs, even leaders of nations, have all to some extent, learned to roll or run from buried fears, having been conditioned by them along life's path. Consciously or unconsciously, they do things, decide things, and think things that are foreign to their soul's imprint of love and goodness because of being at the effect of some conditioning of the world.

It takes courage, boldness, and self-honesty to stop rolling in fear, become still, and embrace the energies of love and oneness. Many have risen above these various kinds of unfortunate programming and counter tendencies to again reclaim their True Self and a happier, freer life. The past is gone. It's over and done. We are to put in motion new patterns to roll toward the good, to move beyond fear that blocks the energies of life that can create anew. Fear focuses on what we don't want when we could be channeling those same energies on what we do want and creating happy, fulfilling experiences. I've found that in many instances, it's as simple as realizing where I've been focusing my attention and being determined to put it on what is good and desirable.

It is surprising how deeply and unconsciously we all can be conditioned to ways of life and living that put us at the effect of our past. We are becoming conditioned to what is most familiar from the time of our birth and particularly through what we are exposed to in our childhood. Even books and fairy tales read to you when you were young can contribute. One's school, teachers, parents, TV, computer games, family, religion, culture, friends you grew up with... all these and more condition us unconsciously.

While I was growing up my mother was at times stressed about having the dinner meal ready to sit down at exactly 5 pm each weekday when my father came home. My father made it very clear he wanted to eat immediately after he arrived home, which was about 5:15 pm and was not happy if it wasn't ready. That was the way it had been at his house while he was growing up. So we kids always knew we needed to be at the house and ready to eat at that time. It was conditioned into us.

When I got married, guess what? I expected the same thing. Why? Did I need to eat immediately upon arriving home from work? No. I had been conditioned by my family life to think that was the way it was supposed to be. I began married life with that expectation. It didn't last for long. My dear wife, Diane, helped me give that up rather quickly. We all have many thoughts, ideas, beliefs, ideologies, biases, prejudices, and limitations conditioned into us. It can be the prison of our own making that takes away our sense of freedom and imposes on others. Actually, just by noticing what our conditioning may be can help us to release its power and control over us.

Most everyone has fears buried in them that they have spent years running from. And the unfortunate part is that unlike my brother's rolling in the night, most of our fears, conscious or unconscious, affect our daily lives. And equally unfortunate is the fact fear is an energy of separation that denies us any experience of love and oneness. Our fears have been conditioned into us... and the good news is they can be conditioned out. A fear is an energy born of some thought that produces a body vibration or feeling of separation. Fear is at the root of feelings of anger, guilt, insecurity and a host of others that pull us out of alignment and separates us from the energies of love, peace, joy, and oneness.

Awareness is key. Becoming a watchdog of your thoughts, especially when you notice these separating feelings, and tracking down the originating thought that has ruled you and taken your power and happiness away, is the inner work we are called to do. Just noticing what thought or stories you've been telling yourself is often helpful enough. Don't condemn the thought or yourself for it being there. Just notice it and the existing inner desire to grow, evolve, and be free can dissolve it and take you beyond it.

Another aid is to realize that when you are in fear, or its offshoots, those unpleasant feelings are telling you that you are in the clutches of your mind and not your heart. It is helpful if you can stop, take a moment to consciously go to your heart, and ask it what it wants to tell you about whatever has taken you into separation. If you allow the heart to rule, you will be taken back to the energies of love, oneness and wisdom.

There is a somewhat familiar Native American story about two young braves who were still learning what it takes to become a chief, a Medicine man, or one who is respected in the tribe. One was named Willie White Feather, and the other was Johnny White Eagle.

A conflict developed between them, so Johnny decided to seek advice about this problem from his wise grandfather. He went inside the grandfather's teepee and stated that he was very angry and needed help. The grandfather asked him to explain what he was dealing with and how he could help. So, Johnny gets red in the face with anger as he tells the elder about a situation that arose between him and Willie. Johnny says, "Willie makes me so angry that I want to hit him. But I know it would just get me into trouble."

The grandfather listens and says, "I hear and see that you are angry and I understand because I can get angry too. Sometimes I feel as though I have two wolves inside of me. One is nice and light and the other is dark and bad. The light wolf inspires me with Love, peace and joy... while the dark wolf creates anger, sadness, and hatred. And sometimes these two wolves battle it out in my heart. They fight each other to decide which one will determine how I will be and feel." Johnny then asks, "Grandfather, which wolf wins the battle?" The grandfather looks into the eyes of the young brave, points his finger to his heart and says, "The wolf I choose to feed." What is it that you feed, give energy to, and keep alive that sustains the darkness, robs you of joy and locks on to a negative from the past?

I've found that in many instances, it is as simple as realizing where you've been focusing your attention and being determined to redirect it onto what is good and desirable. It is to become one in heart-thought and heart-feeling with all that is good and connected to the One, the All, the Source of all good. In that way you identify with your Higher Self and enter into the principle of One + One is One.

Happiness, which is what we all seek, has to do with inner freedom. It is to become freer and freer of our fears. Stop and consider what it would be like to be free of all your fears. In the human experience, it is not realistic. Fear is a human emotion and is going to come up in us from time to time especially when we adventure into the unknown or something new. So in this life you are going to have the discomfort of fear as one of the human emotions. However, the key is learning to step back, notice it, feel it through, and choose to see it only as a thought of the mind and not to identify with it. You are not the fear; it is only an emotion brought on by a thought of the mind. It need not take control over you. There is that in you, the Higher Self, and as you identify with that part of you, it will change the energy. It will transcend this separate self that appears in various situations and wants to be given life in you.

One common fear is to be in resistance to what is. When referring to "what is" we mean whatever is there as a feeling, an emotion, an internal discomfort. It can also be an external condition, circumstance or situation that we may be facing that takes us into fear and other emotional discomforts. It is the "what is" inside that has often been suppressed and pushed down. Much of our fear of life is the fear of emotions that don't feel very good and we want to run from.

Realize that most all resistance comes from the mind. The mind keeps us in the past or future, and out of the moment. That is the way the ego or separate self operates. It is only our mind. The mind is a tool. Either we use the tool in wise, expansive, constructive ways or the tool uses us and chokes off life. There is the Eternal Essence and Spirit of us that is able to witness and observe our mind and thoughts. All fear, resistance, and conflict originates in the mind and is felt in the body.

As has already been shared, it can be helpful to understand that the mind does not have the capacity to experience or feel. For example, when you read a statement like "God loves me," that is a spiritual truth. But your mind alone cannot experience this truth. Only your heart, where spirit lives, can. When you are isolated only in your head or mind, you cannot feel. The mind is not capable of feeling. And love remains just a concept. Mind may intrude and dominate with thoughts from your past conditioning, rebuffing "God loves me" with, "You're not worthy... You're not good enough... What about your past?"

So when you transcend the head or mind, and access your heart, your Spirit, your Essence, there is another flow of higher-vibration energy possible. This connection can be felt when you allow yourself to experience the truth, "God loves me." It actually helps to mentally locate your heart, and connect the two, mind and heart, so as to shift the frequency into that of love. Jesus said, "You shall know the truth and the truth shall make you free." (John 8:32 KJV) But it has to be more than a concept of the mind. Freedom comes when a truth is felt in the heart. So it requires that you begin to learn to think more and more with your heart.

Our feelings are like gurus. They communicate whether what is being passed on from the mind is truth or error. If it is spiritual truth, it is energetically felt as a plus in the body. If it is error, it is a minus feeling or diminishes and blocks the life energy. Every problem has a spiritual solution. Every challenge that imprisons you in some kind of fear or negativity, has a spiritual truth you can turn to that will set you free. If we can inwardly turn to love, faith, forgiveness, or any of the spiritual attributes and truths that are attuned to oneness with God, a shift will take place in our energies. It opens us up to higher frequencies of inspiration by which ideas, solutions, answers, and guidance can emerge.

When you are feeling worried, afraid, lonely, hurt, unloved, angry, or anything that is inharmonious, notice the unpleasant feeling that is being activated in you. Then name it. Tell yourself, "I'm feeling sad right now." "I notice that I'm feeling afraid... angry... resentful" or whatever. Own it. Don't allow your mind to go into blame, or project it onto someone, or get lost in a story of victimhood. Be in the feeling. Experience it. Don't judge yourself or make yourself wrong for having the feeling. We all have positive and negative feelings as part of life. See every negative feeling as arriving to the surface of your awareness for you to learn something about yourself. Ask yourself what the dominant thought might be that is transmitting this feeling. Ask yourself what you can do about it. Is there a higher choice to be made, or a healthier, more freeing perspective to take? Is there something constructive you can do internally or externally that might lead to internal peace and harmony?

Keep asking yourself appropriate questions. In what kind of separation am I? Is it a feeling of being separate from God, from myself, separate from another, separate from some desired good, such as a raise, a person, promotion, prosperity, or healing? Having captured, arrested, and given the particular feeling the third degree, a next very helpful series of questions might include; "What would the Spirit of Oneness have me do? What would the Source of love and oneness have me do with this feeling or in this situation? What spiritual truth would move me into a higher frequency? What alternative thought, idea, belief, perspective or action would my heart, my inner spirit of love and oneness, guide me to?"

All feelings must be felt all the way through. That means you should not suppress, repress, or run from your feelings or project them onto others through blame. That will only cause you greater pain and suffering. We must learn to face the "what is" of life, whether it's a circumstance or an emotion. It is much better to own our feelings, take responsibility for them and learn to neutralize them. The way we can do that is by becoming aware of the feeling, letting it be felt, staying with it, letting it run its course, and letting that energy out to create the space for that of a higher frequency to replace it.

A very good parenting skill is learning to teach your children a healthy way to deal with their frustrations and negative feelings. For example, I was visiting my oldest daughter, Dawn, and their two children in the state of Washington. Brady, who was five years old at the time, had his little sister, Dylan, age three, do something that upset him. She accidentally pushed over something he was building and erecting. He got upset and began to yell and cry in frustration. I watched my daughter calmly go over to him, and without condemning him for his reaction, sat down and said, "Okay, calm down and let's talk. What are you feeling?" She was asking him to check inside and define what emotion he was feeling. If he didn't respond she offered, "Are you feeling angry?" He would say yes. Then she would talk it through with him and validate those feelings, help him own them, stay with them, and let these feelings be noticed as if he were an observer of them. I was quite impressed. Where did she learn that? Rather than shouting at the kids "Stop that!" or giving a message that it is wrong to have feelings, she helped Brady become aware of his feelings as a "what is" that was being experienced in that moment. He was learning to notice "this is anger I'm feeling… or sadness… or whatever." That way he learns to own it, feel it, dissolve it and let it go. When we are taught to bury our feelings, we eventually become numb. It is valuable to realize, all feelings fully felt lead to the feelings of love.

As you've probably noticed, feelings come and go. You eventually realize that you are not your feelings. They are temporal. The Real You that has permanency is witnessing them. In that way they can become your "gurus," in that you trace the feeling to a thought that either reflects truth or error. When it's an error, you get to choose again — higher. We all have an Inner Being. And there seems to be two aspects to our Inner Being. The first is the Authentic You, your awareness, you as witness and observer of life and yourself. The other aspect is that which you are noticing, witnessing or are observing going on in you. The truth of who and what you are is beyond thought and beyond the body. You are more than your mind, although it is a powerful tool. And you are more than your body, although it is the physical garment that you wear and use as a vehicle for a time. You are so much more.

We have already said that we are spiritual beings and that the Spirit of God lives within us. Another name for this Divine dimension within us is the "I AM." In scripture we are told that the name for God is "I AM." We read in the book of Genesis that upon being told by God that he was to lead the people out of bondage in Egypt, Moses asked God, "Who shall I tell the people has sent me?" God said to tell them "I AM" has sent you. So we are to understand it would not be Moses leading the people, it would be the "I AM" of God in Moses that would be doing it. The "I AM" is the Higher Self in us all, and is where the universal principle of One + One equals One is lived.

If we jump forward to the New Testament and Jesus Christ, we find many statements using "I AM". Scholars have told us that "Jesus" was the name of the man, the human part of this great Teacher. "Christ" was not Jesus' last name, but stood for God in Him. Actually, "Christ" and "I AM" are synonymous for the Divinity of God in Jesus. When Jesus used "I AM" in his numerous statements, he was referring not to his human self, but the God in him that dwells in us all. When he said, "I AM the way, and the truth, and the life…" John 14:6, he was saying the God in you, like the God in him, like the God in Moses, like the Spirit of God in us all, is what leads us to the High Way, to the Truth, and to the Life that is meant to be lived. In every person, there is only one living "I AM" from which they derive their existence. No one else can say "I AM" for you.

This concept exists in other religious paths and philosophies. The Hindu Vedas or scriptures call this "I AM" Brahman. Buddhists call it the Buddha Nature within. Jewish Kabbalists call it Einsoph. Many who follow the teachings of Jesus call it the Christ Within. They are all referring to this Divine nature in us all. This "Christ", this "I AM", this true Divine Essence, is eternal and has always existed, even long before Jesus came to earth.

Jesus himself stated in the Gospel of John 8:58, "Very truly, I tell you before Abraham was, I AM!" He is saying that the existence of the eternal Christ dimension predated Abraham. That is why it is called "I AM" in present tense, as opposed to "I WAS" or "I WILL BE." The "I

AM" is the Presence of God, present and available to you now as Spirit's true nature of love and oneness. It is the very core of our own existence. Through all the levels of our spiritual evolution... through all the varying states of consciousness... whether spiritually awake or asleep... we are still "I AM." It is that of us which remains changeless, formless and eternal.

As pointed out in Chapter One, even the Apostle Paul captured this understanding when he stated quite clearly and emphatically in Romans 8:16-17, "...it is that very Spirit bearing witness with our spirit, that we are the children of God... heirs of God, and joint heirs with Christ..." The truth that we are all to awaken to is that although it appears we are all separate, individual beings, housed in our own bodies... all of us have our existence in the same "I AM," the same God, this same Spirit. Whether we are spiritually asleep or awake... whether we are in ego-separation or spiritual love... whether we are experiencing happiness or sorrow... on the grand scale of Truth, we are each part of the Whole of Spirit. We are all part of the ocean of God. Each is a part that contains the sum of the Whole. One + One is One.

This also means we are one with all who have gone before us and have passed on. Death is just another of the illusions we have bought into because we are conditioned to the appearances of a three-dimensional material world. Earlier in this book, we pointed out Jesus' statement, "In my Father's house are many dwelling places." (John 14:2 NRSV) In the King James Bible it uses the words "many mansions". The RSV uses the word "rooms." In all cases it suggests there are other realms and rooms beyond the one only our physical eyes can see. A spirit or soul never dies. It only travels into the next room of God's great house of life.

I've heard the saying, "Out of sight, out of mind" and felt it was true for some applications but not for others. When a loved one passes out of sight and is no longer physically with us, it does not mean they are gone from mind and heart. Out of sight is not out of existence. Relationships never end, they just change form. My mother and father have passed on into the next room of God's great house and into the unseen dimension, but there are times when I may think of one of them or feel their presence. Can I really say with certainty they weren't with me in that moment? A chorus of spiritual masters and enlightened teachers have through the centuries conveyed the same message to us about death. They affirm that we are not our physical body. We are a Spirit and Soul housed in a body. The body is temporal, while the Spirit is eternal. The body is the vehicle or garment the spirit wears for a time.

Biblically, the Apostle Paul called the body "the temple of the living God." Every temple eventually crumbles, but the spirit goes on living. The masses have had a growing acceptance of this idea that the physical body is discarded through death, as evidenced by the significant increasing percentage of people who have chosen cremation rather than burial. Either is fine, of course, and we must respect each other's beliefs. However, in talking with staffs of funeral homes, I've been told that the increase in cremation over the past several decades is staggering. Either it has become the most economical choice or people have come to accept that it's not sacrilegious to cremate, for they understand the spirit leaves the body and never dies.

Cremation is an interesting topic for children to understand. I was in a waiting room of a hospital while a friend and member of my church was in surgery. There were several of this lady's women friends waiting with me and whom I'd never met before. It was a long wait and various topics were covered by this group of three, who knew each other well. I just politely listened.

Somehow, one of them started telling about a conversation she had in her home with a visiting friend while her five-year-old granddaughter was present and listening. They were chatting about a mutual friend who had passed on, had been cremated and had her ashes spread in the mountains of Colorado. They shared where they'd like to have their ashes spread, if they were making a choice. The five-year old girl didn't understand and asked what cremation was. So grandma said, "Well, honey, when a person dies, they can choose to be cremated, which is to have their body burned into ashes rather than put into a grave site. Their spirit lives on. Sometimes people who choose cremation ask to have their ashes spread over a place that they truly loved to go to and be at."

The little girl's immediate response was, "Well then, when I die, I want my ashes to be spread all over 'Toys R Us!'" We all burst into laughter. It was a nice break in our serious time there in the waiting room. And it was interesting to me, this being a true story, that the child was not the least bit turned off by the thought of a body being burned to ashes. Her love of toys was what she wanted to be one with.

Although there is a greater acceptance that life is a continuum, and there are numerous books on near-death experiences to support it, longevity remains a common desire.

We all recall the cigar-smoking comedian, George Burns. In his book, "How To Live To Be 100 or More," there is a chapter titled, "Stay Away From Funerals, Especially Yours." Of course, George is no longer with us, and he had also stated, "If you look in the obituary column in the morning and your name isn't there, go ahead and have breakfast."

I find that people typically understand there is no death of the soul or spirit, that it is a transition to the next realm, whatever the specifics of a person's religious beliefs. For the most part, people believe the loved one is fine and in a better place. But it doesn't mean that they don't deal with a sense of loss. I've watched some people make the adjustment with such ease and grace, while others struggle to let go. We must accept change, and the fact that people experience physical death. But I believe we must learn to accept that our connection to that soul need not be lost while we seemingly remain apart. The Spirit of us is the spiritual Essence of "What" we are and the eternal Self from which the law of oneness is known.

A friend and colleague of mine shared his personal experience around his father's passing. Phil was close to his father, who at age 95 became ill. One day his father said he was ready to go and they discussed together their mutual conviction about life being an ongoing, eternal process. So Phil asked his father if after having left the physical plane, he would somehow let him know that he was all right. His father said that if there was a way, he would do that.

The day came when Phil was informed his father had passed and he immediately called his brother on his land-line phone to break the news. They only got a couple sentences in and the line went dead. So Phil called back and reconnected. After another few moments the line went dead again. Nothing like this had ever happened to Phil before and he suddenly had come over him a sense that this was not an accident. They were cut off one more time before he was able to conclude the message to his brother. Phil said he got an overwhelming feeling that it was his father's way of sending him a message that he was alive and well in spirit.

Phil then called his sister and again the telephone went dead a couple of times. Now he was even more convinced. A couple of years passed and Phil happened to be in conversation with a friend on a topic which caused a significant memory to return. In previous years, Phil had a weekly hour-long TV show in California that had authors and interesting people that he and his wife, also a minister, would interview. Phil was telling his friend about the time he had the famous Buckminster Fuller there for an interview. Phil's father, who was still alive at the time, happened to be visiting that day for the TV shoot, as he occasionally would do. Prior to the shoot, off-camera, with his father standing there, Phil asked Dr. Fuller, a very spiritually insightful man, "What do you think about death?" His immediate reply was "Well, it is no different than if you were talking to your father on the phone," pointing to Phil's father, "and you were suddenly cut off. You wouldn't think he was dead just because the instrument called a phone wasn't working, would you?!" He was implying that you wouldn't think he was actually dead just because the instrument of his physical body was no longer working.

So as Phil is telling this story to his friend, he suddenly realized that his father had chosen this means of communicating with him based on that shared incident and conversation with Dr. Fuller, which Phil only then had brought to memory. Phil said a renewed wave of joy and peace came over him in that moment as he now felt even more certain it had been his father in communication to relate he was just fine. When my friend, Phil. shared this story with me, I was struck with the heightened comprehension that there really is nothing that can separate us. The true reality is that we are all contained in the One, in the grand Circle or House of Life... and that One + One truly is One. Numerous stories abound in which people have shared incidents and events that convinced them a message was being conveyed to them from beyond the veil. It might have been through a dream or the timing in which a beautiful rainbow appeared, a butterfly made itself known, or a stranger momentarily presenced themselves as if to serve as some angelic messenger.

Cindy was in her twenties when I hired her for the church staff. Over almost three decades she has served in a number of positions, all of them well. She is a vibrant, loving, lively, bubbly kind of person that people are uplifted by simply being in her presence. Serving as Director of Volunteers, people are drawn to her and love serving with her. Cindy was extremely close to her mother, who was also an angel of a lady. Her mom was her life, best friend, and someone she always spent much time with. When her mother reached her 90s and her health began to waiver, Cindy's comment was, "I don't even want to think about her ever passing. I don't know what I'd do. She means everything to me."

When her mother passed on at the age of 94, Cindy and her family were bonded together with love and support in dealing with the loss. Cindy, who has a big heart, understandably cried her share of tears upon learning of her mother's death, again at the memorial service, and in between. In time, she began to focus on how grateful she was for the times they had together and was adjusting quite well.

Two weeks after the funeral, after working at our two Sunday worship services, she got into her car to go home. Ordinarily, the next thing she would do was go to visit and spend time with her mother. She was seized by the realization that her mother was no longer there to visit. A powerful wave of emotion suddenly swept over her. Alone in her auto, she wept and wept. After a time, she was able to gather herself, start the engine, and head toward home. She drove several blocks and came to a stop when the light turned red at a fairly busy intersection. Out of nowhere a very elderly African American man, appearing to be a homeless person, came and stood immediately in front of her vehicle. He just looked at her and smiled a toothless smile.

It was a bit unsettling to Cindy because she didn't know why he was just standing there and wondered what would happen when the light changed.

After several moments he maneuvered around to the window on the driver's side and tapped on the window. He then signaled for her to put her window down. Reluctantly, she drew it down half way. Then the man, with a heartfelt smile, looked deep into her eyes, raised his forefinger to his mouth and with the same gesture as one signaling for quiet as if not to wake a baby, expressed a "SSHHHHH." Next, he reached in and gently took her hand, softly kissed it, and just as gently released. He then stepped back, never having said a word the whole time.

Immediately, Cindy had an overwhelming sense that her mother had everything to do with this unique experience. Only minutes prior, Cindy had been sobbing over the loss of her mom. And through this man, her mother's loving nature came through, along with a message that seemed to say she was to quiet those sad emotions, for she continues to remain enfolded in her mother's love. All this was done and clearly communicated with heartfelt eyes and a kiss of her hand, while not a word was spoken. It didn't need to be. Cindy got the message. She was so moved by this experience that she immediately called me on her cell phone to share what had just happened. She was happy, touched, grateful, and comforted by it all.

Signs and signals can come to us in unexpected ways and times. If we are open, and can go to our heart, we are usually able to understand their intent, meaning and message. Surely you will agree that there exists a whole domain of occurrences beyond the limits of what we currently are prepared to fully comprehend. They need not be feared, because they tend to be activated by love and foster a feeling that connects us to an unseen world or dimension that carries compassion and goodness in it.

If you believe yourself to be one with the God of All That Is, then you must also come to understand this means you are one with All That Is in this world and the next, this realm and all others, the seen and the unseen, that which is known, familiar and understood by man and what currently is not. One + One is One is a Universal law and principle that exists everywhere in all space and time. Therefore, it makes us one with all life and all souls that have ever lived, wherever they are as eternal beings.

There are a variety of levels at which one can engage different aspects of all that exists to be experienced. There is at all times a life going on beyond the borders of what our physical eyes can see. Life is not static, but always dynamic, changing, flowing, progressing, in an unseen current of energy that is connected to the eternal stream of life. Let me tell you about just one of a number of events that have contributed to this perspective.

There was a seasoned minister who became a friend and mentor when I was starting out in ministry. His skills as a powerful speaker and teacher were known to many of my colleagues. He was very successful and had an inspiring impact on not only those in his congregation, but to many of his colleagues like myself. His name was Jack Boland. He was devoted to the communication of spiritual truth and sought to live from that Higher Self, the I AM in him.

There came a time when Jack became ill; he was dying of cancer. When he reached the stage of being put in hospice, close friends of his and mine stayed at his side. They later shared with me that Jack had asked that there be no medication administered. He wanted to fully experience his transition process. At times he went in and out of consciousness. They said it seemed at times he was very close to passing, but lingered on for a number of days for some unexplainable reason. When conscious, he would talk to friends at his bedside and share about other-worldly things he was experiencing as he went in and out.

Finally, on March 4th, he made his transition. For most people the significance around the date of one's passing doesn't take on much if any meaning. But in this case it did. All who really knew Jack well recognized immediately that he was delivering another and final teaching lesson to all he knew and loved. His parting message was in two words, "March Forth!" It was the day his soul chose to leave the body.

Some things just are not a coincidence. Jack seemed to be saying he was marching forward as a soul and at the same time telling each of us we were to do the same. In part, I interpreted his message to mean we are all here in this life to learn and grow, to expand in love and wake up to the reality of The One. We are to let duality die along with all sense of separation while marching forth toward a greater consciousness of oneness. I salute my friend, Jack, who continues to live on.

In the ancient writings of the Bhagavad Gita it states, "Beyond the power of the sword and fire, beyond the power of waters and winds, the Spirit is everlasting, omnipresent, never-changing, never-moving, ever One. Invisible is He to mortal eyes, beyond thought and beyond change. Know He is, and cease from sorrow."

Earlier in this chapter I made the statement that we have a mind, but we are not our mind, and this remains the truth. However, never underestimate the power of the mind. As already stated, we must learn to use it or it will use us. If we are not masters of our own minds, then it becomes master over us and can take away our happiness and freedom.

Perspective is a generator of outcome. Ideally we want to be consciously connected in mind and heart to the Whole, the One, the All, whose nature of good is to be living from the universal principle that says One + One is One. Separation consciousness, which is the problem every soul must rise above and beyond, is the inhibitor of the energies of wholeness, goodness and love.

The perspective we carry about ourselves, a situation, a set of circumstances, a challenge, a change, or a day in our lives is of paramount importance in the kind of experience we are creating for ourselves. Sight is not just something conducted by our physical eyes delivering to our brain information about what is out there in our world. True or spiritual sight is of another level and depth that goes beyond the existing linear data. "Insight" is the development of a capacity to deliver to the mind a perspective that transcends what exists in the three-dimensional world. Insight is born of a deeper kind of engagement with circumstances from which one can learn, and where a kind of sorting-out process is done regarding what to focus on and what to look beyond.

Instead of seeing limitation, one learns to depend on a kind of "insight" that sees a greater reality than what the outer eyes can reveal. Insight sees beyond the limits. Insight takes one's focus off the existing problem or condition long enough to see beyond it. It is not ignoring what is there or hiding one's head in the sand, but shifting the creative energies. Insight sees a preferred outcome, and into a field of greater possibilities that exist and can be created. It is very much like Einstein's statement that "the solution to a problem cannot be found at the level in which it was created." It is seeing your way past it.

A few years ago, I had the pleasure of experiencing a day of golf with the famous author and speaker, Deepak Chopra. He was in town to speak at our ministry and had arrived early enough to have the outing. I had invited my friend Rudy Tomjanovich, former NBA star and coach of the Houston Rockets, and a friend of his to join us. Deepak and I were in one golf cart during the round, and Rudy and his friend were in the other. Rudy and his friend are avid golfers, and quite good at the game. Deepak and I, on the other hand, although very much enjoying the opportunity to play, do so rather infrequently due to time demands. Nevertheless, I was quite surprised at Deepak's level of play, being as good as it was considering how seldom he plays. As for me, I will admit, I dearly wanted to play well enough to hold my own, especially with my cart mate, Deepak.

I remember well an experience we had on one of the holes that day. It was a par 4 that had a body of water directly in front of the green. We all had respectable drives off the tee into the fairway that gave us each a next shot that required clearing this body of water. There was little room for error because the water came right up to where the front of the green began.

Golf is an interesting game, in that it often mirrors life. In life, there are times we find ourselves on a clear path to reaching our goal. We are focused, everything is clicking, we're making progress, having success, are in the flow with seemingly no problems. It is like getting all pars and birdies on a golf course. Then there are times when we can seemingly lose our swing groove and find ourselves going from one hazard to another, from the sand trap to the woods to the water. In our lives we can lose focus too, become negative, fearful, perceive the worst, and draw it to us. We lose the flow or the groove of thought in which good can come to us. Focus and perspective are definitely factors that come into play as you maneuver your way through the course of life.

Golf is a game. And in many ways we could say life is a game. When we play it well, we experience health, wealth and quality relationships. While we are learning the game of life and developing skills, we may not score all that well in any one of those areas. In the game of golf, the goal is to hit and steer your ball in the areas where harmony reigns and the path called a Fairway is friendliest. But there are hazards all around. It's fine to see where the hazards are, but better when you commit your focus to executing the shot where you want to go and where you want to end up – rather than where you do not.

In the game of life, the hazards can be difficult people, difficult decisions, attitude, self-image, self-confidence, addictions, negative thinking, procrastination, perfection, fear, unforgiveness, and more. One cannot expect to do well at the game of golf without learning the rules, developing the fundamentals and practicing the intended skills. A person will play the game of golf poorly if he or she is not willing to learn the game and apply the principles.

Part of the game of life is to realize what is causing you to keep ending up in the hazards and to practice the laws and principles of consciousness that can get you back in the fairway of happiness and fulfillment. One cannot expect to find the fairway with the same old swing, just as one cannot expect to find a better life with the same old thoughts, attitudes and beliefs that have been causing pain, suffering and unhappiness.

So, all of us were in the fairway on this hole. Rudy went first and hit into the water. His friend went next and did the same. I was determined not to create a splash with my shot. As I set up to hit the shot, the water was what dominated my mind instead of the green on which I was trying to land the ball. I swung the club and you guessed it, I was the third of the group to hit into the water. Honestly, although we played this hole poorly, we played much better on a number of other holes.

Deepak was the last to take on the challenge of having the success that none of us were able to pull off. Deepak stood over his ball, swung the club he had chosen, connected solidly with his ball, and then watched as it cleared the water and landed softly on the green. It was a pretty shot. We all congratulated him as we walked back to our carts, wondering why we hadn't done the same. When Deepak and I were getting into our cart I said, "Nice shot. You were the only one of us four not to hit into the water." He looked at me, and appearing to be dead serious, said in that wonderful East Indian accent of his, "What water?"

He was saying in his own way that he never acknowledged there was any water there. He gave no power to the hazard. He used a kind of insight, a disciplined way of seeing that comes from within and demands a special kind of focus. In Deepak's mind, there was only the green where he wanted to land his ball and he was one with it. For him the green was the All. Here we have another example of the principle that One + One is One.

One of the well-known quotes from Ralph Waldo Emerson is, "What lies behind us and what lies before us are tiny matters compared to what lies within us." What lies within us is Divinity. Although God is the All, it is helpful for us to think of the Infinite, the Divine in two important ways. One is to embrace the idea of God as a Presence that surrounds us and lives and enfolds us. The other is to think of God as a Self, a Higher Self, that is the Essence of both who and what we are.

You and I are a three-fold being. We are Spirit, Soul and body.

Spirit is the perfect, immortal, divine aspect of you. It is the highest that is in you. It is your True Self, your reality as an eternal being.

Soul is a sort of measurement of where you are in consciousness. You grow your soul, evolve your soul. Soul distinguishes how near or far you have come in mind and heart in relation to the Way, Truth and Life of Spirit. It is a measurement of how much you have been feeding the light or dark wolf inside. It is how far you have come in living from your Divine Self, Higher Self, beyond the ego's ways. You are here in this life to grow and evolve your soul into the consciousness of love and oneness. There are enlightened souls and unenlightened souls. There are what we might call mature and immature souls. There are souls that are consciously connected to Source and others living from disconnect and various degrees of separation. Your soul is on a journey in consciousness, evolving from Adam consciousness toward Christ consciousness and the living of your Higher Christ Self, which you have come into life to be.

The body is the garment of the eternal you. The body houses the Spirit and Soul. The body is the instrument of the soul, in that it is always giving us feedback as to whether we are in the flow of love and oneness or its opposite. It tells us where we have directed our minds. This feedback comes through the feelings and emotions felt in the body that thought creates. These feelings are either freeing and life-giving because they are aligned with truth, or they are depleting, contracting and uncomfortable because they come from thoughts of a separate self we have created. Where you are in your soul progress is determined by how much you have incorporated into your consciousness of either separation or oneness. So, you ARE Spirit. You HAVE a body. You EVOLVE your soul.

And the question becomes, do you identify with yourself more as a body or more as the Spirit of the Infinite? In life we do not see things as they are, we see things as we are. We see through the eyes of our existing level of consciousness. Our Higher Self sees life from a higher place. It carries within it the Light of truth. Scripture calls this Higher Self, "the true Light that lighteth every man (person) coming into the world." (John 1:9) Jesus referred to it in numerous ways and paraphrasing, said, wise is the person who builds his house, (consciousness) on this rock or foundation of Spirit and Truth. He was saying that spiritual truth is rock solid as a foundation on which to build one's life.

The idea of the Divinity of man can be a difficult one for many to accept. One reason is that people know all too well their limitations, shortcomings, weaknesses, failures, and character defects. And when they don't know these things for themselves, they often know them for their neighbors and people around them. Just because much of humanity isn't expressing its divinity, doesn't mean that it isn't there. One can take a handful of flower seeds and place them in a jar and leave them there for years and years. The truth of those seeds is that they are flowers, even while they remain seeds. It is true that much of humanity continues to fall short of fully expressing who and what they are in reality, but that does not keep any one of us from knowing who and what we are in Truth. In fact, it is of utmost importance in our soul's growth.

We began this chapter by stating the need for more of us to realize "I am in the ocean and the ocean is in me." It was in much the same manner that Jesus stated, "I am in my Father and my Father is in me." So what we want to begin to recognize is that, at all times, God, the Infinite, is in you and me. You and I can say as Jesus said, "my Father is in me." But not always can we say, "I am in my Father." Sometimes you and I are into separation consciousness and the small self.

Men are not created great, but created with the capacity to become great. You were not born as a Christ expressing, but your soul was born with the capacity to become Christ-like. The Master Teacher, Jesus, taught a number of things that were designed to lift our image, and help us to identify with a level of awareness beyond the level we are at. He sought to take humanity higher. He said, "If I be lifted up, I will draw all men unto me." He said of himself, "I am the light of the world." Then added, "You are the light of the world. Let your light shine." He said we were the salt of the earth. He quoted from the scriptures of his day stating, "Is it not written in your law, I said, Ye are gods?" (John 10:34 KJV) We find this same message in the 82nd Psalm which reads, "I say you are gods, sons of the most high, all of you."

The ancient Hebrew King, David, also stated in Psalms 8:4-6, "What is man that thou art mindful of him and the son of man that thou dost care for him? Yet thou hast made him little less than God, and dost crown him with glory and honor. Thou has given him dominion over the works of thy hands; Thou has put all things under his feet..." David is talking about you and me, my friend.

The Apostle Paul said, "For all who are led by the Spirit of God are children of God." (Romans 8:14 NRSV) The King James Bible states "are the sons of God." You and I are both children and sons of God, but to experience that level we must become devoted to being "led by the Spirit." Paul also stated, "The creation waits with eager longing for the revealing of the sons of God." (Romans 8:19) Will you be one of those who has made their life a revealing of "What" they truly are and were created to be? It becomes revealed through living the spiritual principle of One + One is One.

Charles Fillmore, co-founder of Unity, has an interesting comment on this matter of God, Christ, and man. He said this, "We cannot separate Jesus Christ from God or tell where man leaves off and God begins in him. To say that we are men as Jesus was a man is not exactly true, because He had dropped that personal consciousness by which we separate ourselves from our true God Self...He became consciously one with the absolute principle of Being. He proved in His resurrection and ascension that He had no consciousness separate from that of Being, therefore He was this Being in all intent and purpose. Yet He attained no more than what is expected of every one of us."

Let us review Jesus' prayer found in the gospel of John, chapter 17:22-23. "The glory that you have given me I have given them, so that they may be one, as we are one. I in them and you in me, that they may become completely one..." If we take this to heart, there is no way for you not to be an offspring of God, but you can forget. You are, have always been, and will always be divine and part of the Divine whole. In your moments of challenge, forget not "What" you are. There is one big reason to do anything in this life, and that is as a statement to the universe that who you are has merged with "What" you are, a light in the world. There is one big reason to undo something, and that is because who you are has fallen short of "What" you are or want to be.

A key factor in the power of prayer has to do with where and with what we identify. There is that question of identity again. The old idea of prayer is one of pleading to God for help, often identifying oneself as a poor miserable sinner. But back of that part of you that has been masquerading as a separate self, is the reality of a Higher Self. Prayer is the identification with God and good. It is to unite in awareness with the one Source which is Infinite, and to which all things are possible. Prayer calls for oneness. It is to know as Jesus affirmed, "I and the Father are one." (John 10:30)

It is stated that the ancient word for prayer in Sanskrit was "palal," which means "judging one's self to be wondrously made." So, when you pray, ask yourself not who but "What" you think you are. In fact, in every experience of life it can be good to ask the question, "What part of me am I identifying with?" The Truth is you are goodness, love, compassion, understanding, peace, joy, patience, forgiveness, strength, courage, a healer, helper, and teacher. You are the child of the Most High God and it is time you come from that which is "Most High" within you.

The principle of oneness is vital to the demonstration of prosperity in one's life. Prosperity goes beyond financial well-being — it also includes health, happiness, loving relationships, friendships, satisfying work and peace of mind. There is a universal creative principle that says, "As within, so without." It is also stated as "the law of cause and effect," "thoughts held in mind produce after their kind" and "what gets your attention gets you." All of these fall under the category of the Law of Mind Action.

The principle of One + One is One, from the prosperity perspective, means that to be One with the One Source is to be One with the idea of abundance. We live in God's universe. The universe is unlimited. The demonstration of prosperity requires that we become open to and one with the very idea of unlimitedness. Our thoughts have creative power and carry a vibrational match to either lack or plenty at virtually all times. It is through a conscious awareness of Oneness with the Source of all good that we become co-creators of the all good. It is true that God can only do for us what He/She/It can do through us. If we want to demonstrate prosperity, we must establish a vibrational match to prosperity. The Divine cannot co-create in and through us when dominated by limitation. We must open to the idea that all things good are possible for God.

We are vibrational beings in which every thought vibrates with creative energy. We attract into our lives that which matches the frequency of what we have sent out. As you give, so shall you receive. So it is important for us to hold in mind a space for which good things can happen and to let that be our focus. Realize we can co-create the good we seek through a relationship of oneness with the Source of all good. We either open ourselves to or close ourselves off from the flow of good that is there for everyone.

Thought and belief have organizing power to act on the quantum fields of invisible "thought stuff." Deepak Chopra in his writings refers to this invisible thought stuff as an "invisible, seamless matrix." Here is what Deepak concludes: "Behind the visible garment of the universe, beyond the mirage of molecules... the illusion of physicality, lies an inherently invisible, seamless matrix made up of nothingness. This invisible nothingness silently orchestrates, instructs, guides, governs, and compels nature to express itself with infinite creativity, infinite abundance, and unfaltering exactitude into a myriad of designs and patterns and forms. Life experiences are the continuum in this seamless matrix of nothingness, in this continuum of body and environment. They are our experiences of joy and sorrow, of success and failure, of wealth and poverty. All these events seemingly happen to us, but at very primordial levels we are making them happen."

Amazing things have happened for individuals who have persistently held a vision and poured their faith into making a possibility become a reality. In his book "The Law And the Promise", author Neville Goddard shares a true story about a lady who demonstrated the creative power of mind working with the Divine to bring about the fulfillment of a desire. From the time she was a young child she had dreamed of visiting far-away places. The West Indies was specifically the place she dreamed of traveling to. She held it as a kind of fantasy, which was carried into adulthood. One year she had to have some surgery done in the hospital and while there spent some of her time reading. She read some ideas about the power of imagination, envisioning your desires and the need to accompany imagination with complete faith that it would become reality. So while recuperating from the surgery, she decided she would spend time intensely imagining with full faith the dream she had been carrying. She secured some cruise-line brochures and pored over them for hours on end, picking out the ship, the stateroom and the seven ports she most wanted to see. She would close her eyes and in her mind walk aboard the ship, feel the movement, hear the sounds of ocean waves. She imagined feeling the warmth of the tropical sun on her face along with the smell and taste of salt in the air.

Confined to a hospital bed for a week, she continued to experience over and over in her mind being on that ship. She was released from the hospital and threw the brochures away. Two months later, she received word she had won a contest she had entered in her neighborhood supermarket. She had won first prize, a Caribbean cruise on the exact same cruise line she had focused on while she was in the hospital. She was given the same stateroom she had imagined being in, on the same ship, which would be stopping at all seven ports she had wanted to visit. Seemingly miraculous things like this actually do happen for those who have faith in the One Source while creating a vibrational match through imagination and believing in the possibility.

A friend of mine named Bob shared a fascinating story with me. It took place some years ago when Oakland was playing in the World Series. He was watching one of the games on his TV in Houston. He said it was a Wednesday night and he decided then and there he was going to attend the World Series game to be played the next night in Oakland. It was somewhat like a challenge to himself that he could co-create this experience with his Source, God. He called a couple friends to go with him but they couldn't get free. He didn't have a ticket and had never been to Oakland or its baseball stadium. Yet he decided to go anyway. He flew out to California on Thursday afternoon. He got a rental car and checked into a hotel. At about 3:30 pm he left the hotel to go to the stadium for the game which was to start two hours later. He said a prayer before leaving his room. He asked that he be able to attend the game with ease, find a ticket to the game also with ease and at a reasonable price as the scalpers were asking for large amounts, and finally that the Dodgers would win. A tall order it was.

On the way in his rented car, he met up with horrible traffic. At some point he realized he was in the wrong lane for the proper exit. He slowed down and motioned for a lady to let him slide his vehicle into her lane in front of her. She let him in. It was bumper to bumper and very slow-moving. Looking in the rear view mirror, he noticed there were two others in the car with this lady. They had Oakland baseball caps on and were obviously going to the game. He thought that they might have an extra ticket. So when the traffic was at a standstill, he put his vehicle in park, got out and had a quick conversation with them. He asked the lady if by chance she had an extra ticket. She said "yes" that she had two! She sold the ticket to him for its face-value price. He got back in his car and followed the lady to the stadium, as she knew the way. When he got to his seat, he knew the guy seated next to him had somehow gotten the other ticket from this same lady. So Bob's first words to the fellow were, "How did you get your ticket? The guy said, "Faith!" This man then shared his story of how he got to the game needing a ticket and somehow met this nice lady who gave him the ticket, totally FREE! Bob was still grateful how well his prayers had been answered and he enjoyed the game with the also fortunate fan next to him. And oh yeah, the Dodgers won the game – and the World Series.

It is really okay to put spiritual principles to the test, to explore what works, to get an internal as well as an outer reading on our relationship to life, spiritual principles and ourselves.

The mind is very powerful and part of our growth in consciousness is to bring it under the direction of that which is the Higher Self where intuition and a deeper knowing originates. Without this connection, the mind on its own can run away with us. Whatever idea you accept with your mind, you accept with your body.

Many years ago I read a story that I have never forgotten. A man was working for the railroad and was cleaning a freezer car in which things were shipped that had to remain cold or frozen. Near the end of the day somebody went along hurriedly and unconsciously slamming doors shut and locked this man in. He tried to get out but there was no way. The walls were so thick that the sound of his voice could not be heard. He was in fear that he would freeze before anyone found him in the morning. He took out a pencil and began to write on the wooden floor of this railroad freezer car. He wrote, "I'm getting chilly now." Then he wrote, "I'm very cold now." A sentence or two later, he wrote, "Feeling numb due to coldness." Eventually the writing stopped. In the morning, he was found, taken to the hospital and pronounced dead. He showed all the symptoms of freezing to death. It puzzled everyone because that particular railroad freezer car had not been functioning properly, but this man had not known it. The coldest it got that night inside the car was 42 degrees. What your mind accepts, your body does also. It could be said that when the mind goes to health and wholeness, the body follows.

It was Hippocrates who explained he would rather know what sort of person has a disease than what sort of disease a person has. It is well known that there is a mind-body connection and that a disturbance of the mind, a conflict in the mind, if extreme and unresolved, can bring conflict and disturbance in the condition of the body. This is why it is helpful to identify with that part of us that is Spirit – that part that is whole and perfect. Unite mind and heart with your Higher Self. The Master lives in the Self that is higher than any other of the selves we have created. In understanding the Higher Self it becomes important to first realize that you have one, and that beyond all self-imposed limitations you are one. Michelangelo, the famous artist, said that the way he created the magnificent statue, David, was by chipping away all that was not David.

A respected well known author and spiritual teacher from Germany, Rudolph Steiner, stated in his writings; "For every human being bears within himself, beside what we call the work-a-day man, a higher man. And each individual can only himself awaken this higher being within him. As long as this higher being is not awakened, the higher faculties slumbering in every human being, and leading to supersensible knowledge, will remain concealed... (but) to all who persevere, the day will come when spiritual light will envelop them, and a new world will be revealed to an organ of sight of whose existence, within them, they were hitherto unaware."

We are all to persevere in the process of becoming unified in consciousness with our Higher Sacred Self, the Divinity or Christ within us. This is a process that is helped through meditation, and remembering to identify with this part of you that is of God. It is also a matter of self-awareness and self-honesty by which we are able to chip away all that we see that is not true to our spiritual character. Without judgment, we let go of a surface sort of self-image and go deeper to align with our inner truth.

Emmet Fox, a great metaphysical writer and speaker, tells about an old legend that he says was quite strongly believed in the artists' colony in Paris. Many years ago a struggling artist was so poor that he didn't even have enough money to buy a piece of canvas to paint a possible masterpiece. Walking along one day he happened to see an old, crude painting, selling third-hand for just a few pennies, including the frame. It was supposed to represent Napoleon III in full-dress uniform. This artist decided he could clean off the existing picture and use the canvas for a work of his own.

He went home, removed Napoleon III, which was an unsightly painting. As he did so, to his astonishment he found there was another painting underneath. The last artist had not taken the trouble to remove the original and had simply worked over it. When Napoleon was cleared away, he was amazed to discover what looked like a very fine work of the famous artist Corot. Experts pronounced it to be precisely that and his days of poverty were over. Whether a true story or fable, it is a perfect illustration of the masterpiece you are. Underneath all the thoughts, ideas and beliefs that we have held of ourselves is the master work of the Great Creator. Beneath the surface we must go to find the Divine image, the work of God that we are. We have tended to sell ourselves short. Many times we know more about what we think we cannot do than what is actually possible. Often times we convince ourselves of limitations that hide our true capabilities.

A good friend of mine told me about a time, some years back, when he was still a single man, and went out to a dinner show with some friends. Following the dinner, the show involved a hypnotist who came out and put on a demonstration. He and his friends knew this would be part of the evening. One of the fellows in the group was an extremely shy introvert and very frightened of being in front of large groups of people. The others conspired and decided that when it came time for volunteers to go up and be hypnotized, they would all volunteer their shy friend. When the hypnotist asked for a subject, they made sure their friend was chosen and helped almost drag him to the front. The hypnotist asked the fellow to say a few words about his favorite subject. He was so nervous he just mumbled a couple sentences under his breath. So the hypnotist asked a few questions he could answer with "yes" or "no."

This hypnotist was very skilled and put the shy fellow into a relaxed hypnotic state, then made suggestions to him that he was a calm, confident person who had a right to share his good with the world. Eventually he told the man to go to the microphone and make a brief speech to the audience on something he felt strongly about. This fellow got up and delivered a beautifully thought out, well-articulated and well-presented message. The audience was impressed and his buddies in the audience were amazed. The hypnotist then stated to the audience, "I DID NOT hypnotize this man. I de-hypnotized him. He has great ability and potential within him and he has become hypnotized by his own fears and limited beliefs. He has always had the ability to do this, but he has hypnotized himself into believing that he couldn't." The question becomes, could it be that you have been doing the same to yourself? In what ways have you hypnotized yourself into limitations?

One of the old Greek philosophers, Xeno, said, "The most necessary part of learning is to unlearn our errors." There is an unmistakable shift in a person's energies when they learn to live from their true identity, their inner divinity, the I AM, their Higher Sacred Self. This is where love lives in us, and is the light Jesus said we were to let shine. It requires us to rise above ways in which the world may condition us to its limitations and fears. We are not our mind and we are not our bodies. Yes, we have a mind and have a body, but we are spirit. We have within us the spirit of the living, loving God. Let us learn to step back and observe what is coming into our minds and determine what is truth and what is error. The ego mind and its ways of fear and limitation only build a bigger false self to separate us from ourselves, others and our good. Learn to identify with the Higher Self that you are, the Sacred Self, the Real You that you are held to be in the mind and heart of God. It is where love, peace, and joy lives in you. It is the true teacher within. It will guide and direct you. It will remind you of your truth and your True Identity. It will align you with the inherent qualities that resonate with the character and likeness of the Infinite. It is God in you.

106

The words of Paul are helpful here, "And because you are children, God has sent the Spirit of his Son into our hearts, crying, 'Abba! Father!' So you are no longer a slave, but a child, and if a child then also an heir, through God." (Galatians 4:6-7) The Divine dwells in us and has made Its home in us. Paul called it the Christ in you. It is the glory of God in us that waits with eager longing. It appears that even the great writer, William Wordsworth, was referring to it when he wrote:

"The soul that rises with us, our life's star,
Hath had elsewhere its setting, and cometh from afar,
Not in entire forgetfulness,
And not in utter nakedness,
But trailing clouds of glory, do we come
From God, who is our home."

All of us are "trailing clouds of glory," for we all have this Higher Sacred Self, which is the image in which we have all been created. We can ask ourselves, is the sky only the part that is blue or does it include the clouds, or both? Is the sun only its core at the center, or also the rays that beam their way to earth, or both? Is the ocean only that which is the body of water as a whole, or is it also the many drops that splash upon the shore, or both? There is a place within you that knows the clouds are part of the makeup of the sky, that you cannot separate sun beams from the sun, nor can you consider a drop of ocean water separate from the whole ocean. They are one.

How, then, can we fail to realize that like the sunbeam and the drop of ocean, we are part of the Whole? A person walks to the ocean shore with a bucket, scoops up some water and carries it home. Can we now say the water in the bucket is no longer of the ocean? Or, are we caught in an illusion that is blind to its original home and true makeup? You and I live in an ocean of life and love. And it lives in us. Like the fish searching for water, we often fail to realize its Presence is all around and in us.

Know in your heart that this Presence is with you and within you at all times. Your awareness of it grows and it takes on life, energy and power to the extent that you sincerely acknowledge it is there, ready, and able to guide, empower and love you into your next highest good. For the truth remains, One + One is One.

CHAPTER FOUR
From Me To We

So far, we've said the universal spiritual principle of One + One is One plugs us into the power, energies and consciousness of heart-centered love. As you continue to grow in this awareness that you are a part of everyone and everything, and it is all a part of you, it softens you into the realization that there is a relationship of oneness within humanity to be upheld and from which you can live. As you come to realize that it's all God, that no one and nothing is outside the Circle of God-Life, then you begin to expand into a deepened understanding that we all really are one in God. Humanity really is all one family. In the grand scheme of things, the truth is we really are all brothers and sisters.

Jesus' teachings made it clear that most importantly we are to love God, which in essence means we are to have an all-out love for Love Itself, which God is. Then Jesus said, that like unto it, is the love of our neighbor as our self. Why? Because within the principle of One + One is One, our neighbor, IS our self. Inside this principle one's life is no longer just about "me", but becomes a "We." "We" are in this life together. "We" are one. "We" are spiritual beings. "We" are eternal souls. "We" are bound together by love in the web of life. Only the illusion of separation seen through the five senses says otherwise. "You and me" equates to "We," which is family. As I help you I am helping me, because in truth we are not separate. Of course, we are establishing that our "neighbor" includes all of humanity. At a deep level we all know this to be true.

A few years ago at the Seattle Special Olympics, nine contestants, all of whom had some physical or mental disability, were assembled at the starting line for the 100-yard dash. The starting gun sounded and all were off with the desire to run the race, finish, and possibly win. There was one boy who lost his footing, stumbled on the asphalt, and tumbling over several times, began to cry. The other eight in the race heard the boy cry. Amazingly, they all slowed down and looked back.

Then, equally amazing and heart-warming, they all turned around and went back, every single one of them. One of the runners in the race, a girl with Down Syndrome, bent down and kissed him and said, "This will make it better." Then, something happened that brought tears to many eyes. All nine of them linked arms and walked across the finish line together. Everyone in the stadium stood and cheered. It went on for several minutes. For many days after, those who attended told others the story of what they had witnessed, for the power of that scene stayed with them.

Why was this such a powerful event for those who were there? It has to do with the principle of "one + one is one." Deep inside, we know that what matters most in life is more than winning for ourselves alone. What matters most is winning together because on some level we know we are truly one. We know that united in a collective oneness, the win is always bigger and more fulfilling. As a person grows and evolves in consciousness, there is a broadening of his or her field of reference. One starts with the mentality of survival and a person's reference field may not go beyond home and work. There is a sense of being tied to one's immediate family, close friends, the clan, the brotherhood, the tribe. All others can seemingly fall outside the circle of feeling connected. But we are meant to evolve into the bigger picture of an all-inclusive oneness within the family of humanity.

Oneness is to be revered as your most important spiritual value. From it, all other spiritual attributes emerge. All love, faith, forgiveness, understanding, peace, patience, kindness, joy, and goodness of all kinds is the product of living from the awakened awareness that you are one with the One, the All That Is. Our manifestation of prosperity, health, wholeness, and fulfilling relationships is the result of a co-creative process that reflects a consciousness of oneness to the Source. It is to live, move and have your being in oneness.

We know Jesus was one of many spiritual masters and teachers that sought to bring oneness to the forefront of our awareness. When he stated, "The Father and I are one" (John 10:30 NRSV) he didn't mean this state of being one was for him alone, an unattainable reality for all others. He was a model of that state of consciousness so we

110

could learn to make it our reality as well. His prayer was that we know and experience this same oneness with the Divine that he knew. Jesus taught us to pray what has come to be known as "The Lord's Prayer" which begins with the two words "Our Father..." indicating the connection that exists between you, me and humanity as "our" Father, and not the Father of Christians alone — or any other exclusive body of people. There is one Father of all as the One True Source we all share and draw upon.

Jesus said, "I am with you always..." (Matt. 28:20), solidifying an eternal relationship of oneness with the Christ. He also stated, "...all that is mine is yours." (Luke 15:31), which implies all that he had attained in spiritual consciousness was there for us as well to step into and become one with.

In this book and this chapter in particular, I place emphasis on the truth that humanity is a family and that we are all brothers and sisters. I'm certainly not the first to convey this concept, but perhaps you've wondered from where this idea comes or is supported. Again, it was Jesus who made a definitive statement that indicates its validity. When he was addressing the issue of "who is my mother and who are my brethren", to paraphrase He pointed to those who were with him and declared that whoever does the will of my Father is my brother, sister and mother. (Matt. 12:48-50)

So, there you have it. It couldn't be more clear that with Jesus' arms extended out in reference to all of us, He is at the same time offering encouragement that we all follow the Father's Will to live as beings of universal love and oneness, thereby demonstrating the divine ideal that in reality we are one family. Understanding that the spiritual principle of One + One is One and building it into our awareness opens the way to a deeper knowing that in truth anyone and everyone is our mother, brother, and sister. We did not have to come from the same womb, or household, or community, or race, or culture, or nation, to qualify spiritually as family.

We know there are those people in the world who are easy to love and those who make it hard. I can admit to that along with you. However, Jesus conveys that we are to offer energies of love even when the mind finds a rationale to justify a shut-down. I defer to the

King James Bible for its thoroughness on this point. It is here that Jesus said, "But I say unto you, Love your enemies, bless them that curse you, do good to them that hate you, and pray for them which despitefully use you, and persecute you." (Matt 5:44 KJV) Wow! That is a big ask... a big stretch for the individual to make. Why does Jesus make this important? Because One + One is One and everything we do is meant to take us toward expanding oneness, not strengthening polarities, division and distancing. He is essentially saying that everything that comes at us calls for a reaction and that the level at which you respond is to be of a much higher quality of energy. We don't always know what internal charges other people are experiencing, the result of having been imbedded from their past. But what we do know is that to match their energies, if negative, and give back the same, in no way helps the world move forward, nor does it help us or another move out of a painful past. It holds it all in place.

It can help to think of the workings of our bodies as a parallel to what is being called for in our world. Your body is a creation of God. It is a masterpiece and in some obvious ways reflects universal truths. Every human body is said to be made up of approximately 50 trillion single cells. In this analogy, it helps to think of cells as miniature humans. We are in truth a cooperative community of around 50 trillion citizen cells.

Biologists tell us that each nucleus-containing cell possesses the equivalent of our nervous, digestive and respiratory system... our excretory, endocrine, and circulatory systems, our muscular and skeletal systems, as well as an immune system. So each cell is an intelligent being that contains all systems necessary to survive on its own. In fact, scientists have proven this to be true, having removed individual cells from the body and grown them in a culture. We are also told that single cells are capable of learning and able to create cellular memories they pass on to their offspring. As we walk and talk and live our lives it is all because of a highly organized, cooperative society of millions, billions, and trillions of cells within us. Our body is a microcosm of the world in which we live.

Science is now beginning to support what spiritual masters have been saying for centuries, that the earth, its humans, and other species are all one living organism. Our bodies are an example of one interconnected, cooperative community of cells. As souls, we are to grasp the truth that spiritually we are all interconnected expressions of One Intelligent Life.

The same principles that equate to health in the body equate to a healthy, peaceful world. It is by consciously being in the flow of the One Divine Intelligence of oneness, which results in a cooperative inner harmony in both body and the world.

The Apostle Paul speaks to this very idea when he states, "For in the one Spirit we were all baptized into one body - Jews or Greeks, slaves or free - and we were all made to drink of one Spirit. Indeed, the body does not consist of one member but of many. If the foot would say, 'Because I am not a hand, I do not belong to the body,' that would not make it any less a part of the body." (1 Cor. 12:13-15) He was saying that we are not to say of anyone who looks different, thinks different, or worships different, I have no need of you, you do not belong to the body because the spiritual truth is that we are all members of the one body of God.

It was the great poet Rumi who said, "In things spiritual there is no partition, no number, no individuals. How sweet is the oneness – unearth the treasure of unity." When the energies of oneness and love begin to grow in us, we also begin to change. These ideals have been around a long time. However, they have to become conscious in us, reflected upon, integrated and embraced as truth, overriding the ego mind that has conditioned us into ways of separation, exclusivity and division. Most people have learned a kind of love that is "conditional." It's the kind of love that requires it be earned on the basis of how well others treat us. It's a love that has to be won and is often easily lost. What was said to be love today can be gone tomorrow because certain conditions are no longer being met. This conditional love reflects the very human side of our nature.

However, as we evolve spiritually and align more with our True Self we come into the realization we are love regardless of the conditions and who or what we are confronted with by life. Our love then becomes unconditional. As stated earlier, it is causeless, meaning our heart remains open and centered in love and does not require some condition outside ourselves be met as a necessity to cause it. You embrace the idea that love is what you are and your purpose for being. In our minds we can become conditioned to leave love behind, withdrawing it in various ways for a variety of reasons. We can blame others and the world for our unhappiness. We can create in mind a story to support our remaining in resentment, anger, or unforgiveness and even feel justified. Misery is maintained when giving our power over to a negative past.

You and I are meant to go the other way; to learn to love no matter what. The seeds of love are there inside you. God's seeds of love are in you waiting to bloom. I recall reading about a place somewhere in Texas that went without rain for seven years. There were deep cracks in the ground. The soil appeared ruined; people were convinced nothing would ever grow there again. Then one day the skies opened up with five inches of rain in a twenty-four-hour period followed by a return of the sun. Before long, bluebonnets and other native flowers began to rise up, cover the area, and burst open with beautiful blossoms. No one had just planted these flowers. The seeds had been there through the seven years of drought, waiting to be given expression and the opportunity to bloom.

Sometimes it can seem as though you and I live in our own little world, seemingly with our own self-made seasons, climate and weather, controlled by our moods, attitudes, thought patterns, and belief systems. Sometimes we can go into our own period of drought. Some area or phase of our life dries up and seems to become lifeless or loveless. Yet, it would be important and helpful to remember there are seeds of good all around and within us, even though we may not see them or know it. These seeds of good are like beautiful flowers that are just waiting to break open. You and I bring the water and the light to nourish, activate and foster the bloom. You and I set the tone and create the conditions that allow the seeds of love and good to be realized, rather than be swept into a dusty, dry corner of life because some problem or condition has taken us away from our heart for too long and has conditioned our mind to sustain the drought. I have found that no one in this life goes without having to face problems, challenges and loss. And yet, our response need not allow circumstances to shut down our true nature of love.

Some years ago I experienced a powerful example of what a deep commitment to unconditional love can look like. There was a young couple in our church who had a beautiful two-and-a-half-year-old daughter. It was the couple's only child at the time. Knowing the family, I had heard this child referred to by family and relatives as an angel, for she exuded such continuous love and was a true light in all of their lives. They had shared stories with me about this child and how she displayed a seemingly mature kind of love and giving spirit beyond her two and a half years.

Suddenly she became ill, showing signs of serious discomfort. One day later she had grown listless and had a loss of balance to the point that she could not walk. Things rapidly got worse and they flew her by helicopter to the hospital emergency center. It was soon discovered the child had a brain tumor at the base of her skull and immediately they did a procedure to drain fluid. That was on a Tuesday. Wednesday she was worse, and on Thursday, late in the morning, she passed on. It all happened so quickly. Just a few short days before she had been fine, and a light in their world. I arrived at the hospital shortly after learning their only child had passed on.

On the way there I wondered how I would find the couple to be, in what state… knowing how devastating something like this can be. I went into a small room where the young mother and father were alone with the great-grandmother, who had a close bond with the couple and their child. It was obvious they had been crying. There was a sense of grief and loss clearly apparent. We greeted and hugged each other before sitting back down. A conversation ensued that consisted of all three sharing delightful, happy remembrances of the way she was, things she had said, her loving ways… causing all three to take on teary smiles filled with love and appreciation for what she had brought to them. The magnitude of life and goodness she had delivered could not be measured in the short two and a half years she had been with them. There was such a heart-filled, love-filled exchange of gratitude. They had already completed the paperwork with the hospital before I had arrived. After our time of sharing, we had a sense that it was time to leave and be on our way.

What I witnessed next was rare indeed. I observed this young mother, in the midst of dealing with the loss of her precious daughter, turn to her husband, look deep into his eyes for an extended moment, and with a soft smile, ever so sweetly say to him, "I love you." He smiled back and in a gentle tone, immersed in heart energy, said, "I love you, too." That scene will always be with me. The mother demonstrated to me such a conscious, attentive, commitment to remain love, no matter what. In the midst of this tremendous loss, the couple chose not to have the love in them be broken apart, but remain whole and true to who and what they were... love. I was moved and touched by what was for me a sacred moment in which two parents were being true to themselves as a tribute to what their daughter had brought in love and light to their lives. I knew they would go on in the strength of that love for they would not permit the principle of "One + One is One" to be denied.

It is easy to get caught up in the mind and paint a story that locks us into something painful from our yesterdays. Love and Oneness are found in the now moment and never in guilt, shame and blame toward ourselves or another about the past. It is true that we must learn to let go of former mistakes and not punish ourselves. Unconditional love is to be directed not only toward others, but toward ourselves. One of the most common ways in which a sense of unity with yourself can fade and disappear for a time is by heaping guilt on yourself for an accident or mistake you might have made and allowed to loom large. It's like putting a boulder in your mental-emotional backpack. It can weigh you down for miles and years if you let it. Realize that in this life you are going to make some mistakes. You are not going to get it all right or perfect from the get-go. Part of learning is making mistakes to which adjustments and new choices can be made. And yes, some mistakes can be harder than others to get over.

I grew up in a family of avid hunters and fishermen. My father hunted from the time he was a boy. My brother, four years older than I, also loved to hunt and fish. Both were very adept at it and it was what they did on most weekends during the hunting season. From the time I was six we lived on what was then the outskirts of town with lots of woods in the backyard to hunt in. We had two freezers in the basement and each one was filled with wild game. Most of it was venison, rabbit and pheasant. My mother was known for her abilities to cook wild game in a variety of tasty ways.

As for hunting, I wasn't as into it as my father and brother, but it was a way to feel included and spend time with them. I just loved being out in nature, which I know was true for them, too. We had a number of Beagle hounds trained to bark on the trail of rabbits when we were hunting them. We had as many as eight at one time to go along with fox hounds, coon hounds, a Springer Spaniel or two and usually a Labrador. Some of the dogs didn't stay with us too long as my father would buy, sell, and trade some of them.

However, there were two very special prize Beagle hounds that were beloved by my father and brother and belonged to an elite class of their own. Brownie and Bozo had been with us from the time they were pups. They had brought home trophies from competitions called Field Trials that they'd been entered in, and over the years had allowed my father and brother to bag lots of rabbits for the dinner table. When the names Brownie and Bozo were mentioned or talked about by my father or brother, it was with pride, affection and an admiration for the heart and quality of these two dogs.

One wintry Sunday afternoon, when I was sixteen, my father and I took Brownie and Bozo out hunting rabbits. It had been an enjoyable several hours in the woods and the dogs had performed well. Late in the afternoon, as dusk was setting in, we began to head back home from deep in the woods. We'd already bagged three rabbits. We were walking through an area of large fallen trees and thick brush. I climbed up on the horizontal trunk of what had been a large tree and could see my father who had upped his pace for home and was about a hundred yards ahead. I hadn't seen or noticed the dogs for a while and decided they must be up ahead with him. A few moments later, while on top of the trunk of the fallen tree, I saw a flash of white and grey-brown scurry through the brush to my right. Assuming the dogs were with my father, my mind quickly and carelessly was convinced in the dimming daylight that it was a rabbit making a dash from where it had been hiding in the underbrush. I rapidly raised my twelve-gauge shotgun and fired.

Suddenly, the most horrifying sounds came thundering to my ears. It was the loud howling of dogs in pain. Both Brownie and Bozo had been hit by the spray of buckshot from my gun. I couldn't see them in the underbrush, but I knew the repetitive howling was of pain. It seemed as though my heart leaped out of my chest in agony. It is very hard to put into words the horrible feeling that came over me. I recall the words I yelled to my father… "DAD!!! I think I've shot one of the dogs!!!" I also remember the sick feeling that went with hearing those words come from my mouth. My father came rushing back and together we discovered both dogs had been hit by the spray of pellets and were lying on their side next to each other panting. We petted them, talked to them, and tried to comfort them until they both died there before us in the woods. I still get emotional as I write about this sad event.

My father never once scolded me, gave me a harsh look, questioned me, or raised his voice about the matter. He had to know just by looking at me how distraught I was. He calmly knelt down by the side of the dogs, our heroic Brownie and Bozo, and gently spoke to them. I remember bits of the message he communicated, thanking them for what great dogs they'd been, the fact that both had been with us a long time, had seen many years in the woods they always hungered to be in, and that it was fitting that this is where it would end… in the woods doing what they loved. Brownie was my brother's dog, which he had raised from a puppy, and I dreaded the thought of him learning what I had done. Whether he had been coached by my mom and dad, or responded on his own, I do not know. But he said nothing to me about it, perhaps a combination of his own grief over the news and a bit of compassion and respect for mine.

People who have pets and especially those who have had dogs as their pets for a substantial period of time would know that this kind of unfortunate happening is the closest thing to an accidental shooting of a family member. It is one thing to have your pet die, which is bad enough. But to have two be taken out in this manner somehow adds another wave of hurt inside. One doesn't know what to do with the feelings that something like this produces, but all you want is for the feelings to be over and gone. There is no way past them except to be with them until the pain is spent, breaks up, dissolves, and you direct the mind back into moment to moment living.

It was very quiet around the dinner table that evening. Looking back on it, that was exactly what was best for me at the time. There was nothing that needed to be said... just feelings to be felt. It may sound strange, but there was a sort of oneness about what took place there at the dinner table. It seemed as though the silence was the way we all were respecting each other and each other's feelings of sadness, grief and loss. I felt no blame energy coming at me. Looking back, the somber silence seemed the right thing. It was a soft and gentle energy. We each were dealing with it in our own way and respecting each other in the process. I'd like to believe that somehow we were linked together by our mutual shared love for those dogs and by my dad and brother's compassion for me in dealing with what I had done. Whatever it was, somehow it helped the pain to dissipate, and kept it from lingering.

After a couple of days, I was able to let go and move on from the experience. There was no need for me to punish myself. It's often what we do to ourselves. We make ourselves a victim of our own mistakes and prolong the pain almost as though we believe that we deserve to be punished. In this world, accidents can happen as much as we want to avoid them. And we are going to make mistakes. A powerful and important teaching to learn in regard to our human errors in life, is that mistakes call for correction, not punishment.

My father and brother were not into punishing me. I don't believe God punishes us, either. We punish ourselves and each other. It doesn't come from God which we know is only love. I was the only one who was going to punish myself if consciously or unconsciously that was my decision. How much better it is to come back to yourself, to loving yourself, to forgiving yourself, correcting whatever you can, and getting back into the present moment as one, whole, healthy being. At some point, in these times of pain, loss and sadness, you will learn to be there for yourself as much as you want others to be there for you. Have compassion on yourself. You can be assured that the Divine will never desert you. But at times you may have deserted yourself. That is why you must try to remember to seek and live the principle of "One + One is One." No matter what has happened in your life, you and God remain one. Although you may step away from yourself, Spirit never steps away from you. Knowing this at a deep level is the Truth that sets us free.

We've been told many times by those who have attained some degree of enlightenment that a big part of evolving spiritually and progressing toward the freedom of oneness is to unlearn much of what we have learned and had conditioned into us that is of separation consciousness. We are to let go of what our mind has accepted that does not serve us. Forgiveness is a spiritual principle of letting go that falls under the Divine formula of One + One is One. Forgiveness, when applied, restores oneness where separation has set in.

In the Spring time of the year, I find a day off to do a lot of cleanup work in my backyard. I do trimming, pruning, digging, planting, mulching and get quite dirty, sweaty and grimy after six or seven hours of physical activity in the yard. I love it when I'm done and able to go in and take a refreshing shower. It feels so good to have the water wash all that away and have that clean, fresh, alive feeling again. That is what forgiveness can do for your soul. When you are able to wash away all that has clung to you having to do with a negative past, such as things that have happened, that you've done, that have been said or done to you, while working in the schoolyard of earth-life, it is very enlivening. It's very easy for your mind to have picked up and carried around for a time some buried anger, sadness, or unforgiveness. Like stepping into a shower, forgiveness washes away any mental, emotional dirt, grime, or residue that wants to stick and cling to your consciousness, weakening your energies by tying you to the past.

As you make a practice of pausing and even momentarily checking in with the Spirit that resides within, you can draw upon the power of Its Divine Intelligence guiding you to let go. You draw on this power and energy by allowing it to steer your thoughts, words and actions to higher ground. With the choices and decisions you make related to both the outer world and the inner world of consciousness, you facilitate whether this energy will drain or sustain you, whether it goes to empower or disempower you, whether its flow is blocked or set free.

It is helpful and valuable to realize there are a multitude of experiences you face or encounter in your life that are important and necessary to your soul growth and development. Spiritual awareness includes the ability to identify behaviors and thinking in yourself that operate in opposition to the true spiritual nature of your soul. It is like an internal radar screen that detects negative elements you want to rid from your soul. When you are in fear, anger, jealousy or unforgiveness, you are energetically vibrating at a frequency that needs to be healed and altered. Aspects of personality can keep you stuck. The soul of you wants to rise above it and be made free to be love and light. If ever you notice you are carrying ongoing anger or resentment, then at a soul level you know there is inner work for you to do. Affirmations of letting go, prayers of release, and meditations to sooth the soul back into the Presence of peace and well-being are the way to go. Everyone has times when some element of consciousness is hurting and in need of healing.

Years ago I came across a story told in Spain about a father and his teenage son who had a relationship that had become strained. So the son ran away from home. His father began a search for his rebellious son and couldn't find him. He looked everywhere. Many months passed. Finally, in Madrid, in a last desperate effort to find his son, the father put an ad in the newspaper. The ad read, "Dear Paco. Meet me in front of the newspaper office at noon. All is forgiven. I love you, your father." The next day, at noon, in front of the newspaper office, over 800 "Pacos" showed up. They were all seeking forgiveness and love from their fathers. I am uncertain whether the story is true; however I am certain that the need for forgiveness and this kind of internal healing is universal.

Are you a "Paco" in the world? Is there somebody you long to have forgive you? That, my friend, is out of your control. Notice if the return to loving yourself hinges on receiving the forgiveness of another. You must break free of the binding that this places on you. It is only a cause for power and life energy to drain from you. It is not callous toward others to work toward the restoration of your own wholeness. It is not insensitive to cut yourself free from someone else's established conditions by which you get to be loved. No one can keep you from loving yourself without you agreeing to it. Instead, have compassion for the person who refuses to forgive, and compassion on yourself enough to be free of yesterday's errors, if any. Not everyone is able to go there with ease all the time and under all circumstances.

A truck driver parked his rig out front and went inside a roadside restaurant. As he sat drinking his coffee, three roughneck motorcyclists parked their bikes out front and came inside. They saw this truck driver and although not all motorcyclists are like these guys, these fellows had some mean intentions. For whatever reason, they decided to pick on the truck driver, who was minding his business. One came over and put his cigar in the truck driver's coffee and said, "How do you like that?" The second cyclist took the truck driver's coffee and spilled it over his lap. The truck driver just gave a faint smile, nodded his head, and tried to ignore them. The third cyclist said, "What a wimp. He doesn't even know how to defend himself." The truck driver got up, paid his bill and walked out. A few moments later, the waitress was looking out the window and said, "You know, he really doesn't know how to drive a truck either. He just ran over three motorcycles."

I share this story with you partly for fun and partly for you to notice if something in you cheered the truck driver? Was there some sense of satisfaction that maybe they got their just due, a little of "an eye for an eye" kind of energy? Come on, be truthful. I did when I first heard it. It is a common human temptation. There are going to be times when you and I encounter unenlightened people and the potential hurt and pain they can bring. However, there is a rewarding internal feeling that comes with the soul satisfaction of choosing not to meet low with low, but instead choose the high road of aligning with our Higher Self.

Mahatma Gandhi said, "An eye for an eye makes the whole world blind." Revenge or getting even blinds us to the ways of the heart. You can see that we live in a world in which the imperfect are being perfected and sometimes rather slowly. You and I slow ourselves down considerably in our path toward spiritual progress if we are not able to move in consciousness to where we rise above the pain others have seemingly brought to us. There are behaviors that in no way deserve our approval. However, our response is another matter. It has to do with being in the world but not of it. It is learning that no problem is solved by remaining in the energies that created it. We are not to make our returning energies match the low energy that we received. Whatever negative energies are coming toward us, rather than match them, we want to learn to rise above them. It may not be an easy thing to do, but if we can think in terms of "I am you and you are me" then we will be led to do what is best in most situations.

From his essay entitled *Nature* Ralph Waldo Emerson said, "We live in succession, in division, in part, in particles. Meantime, within us is the soul of the whole; the wise silence, the universal beauty, to which every part and particle is equally related; the eternal ONE." No matter how things appear on the outside, how great the division, how inappropriate the behavior, or how small and removed you may be from your True Self being fully activated, within you is the "soul of the whole." There exists within you that which is of the One Spirit, offering the wisdom found inside its silence. It connects you as a "part and particle" that is "equally related" to the eternal One. It is in this vibration that you move toward a greater spiritual wholeness of compassion, understanding, and inner peacefulness.

It is not always easy to accept others who may not think the way you do, who convey ideas you cannot align with or whose behaviors you may deem inappropriate or unacceptable. Sometimes when faced with an annoying or difficult person you are encouraged to stop and ask yourself what it is that may have caused this other person to be the way they are. What might the formative years of their childhood have been like, what kinds of people might they have been surrounded by, what experiences did they have that influenced them, what conditions might they have met up with that caused a deep inner wound yet to be healed. You can't know these specifics but you can be sure they, like you, are a product of these and many factors from their past. This is not a kind of excuse, but a reason to give pause to any tendency you, I, or anyone may have to quickly cast a fellow soul aside without even a glimmer of compassion. It helps to be less condemning and more understanding if we can remember that every person is a product of their past. So many factors can come into play and contribute to the molding and making of a person's personality, make-up and level of consciousness.

Feral children offer an extreme example of how we become like the character and nature of that which we have been surrounded. A feral child is a human child who has lived isolated from human contact from a young age and has little or no experience of human care, social behavior or even human language. Some feral children were confined in isolation or abandoned by parents. Just over a hundred incidents have been reported through the years and you may have read or learned about one or more of the most well-known cases.

In 1990, a boy was found in the Andes, Peru, and was said to have been raised by goats for eight years. He survived by drinking their milk and eating roots and berries. He had taken on the characteristics of the goats with which he lived. He tended to walk on all four limbs, causing his hands and feet to be hardened due to scar formations and they became almost like hooves. He had adapted to the company he kept and was able to communicate with the goats he lived with. This was one example of a feral child.

Another and perhaps the most famous of these cases documented had to do with two girls found in 1920 in the Bengal jungle near Midnapore in Northern India. They were eventually given the names of Amala, who was 18 months old when found, and Kamala, who was eight years old. Although it was determined they were not sisters, their behaviors were exceedingly similar. A missionary named Joseph Singh, having heard stories of two strange figures accompanying a band of wolves, decided to look into it and hid in a tree top over-looking the den. Singh wrote about the experience in his diary. As the moon rose, he saw the wolves come out one after the other sniffing the night air. Then out came two hunched and horrible figures. He wrote they were "hideous looking... hand, foot and body like a human... their eyes were bright and piercing, unlike human eyes... both of them ran on all fours." He continued to describe that the girls seemed to have no trace of humanness, as if they had the minds of wolves.

Eventually they were captured and attempts were made to rehabilitate them. Upon capture, they were just like the wolves by which they had been brought up. They tore off any clothes put on them and would eat only raw meat. They curled up in a tight ball and slept next to each other, twitching and growling in their sleep. They would awaken only after the moon rose and then would howl to be set free from their confinement. Having spent so much time on all fours, their tendons and joints had shortened, making it impossible for them to straighten their legs or attempt to walk upright. They never smiled. The only emotion they showed was fear, often with a growl and display of teeth. Even their senses had adapted to becoming wolf-like, having amazingly sharp eyesight at night, heightened hearing, and the ability to smell meat three acres away in their enclosed space. Singh felt the wolf habits acquired by Kamala and Amala had blocked the free expression of their inherent human characteristics.

I share these amazing stories and their fascinating details so as to amplify the realization that we and our fellow human beings can be and often are profoundly affected by our immediate environment and surroundings, especially during the early years and through our youth. Amala and Kamala vividly displayed the extent to which a human can be conditioned by what comes unfiltered through our five senses. The constant images their minds were given, the inhumane life being modeled, and the consistency of their exposure to an animal-like environment became accepted as the norm.

When we consider the world in which we live, the many different levels of consciousness and systems of thought that get established in individual minds, we come to understand that most everything is learned, and depends on the nature of what we have been exposed to. You and I can gain an awareness about ourselves by reflecting on the den from which we have come. Although not a den of wolves, it may have been a haven of angels or myriad possibilities of good, bad, or in between. What have we picked up consciously or even subliminally from the people, surroundings and circumstances of our earliest and most formative years that represented oneness or separation, love or fear?

I grew up with an uncle who lived next door and loved to work in his yard. It was kept beautifully groomed and manicured. I have wondered if my love of flowers and appreciation for a beautifully kept yard came from the many appealing mental pictures of what I saw my uncle create. It is true that you can be inclined to take on characteristics of your parents – or relatives – both positive and negative. The company you keep throughout life can have a definite effect on you, for good or ill. There is a definite advantage to surrounding yourself and spending time with those you look up to and admire. Every parent should realize the incredible influence they have on their offspring. Fortunate are those who are brought up in a home where love is taught and demonstrated. The seeds of love go a long way to provide the harvest of many happy returns in life. Fear, hatred, prejudice, biases, labels, judgments and the consciousness of separation are a learned system of thought and behavior… but need not be retained. For that is not who or what you are or have come here to be.

As the missionary, Singh, pointed out regarding the two girls, the free flow and expression of innate human characteristics can somehow be blocked. This can help explain that a person's past can be and often is a factor in blocking the flow of inherent spiritual attributes and characteristics until these aspects of separation consciousness are unlearned. When you are dealing with what might be considered a person's negative characteristics, you are not meeting the real person, but elements of their personal history. This is not a reason to give them a pass on what is unacceptable, only to help you pass from overreacting negatively, and to not take personally any unkindness that may be directed toward you.

As I have stated before, life is relationships. All relationships are valuable and important. However, our personal relationships with others are the ones where we can learn the most about ourselves. Relationships play a key role in our soul's development in at least two very important ways. Relationships give us opportunities for learning to love, and for healing our past. You, like me and many others, likely have buried pain, hurts, wounds, and issues. These all typically have to do with unresolved issues from our past, usually from childhood. They can keep us in some state of disconnect from ourselves, others, life and even God.

The order of the universe is such that in addition to having people in our lives who add happiness, we often tend to draw to us exactly those who will help us learn what we most need to learn about love and heal what most needs to be healed. That means whether either party realizes it or not, some people help us uncover our wounds. People show up from time to time and may unintentionally seemingly pick the scab on our internal wounds. They will say or do things that trigger an issue, wound, or limited belief we hold about ourselves. It may cause us to have an emotional outburst or to just stew inside for who knows how long. It is crucial to realize when this happens to you, the emotional charge or strong reaction in you wouldn't be there if there weren't something to be healed and released. As you do so, it is a very freeing feeling and can reconnect you again with the energies of love and oneness. Over-reactions are reminders that we may have a hurt, inner wound, or unhealed issue from our past. Anything unhealed with our parents, with people in authority or wherever we felt rejected, unloved, or heavily criticized, can become a recurring issue in relationships going forward until we get healed. It is the order of God's universe, attempting to help us clear a path for love, to help us release and move out of the way all that internally stands as a block to love and joy. Our true nature is love and that is who and what we truly are, even beneath the layers of pain that may cover over it.

Psychologists tell us that, whether we are aware of it or not, much of our unhealed pain from our past comes up in our relationships with present-day people. It could be that your co-worker, spouse, or boss reminds you of your father who was emotionally absent, controlling or critical. The Course In Miracles says, "We are never upset for the reason we think." This is because we usually don't see our upset as being something other than what is current or directly in front of us. We don't think to ask ourselves what is in us that could be causing this strong inner or outer reaction. We don't realize it could be about an issue or person from our past. We don't realize that by forgiving our father, if this was the issue, it will help heal the relationship with our current husband, or boss. Understanding this can help you keep from over-reacting to another person's charge, especially when it is directed at you. It can help you be more understanding and compassionate. You can learn to see it as something coming to the surface for healing, or as a cry for love.

The strong intention to own and take responsibility for our own feelings can help to remove the rigid reaction of rejection we may have of a person or persons. It can contribute to diminishing any sense of distance between us and others. When any two people can strip away the effects of their past and stand in the moment, owning their own feelings without blaming another, they become free, left with only that of themselves that knows love and oneness. It then has the opportunity to become a powerful and beautiful soul-to-soul, spirit-to-spirit exchange.

So, there is much you can learn from your relationship with yourself, others, situations, circumstances, and God. Rather than judge yourself for having a negative feeling, and rather than repressing or suppressing your emotions, learn to notice them, dialogue with them, seek out their origination, and feel them through. Recognizing that they are coming from you and not that somebody else has given them to you is a factor in accelerating your healing and returning to love. It should be noted we aren't likely going to love, or even like, everyone. However, we need to notice any biases, prejudices, or negative judgments we might have. These are notorious for throwing us into separation consciousness and sustaining the vibrations that divide us. As we grow in the energies of oneness, we learn to make a distinction between disliking people and disliking unacceptable behavior.

In our relationship with ourselves, any kind of separation we experience is a factor of the mind ruling over the heart and spirit. The egoic mind can cause us to get lost in fear and separation. It takes us into comparing ourselves with others and causes feelings of superiority and inferiority. Remember also that the separate self is the ego mind that sees only twoness, and always is focused on externals by which to measure ourselves. Your Higher Self is connected to and identifies with the All Knowing Spirit within you and sees from the Divine Reality of oneness. Jesus spoke of this as the "single eye." Your Higher Self sees with the single eye, which is the eye of oneness, the eye singularly directed toward spiritual truth, which has the laser focus of knowing that no matter how things may appear, One + One is One.

Jesus said, "No man can serve two masters." (Matt. 6:24 KJV) We can take that to mean you cannot serve both oneness and two-ness. You cannot serve both your Higher Self and your separate self, the ego. "…if therefore thine eye be single, thy whole body shall be full of light." (Matt. 6:22 KJV) Whatever you may be facing in the way of emotions of fear, anger, loss, sadness, resentment, or others that disconnect you from peace and harmony – when faced with times you get down on yourself… times you are dealing with a challenging relationship… times when a situation or set of circumstances overwhelm you and take you into separation – the way to re-connect in consciousness is to cultivate the single eye that has the single focus of oneness.

The mind is capable of shutting down the heart. The mind, acting alone, apart from the heart, can activate the ego which pulls from old learned ideas, biases, and behaviors of the past, causing a person to be quick to judge, condemn and de-value another, leading to a loss of listening and compassionate understanding. Every one of us has had our own unique life path, having been exposed to people, cultures, religions, ideas and systems of thought that have contributed to the person we have become. Only you know where you stand in relation to being affected by the past and what is best to release. Step into a process of being transformed by the renewing of your mind and restoring a conscious connection to the heart. The heart knows that no matter how things appear, the truth is, One + One is One. You are one with the All That Is. Move beyond the sense that there is a "me" and a "not me" where you see everything as being apart and separate from you. Instead, begin to see everyone and everything as connected and part of you.

Albert Schweitzer said, "Until he extends the circle of his compassion to all living things, man will not himself find peace." The rule most all of us learned growing up was said to be golden, "Do unto others as you would have them do unto you." It reflects the principle of oneness in which we realize that "I am you and you are me." If we can remember to think in terms of "I am you and you are me" then we will be led to do what is best in most every situation. We will learn to go the extra mile, as they say. What we give out will seemingly always come back to us.

There is a true story of what going the extra mile can look like and mean in a person's life. Helping a stranger, a neighbor in need, or simply putting love in action will always work in our favor, sometimes in more significant ways than we could have imagined.

One stormy night years ago, an elderly man and his wife entered the lobby of a small hotel in Philadelphia. They were trying to get out of the rain and find shelter for the night. They went to the front desk and the husband asked the clerk if he could give them a room. The clerk told them he couldn't send a nice couple like them out in the rain at one o'clock in the morning. He went on to explain that there were three conventions in town and all the rooms were taken. But, with a warm smile, he offered that perhaps they would be willing to sleep in his room. It wasn't exactly a suite, but good enough to make them comfortable for the night. When the couple declined, the friendly young man working as a clerk tried to convince them he'd be fine and not to worry about him. Finally, the couple agreed.

The next morning, as the elderly man paid his bill, he told the clerk what a fine manager he was and that he should be the boss of the best hotel in the United States. He went on to say that maybe, someday, he would build one for him and make him manager. They had a laugh together and the couple left. Two years later, the clerk, who had almost forgotten the incident, received a letter from the same elderly man referring to the stormy night they'd spent there. In the letter was a round-trip ticket to New York with an invitation to pay them a visit. When the clerk arrived in New York, the older gentleman met him and took him to the corner of 5th Avenue and 34th Street. And there he pointed to a beautiful new building and told the clerk that this was the hotel he'd just built for him to manage. The young clerk thought the man had to be joking, but he was not. The older gentleman's name was William Waldorf Astor, and the lovely new structure was the original famous Waldorf-Astoria Hotel. The young man was George C. Boldt, and he became its first manager. Being in loving service and treating others as we would like to be treated can put into motion a dynamic that opens us up to opportunities by which life loves us back. It won't always be on this kind of scale, but love put into action will only cause a return of good on some scale, for love unites us with the Source from which all good comes. One + One is One. Love + love is love. Good + good is good.

Love has a pure and lasting quality. Three of the most powerful words one can speak to another or hear spoken to them are "I love you." When I receive holiday and birthday cards from my wife and children, signed with "Love" followed by their signature, that word "Love" they have penned to the page kind of leaps into my heart. People are afraid to "all-out love" with nothing held back. With adults the fear can be it might not be received, it might not get returned, or it might get misunderstood. There are all kinds of silly thoughts and fears around letting love flow freely. It typically can be so easy for adults to share their expressions of love with babies and children. And it is usually a very natural thing for a young child to express love and to let it in. The older one gets, factors can set in, the mind begins to hold the heart back, provide reasons and conditions to temper the giving and receiving. It can be so special to experience the spontaneous, authentic love of a young child. They are an example to us and demonstrate this is the way it is meant to be for all of us.

Two of my grandchildren were visiting from the Northwest. It had been approximately three months since we'd been together. Brady, my grandson was five; Dylan, my granddaughter, was three at the time. They are very dear to me and I cherish every minute we have together. It was only hours after arriving at our home and the precious three year-old Dylan, who is a ball of endless, happy, effervescent energy, had found her way to our small upright piano in a room just off our entryway. Everyone was visiting in the main family room except Dylan, who was now slamming on the piano keys with her hands and little fingers. There was nothing musical about it, but she was having a joyous time seemingly rewarded by the loud sounds she was banging out.

I went into the room where she was, and sat down next to her on the piano seat. She stopped briefly. We looked at each other momentarily, but said nothing. She gave me a cute welcoming smile as if glad I had joined her. Then, because I don't play the piano either, I joined her in striking the keys in a similar robust fashion. We were pounding out a storm. It sounded atrocious. However, after a minute or so, we both paused, she leaned into me with an angelic smile, looked up into my eyes and out came the words, "Pappa... I love you" with feeling and authenticity that melted my heart. Here I am a couple years later, recalling the moment and still emotionally touched by the memory. In the years ahead, as the world and its ways get hold of her, my hope and prayer is that she maintains that purity of sweetness displayed that day on the piano bench. It was so precious and natural.

It has been stated over and over by many through the centuries that love is the greatest force in the universe. Nothing can match it in its capability to join, unify, and bind together as one. When you are in the energy of the heart you know it, and your life is different, better, and enhanced. Love is a wonderful energy to feel moving through your being. I ask myself the question, "When I'm not in my heart, and not coming from love of life, people, Creator and creation, where am I?" My simple answer is, "I'm in my head." It is so easy to get caught up in the mind and its dominant communication of thought, which is often driven by experiences and conditioning from a personal history that has so much stored in the subconscious. My mind can also take me into the future with possible concerns, projects, deadlines and events. When I allow that to happen, I'm not in my heart either, but lost in linear thought. Captured by the mind, you and I often place ourselves in the prison of the past and future, out of the present moment, where the heart can be engaged and love is free to flow.

When communicating with others, I've learned that our words, spoken or written, carry power. A dear friend has shared with me that for those who admire us and look up to us for encouragement, love and support, "our whisper is a roar." In other words, it sometimes takes very few words to have a powerful impact on another. It is a truth that communication is creation. Communication carries a current of energy. Thoughts carry creative power and spoken words add the vibration of sound as well, bringing another energy level to that which is communicated. What, when, and how we say what we say, along with to whom, can be an important factor in our communication.

I heard a humorous story about a husband and wife who were dressed and ready to head out to a New Year's Eve party. They had remembered to do all the things necessary to being out for the evening. The night light was turned on, the thermostat adjusted, the parakeet cage was covered and the cat put out in the backyard. Playing it safe and conservative, they had arranged for a taxi to drive them to and from the party. When the cab arrived and they were walking out the front door to leave, the cat had come around from the back yard and slipped past them back into the house. They really didn't want the cat in the house because it goes after the parakeet when they are away. So the wife went to the taxi and got in while her husband was chasing the rather elusive cat, which had run upstairs to their second floor. Waiting in the cab, the wife, not wanting the driver to know that no one would be home all evening, made up a story that her husband would be out soon and was detained briefly so he could go upstairs to say goodbye to his mother who was staying with them.

After a few minutes, her husband got into the taxi and as they are driving away he says, "I'm sorry I took so long. That stupid idiot was hiding under the bed. I had to poke her with a coat hanger to get her to come out! She then took off running, so I grabbed her by the neck, and wrapped her in a blanket to keep her from scratching me! But it was effective! I hauled her fat butt downstairs and threw her out into the back yard! About then, the taxi driver hit a parked car. Granted, he was talking about his cat, not his mother, but the point is, words communicate an energy for good or ill, and can move us toward love or away from it. Remember, it was the Master Teacher who said, "For by your words you will be justified and by your words you will be condemned." (Matt. 12-37)

Sometimes, we can find unique ways to convey a message of love to another. I knew of a lady who always put love notes in the suitcase of her husband before he left for any business trip. Unpacking at his destination he'd find the note of love tucked inside with his clothes. He learned to reciprocate and leave behind a note for her under her pillow or somewhere she would find it after he left. When we make the decision to live from love and oneness, we can find many new ways to express and communicate it.

Some people still remember the late Paul Harvey, who for many years had a national radio program, usually airing around noontime. He would highlight news and stories from around the nation. It was very popular in its time. One day he shared the story about a man named Carl Coleman who was driving to work one morning when he bumped fenders with another motorist. Both stopped their cars and he and the woman driving the other vehicle got out to survey the damage. The woman was distraught, for it was her fault and she admitted this along with the fact her car was brand new, only two days from the showroom. She dreaded facing her husband about this.

Coleman was sympathetic, but he had to do the usual exchange of license and registration data. The woman reached into her glove compartment to retrieve the documents that were in an envelope. On the first piece of paper to tumble out, written in her husband's distinctive hand, were the words, "In case of an accident, remember, Honey, it's you I love, not the car." Wow, you say. How sweet. So of the heart. So loving and creative. What woman wouldn't have love for a husband as thoughtful as that? There are lots of ways one can get creative in conveying the message "I love you." Communication is creation. Whether located physically near or far from another, love communicated from the heart diminishes all distance and makes One + One be One.

At a deep soul level each of us is being called to transcend the ways of the world. It means to lay aside the "not me" and return to the big "Me" that at its core is love, thereby entering the energies that create the "We." As part of your soul evolution, you are always being challenged to show up in a way that demonstrates a love and oneness for your neighbor, wherever they live in the world. We are all part of the human family and the spiritual reality is that we are all spiritual brothers and sisters as children of the One same Spirit. Some have had this realization come to them in subtle ways and some in rather dramatic fashion.

I've had the good fortune of visiting places like Rome, Sienna, Florence, and Assissi, where St. Francis lived. The life of St. Francis is amazing, fascinating, and revealing in many respects. On one occasion, when he was about twenty years of age, he was headed toward fulfilling his patriotic duties and was about to enter the fight against neighboring Perugia. Before seeing or experiencing any battle he was captured and put in prison for about a year. Two years later, he set out again with an army bound for the Crusades. This time, on the way, he was captured by a vision. It took him about a year to grasp the full understanding of what was going on inside of him, but the inner process led him to a deep faith and a commitment to live the spiritually awakened life. It completely turned him from the pursuit of warfare to the practice of peace. We are not sure what went on within him, but his heart was touched and opened in a big new way. Something inside moved him to a vision of how his life was to be a contribution to others. He broke away from the conforming ways of separation and was transformed internally. His life totally changed. The communication that he went on to cultivate with all life forms was astounding and many of us have read about this. His famous prayer states so well his life purpose: "Lord, make me an instrument of your peace; where there is hatred, let me sow love..."

You have all come into this life to learn how you can be an instrument of love. That is your mission and spiritual destiny. St. Francis had the seed of the Divine grow in him and become a living truth. He came to realize that we are brothers and sisters of the One Source and this turned him from the ways of war to the ways of peace. Something happened inside him that he could not deny. His Higher Sacred Self became activated and came flowing freely into greater expression through acts of service, kindness, love, and goodness. He found the spiritual "Me" beyond the "not me" and it launched him into a life of "We" where One + One is One.

Some of us have had moments given to us when the spirit inside seems to take us to our heart and reveal a kind of connection with another soul we may have encountered for the first time or even for a brief few moments. Maybe you are led to help them in some way. Maybe you are led to share just a few words with them. Whatever it is, there is a kind of sacred exchange that can take place in which you have an undeniable feeling come over you that knows you and they are one.

We were in Italy, on our final day in Rome before heading back home. So my wife, Diane, and I walked all over Rome and soaked in the rich history of some of the oldest parts of the city. We sat down for lunch at an outdoor table of a little restaurant located down a narrow back street. While having our lunch, I looked up and saw a boy of about twelve or thirteen years of age who had some serious birth defects. He had no feet or hands. They were only stubs. He was seated on a skateboard… and had an old shoe over one stub, which he used to push his way through the street. He was obviously quite low to the ground… but it was clear to me that he was not low to life. Yes, he was begging to meet his needs, having a small can to accept coins. But there was a faint soft smile on his face, along with an expression and presence that seemed to convey to me a depth to his soul. Sitting there at an outside table, my heart went out to him, not with pity, but with admiration for what I somehow felt coming from his Being. He did not stop to extend his small can, but made his way up the street. My wife and I conversed about the plight of this teenager. We agreed that there was a countenance about him that was seemingly sacred.

As each moment passed, watching this soul maneuver along and out of sight, a feeling of love and oneness swelled in me. I felt a strong desire to go and engage him, if ever so briefly. I got up from the table and went up the street looking for him. He hadn't gotten very far. When I caught up to him, I stooped down to get as close to eye level as I could. Our eyes met, we smiled, and I put some money in his can. He had deep penetrating eyes in which I saw no pity but such goodness. I thought, this is my brother in life, finding a way to make it through each day. He gave me a big grateful smile and said, "Grazie, grazie." A sweet feeling came over me from our brief connection. My one regret was that I didn't speak Italian and he didn't speak English. And yet, after that thought came another that said we had communicated on a level well beyond any spoken language. Once again it was proven to me that One + One is not two, but ONE. And love is what gets it done. There is something special that takes place inside of us when we connect at what seems to be a spirit-to-spirit level. It is kind of magical. It is possible for this to happen between any two people or two bodies of people. The spiritual vibrations around oneness carry a wonderful feeling.

During the months you were housed in your mother's womb, and until your birth into this world you were literally joined, connected, united, one with your mother. Then, when your body was formed and you reached the time of birth, you came forth from the womb, the cord was cut, and you became separated. But separate in physical body only. Prior to birth you were spirit and after birth you were of spirit, the same as your mother. You left the womb of your mother at birth to enter the womb of the earth. It is all God. During your life in a physical body you are spirit, although it carries the illusion of separation. At physical death you release the body and remain spirit. At the spiritual level, you are one with the Spirit of All That Is. If you agree, then you accept that you are an eternal spirit, as is everyone, and it is the same spirit of love and oneness that lives in you, me, and everyone, and makes us One.

The spirit of you knows only love and oneness. It is the most natural thing in you. It is spiritually instinctive to know your oneness. Yet somehow the world in which we live conditions us to the illusion that we are separate. Your soul is in this life to awaken into oneness and learn to love. It's true that we are spiritual beings having a human experience. The human experience can tend to push many into their minds and away from their heart. When we quiet the fears in us and return to the heart, we begin to grow back spiritually into the truth of our being. We begin to see with new eyes. Beyond our outer physical eyes are our inner spiritual eyes or what we referenced earlier regarding Jesus' teaching on the "single eye." He said, "The light of the body is the eye; if therefore the eye be single, the whole body shall be full of light." (Matt. 6:22 KJV) The single eye is the eye that focuses solely on spiritual Truth. The Truth is that we are all one. Wherever the single eye looks it sees one, not two. Everywhere it looks it sees with a spiritual knowingness that One + One is One. God's light shines mightily where love and oneness lives in the heart. The heart-centered single eye is what can heal a person's life. It is badly needed throughout our world.

It is a kind of loving, compassionate understanding that looks on all others and sees them as one. It is seeing past any and all differences that may exist and knowing that beyond it all, we are one. Although

137

we may not have the same religion, we have the same God, we are all of the same spiritual family, we are brothers and sisters because we share the One True Spirit of All. Let us learn to live from the heart, see with new eyes, and function in the energy zones of peace, love, and joy. In that way we make a contribution to our world in ways we may know not of. Let us be an example of the principle that One + One is One.

We have witnessed in times of crisis, a coming together of humanity in ways that have clearly demonstrated there is an innate oneness of the Spirit that exists at the soul level. It is that place deep within where a compassionate cooperativeness emerges from both a conscious and unconscious knowing that we are interconnected. The awakened heart lives from the inner wisdom of a universal inclusiveness that embraces all. It is a powerful thing to behold.

Perhaps you would agree that one of those times was in response to the horrific tragedy of 9/11. There is a beautifully inspired piece of writing by novelist Cheryl Sawyer, which captures the power of one. Not having been a writer of poetry, she sent the inspiration that came through her only to her mother. However, due to its potent, moving, universal message, it was passed along to others until it found its way into national and international use. Although it was written for our nation, it has a classic spiritual message for the world as a whole. It is appropriately titled, "One."

"As the soot and dirt and ash rained down, we became one color.
As we carried each other down the stairs of the burning building, we became one class.
As we lit candles of waiting and hope, we became one generation.
As the firefighters and police officers found their way into the inferno, we became one gender.
As we fell to our knees in prayer for strength, we became one faith.
As we whispered or shouted words of encouragement we spoke one language.
As we gave blood in lines a mile long, we became one body.
As we mourned together the great loss, we became one family.
As we cried tears of grief and loss, we became one soul.

138

As we retell with pride the sacrifice of heroes, we become one people.
We are one color,
one class,
one generation,
one gender,
one faith,
one language,
one body,
one family,
one soul,
one people.
We are the power of one.
We are united.
We are America." (WE ARE THE WORLD)

As we seek to live the life we have come to live, and to be the people we have come to be, it would serve us well to embrace the truth of oneness that says I am you and you are me. It opens the way to greater understanding, compassion, and forgiveness. It makes you one among those on the planet who are healing all internal conflict, and pursuing the kind of love that is causeless, unconditional, and binds all together in unity. Although when looking with your outer physical eyes, you may see two of us, with the internal single eye of spiritual Truth, you see and know that we are one. In so doing, you become a true peacemaker in the world, one who seeks to know and live the principle of One + One is One.

CHAPTER FIVE
The Circle of Life

You and I live inside an Infinite Circle of Life that is all God. It is infinite and without boundaries. Evidence of its vast existence can be found by looking as deep as you can into a microscope and as far into space with the most powerful telescope. You and I came into this experience of life with much still to learn, to understand and to experience. No one is alone in this process of evolving in consciousness. In some areas of life we are asleep to the reality of our divine connections. Yet we are slowly waking up to the expanded perspective of the true relationship that we are meant to have with it all.

In the previous chapter, the emphasis was on the relationships we have with our neighbors, with other people, and the reality that we are all one in God. As sons and daughters of the Most High, in spiritual truth, we are all brothers and sisters of the one same Spirit. We are a spiritual family. Everyone at their core is divine. Therefore, one + one, you + another... any other, are one, and part of the All That Is.

This chapter places emphasis on expanding our awareness of our relationship with God and all its forms found in Nature. This means developing a deeper bond with the spirit and energies of earth, sea, and sky, and all that is in them. The earth itself is a living being. Everything in it is alive with God and provides numerous channels of wisdom, assistance and truth to help us grow and expand in consciousness.

In this chapter you will find some of my experiences and that of others which relate to the energies of nature as a most powerful avenue of dynamic oneness with the Source of All That Is. If you are to grow in oneness, you are to continually take steps in expanding your awareness of the one life and intelligence in all things, including nature. As Henry David Thoreau put it, "My profession is to always find God in nature." Nature has a language of its own that can speak to the heart and soul of us all. You and I have lessons to be learned, questions to be answered, solutions to be found, and a knowledge that nature is there for us. You may find yourself at times feeling alone, sad, frustrated, searching for answers and not knowing where to turn. God's helpful messages of life and wisdom can be found everywhere around you in nature.

As scripture states, "But now ask the beasts, and they will teach you; and the birds of the air, and they will tell you; or speak to the earth, and it will teach you; and the fish of the sea will explain to you. Who among all these does not know that the hand of the Lord has done this, in whose hand is the life of every living thing, and the breath of all mankind?" (Job 12:7-10) Nature is your friend; when you let go of mental distractions, become fully present and give yourself over to it in consciousness, it can gift you with tremendous beauty, power, inspiration, energy and insight. In many ways we are infants in understanding and comprehension regarding the sacred relationship that can be experienced with the many forms of nature living inside the All That Is.

A line from the writings of Shakespeare taken from "As You Like It: Act II, Scene 1" states that we can "find tongues in trees, books in running brooks, sermons in stones and good in everything. I would not change it." What Shakespeare writes is true. In the Circle of Life, inside the Whole of God's creation, everything is in relationship with us and contains its gifts and messages. It is safe to say that Shakespeare is not alone and that others would also argue along with him that there truly are tongues in trees that seemingly talk to us, that there are books of wisdom to be found in the currents of running brooks, that even the stones are alive, and that we are connected to the good in everything. I, too, would not want to change it, for nature has a propensity to promote feelings of a sacred oneness when we learn to open to them. As a child of God you have an inherent covenant of oneness with all of God's creation.

Most all forms of life and nature seem to convey a message that we can learn from. Flowers seem to say, "Open your heart to the beauty within." Stars tell us to look upward and be guided. Mountains speak to us of majesty. Sunsets communicate beauty and closure. Rainbows speak of hope, and butterflies of transformation. When you are alone in nature and able to become quiet, fully present, receptive and reflective, it can be as if a door of your soul opens, curtains part, and you feel the pure life energies of nature entering, touching and lifting you up. It can be very powerful in that moment to realize also that it's all God, that Its presence is surrounding, enfolding and loving you through all Its myriad forms.

I recall very vividly a time in my life when I was 15 years old. We lived along the edge of a body of woods that extended for miles. It was in the late afternoon of a brisk autumn day. I had come home from school, changed clothes and stepped outside into the cool autumn air. It was a day in which nature seemed to be calling me out... to come be in it and romp with it. So I went for a walk, by myself, along the edge of the woods.

I walked for a long time. I don't recall exactly what my thoughts were, but it felt good to be outdoors strolling through nature. As I continued along, at some point I felt my heart opening and a profound sense of not being alone. It was as if I were embraced by a Presence. It was all around me, manifesting as the Source of life, beauty, and energy flowing to me. It was nearing dusk; the sun was slipping into the woods behind the tree line. All along the edge of the woods there were fields that went on and on. Some were farmers' fields with browning corn stalks and other fields were not farmed, unattended and covered with weeds, wild clover and grasses. It was in one of these fields that a large hill rose up with a single, grand, old oak tree at its peak. I went to the top of that hill to watch the sunset. It was the moments that followed that are imbedded in my memory.

I stood there on the top of that hill, all alone with nature surrounding me. As the sun inched its way into the woodland horizon I could see that most of the trees had half their leaves gone, having given way to the season of change. There was just the right proportion of clouds mixed into the sky and setting sun to make for a beautiful sight in the concluding day. There were sounds brought on by brisk winds that swept across the woods in fluctuations of intensity. You could hear the wind forcing its way through the trees and their remaining leaves, where clinging gave way to surrender. With a big gust, many leaves having met their moment of release came fluttering down. It was magical to watch these descending showers of red, orange and golden leaves raining down amidst the near and distant woods. They even fluttered down around me from the tree I stood beneath.

I remember the feel of strength in the wind. I felt it chill my cheeks and blast against the length of my body with varying strength, sometimes testing my ability to maintain balance. I just stood there, lost in time, staring in a gaze, not blinking an eye, beyond thought, fully into feeling, all my senses open with raw and awesome wonder. I felt the energies of my heart expand into a feeling of the Presence like I had never experienced to this depth in my life. There was no real message being communicated beyond the overwhelming sense of "I AM HERE! FEEL ME!" Indeed, the Divine was there. I was totally "out of my mind" and fully into my heart to such a degree that tears of gratitude began to flow. The only thought that had any validity then and there was "How Great Thou Art." I felt an amazing oneness with the grandness of it all.

As I said, I was fifteen years old at the time. There were no heavy burdens or problems that I was carrying. I wasn't worried or anxious about anything going on in my life. If I had been, those concerns would have been swept away in this special moment. It was simply a wonderful experience that just came to me. It was a gift for which I remain grateful to this day. It may surprise you to know I have never told anyone. It was too personal. And at fifteen, who are you going to tell? It gave me a tantalizing taste of the truth that God was the one life that was everywhere and in everything. The experience has stayed with me to this day.

John Muir, the great naturalist, conservationist and lover of nature, said it best: "Climb the mountains and get their good tidings. Nature's peace will flow into you as sunshine flows into trees. The winds blow their own freshness into you and the storms their energy, while cares will drop off like autumn leaves." Whether you are drawn to the mountains, a walk in the forest, or the water's edge, it is all alive and offers up a healthy, clean vibration. Mountains, lakes, trees, and flowers have no emotional fluctuation. They are examples of pure beingness. They are just authentically being what they are. A mountain is not vulnerable to the ups and downs of being happy or sad and you don't have to hope you are catching it on a good day. The mountain is consistently in the purity of its mountainness. When walking in nature we don't meet up with trees that are having a bad day, that are angry, worried, or emotionally depressed. A tree stands in the purity of its life giving energy of treeness. A flower is in its pure purposefulness of extending beauty. God's many forms of nature are a wonderful example of just being, offering their true essence, their authenticity which emits an energy that feels so clean, fresh and invigorating.

Even Jesus suggested we look into nature as an example; "Consider the lilies of the field, how they grow; they neither toil nor spin." Although you may not realize it consciously, the many forms of nature often act on you subliminally, reminding you of who you really are, of your True Divine Self that lies beneath all the layers of foreign worldly conditioning. Nature offers you a field of energy that is so unique, strong, and nurturing that when you depart from its heightened presence you notice its absence. After having been in it and close to it for a substantial period of time and then removed, you can get the effect of feeling there is a void, as if something is missing. I had my own profound experience of how unyielding it can be to leave the arms of nature after a period of years in its close embrace.

As I have shared earlier, my first ministry was in Olympia, Washington, where I was senior minister for seven years, and where I felt the energies of nature all around. The church was tucked back in a wooded setting at the end of a dead-end street. There was the usual yellow city sign with black letters saying "Dead End" that was immediately visible as you turned onto the street. I had another sign just like it installed about twenty yards farther down the street, except the words on it were "The Living End." I thought it was appropriate, for the street came to a beautiful conclusion. The church was surrounded by acres of beautiful massive fir trees. We cleared a path that meandered through the woods and provided a beautiful place for people to walk through its tall timber. I often brought a bag lunch and ate it on a log, well down the path, amidst a canopy of fir trees, while birds sang to me and an occasional deer romped through, sometimes a doe with its fawn.

Most lunch appointments that I had away from church were almost always at the Falls Terrace Restaurant, which was perched above a rapidly flowing stream with a six-foot waterfall in view. As you ate your lunch, you could look out the window and watch salmon jumping the falls. After lunch you could walk the gravel path alongside the stream or stroll through the adjoining park. The home my family lived in the final three years in Olympia was located high enough in a housing development to have a clear view of Mount Rainier and St. Helens (before it erupted) from our deck. Our family outings were to nature's numerous beautiful sights throughout the surrounding area. It seemed like everywhere you turned nature took your breath away.

You see, for a number of years I had been soaking in the energies of nature to such a degree that without realizing it, my body had actually formed a kind of dependency. When we moved to Houston to take the ministerial assignment there, I literally went through two years of withdrawal. I don't wish to take anything away from all that Houston offers, for it has its own beauty and wonderful people. However, the energies of nature that I was now exposed to by moving there, was a dramatic drop-off from what my body and soul had known, and not only become accustomed to, but literally dependent on.

Sporadically throughout the day during my first year in Houston, although loving my work there, I would find myself being overtaken by a strong craving to leave what I was doing and go find a place to get a fix from nature. It could happen anywhere at any time of the day. It wasn't mental, but physical, as if my body were signaling a hunger for the energies of nature. Quite honestly, it was both surprising and interesting for me to notice that such a strong recurring urge existed. My body and soul had developed a sensitivity to experiencing a quantitative measurement on the energetic frequency of my surroundings.

I found myself periodically having to locate a park to go take a walk at lunch time or would sometimes visit the nearby arboretum on my lunch hour, just to satisfy the appetite for nature that would overtake me. During my second year there, it gradually subsided in intensity. However, the experience convinced me, with absolute certainty, that different environmental settings surely do have their own energetic vibrations and that one of the most powerful and nurturing is to be found in the purity of nature.

This is not to say God's power and presence can't be as fully experienced in the city or anywhere seemingly away from the greater expanses of nature's beauty. For it can. Spirit has no limitations. However, we are capable of picking up on energies around us, whatever they may be. Many people are sensitive in this way, so much so that they can step into a room of angry people and without a harsh word being spoken by anyone, still feel the vibrations of conflict that are there, much as they can step into a room full of loving people and feel the energies of harmony. Likewise, there is a vibrational difference to be felt when surrounded by brick and mortar, steel and pavement, versus nature's forests and mountains.

Obviously, not everyone can live near mountains and forest. However, the teaching here is that everything is alive, everything has energy, and you can expand your awareness of and sensitivity to whatever there is of nature that is around you. It might be a single tree in the yard or neighborhood, potted plants and flowers, a nearby park, a sunny day, the breeze on your face, a bird singing or the stars at night. It's all God.

The Apostle Paul makes an interesting statement in keeping with this thought: "For since the creation of the world God's invisible qualities – his eternal power and divine nature – have been clearly seen, being understood from what has been made, so that humans are without excuse." (Romans 1:20) He is politely communicating that we have no excuse for not experiencing the qualities and attributes of God all around us in nature.

As you become more attentive, pause to notice more often, and internally affirm its life to be akin to yours, you are continually growing in consciousness toward living in heaven's delight. It is to live, move and have your being in oneness, and the deep knowing that One + One is One. You and that tree are one. You and that flower are one. You and that star are one. You and your pet dog are one... that example is easy for pet lovers to understand.

The earth is a living being and the Divine Intelligence that created it is everywhere to be found. You may have noticed that there are many ways in which nature offers up lessons in life for humanity as a whole and all of us individually. Birds are just one example. I have a hobby of creating a colony of birds called "Purple Martins." I currently have three bird houses in my back yard. They have multiple levels with openings going around the circumference of each level adding up to a total of about sixty compartments for the birds to nest in and raise their young. Purple Martins are happy birds with a lively sound and live together quite harmoniously in colonies. I like to watch them swoop and fly as they catch insects and return to feed their young. After the eggs hatch and babies have grown it is fun to observe them learning to fly.

I was home one evening before sunset when one of the young adventurous Purple Martins was taking off from its porch to fly for the very first time. There is a danger they face on their maiden voyage into the skies, for the backyard of our home is on the edge of a small lake, and there is at least a 50-50 chance the young bird could try to fly in that direction. If it does, it might land in the lake and drown.

While watching one of the young push off from the bird house on what was its first flight, I observed something that was rather inspiring. Initially I was quite concerned because the young bird flew directly out over the water at about fifteen to twenty feet above it. As it flew into this danger zone, not only did the parents fly along with it, trying to guide its direction, but a whole flock of ten or more other parents got involved. This whole group became active in flying out over the water, chirping and assisting the process of steering this young bird back toward land before it got tired and fell into the water. They were successful and the baby bird actually made it back to the birdhouse, landing with an awkward thud on one of the decks. I watched this same process unfold for two other young ones on their first solo flight. In each case the community got involved, helping and supporting the parents. It warmed my heart to watch this dynamic of alert conscious caring take place. I thought to myself, "It takes a village, even in nature." The idea of oneness and all being family was exhibited in this colony of Purple Martins. They showed it can be a beautiful thing when we can all work together in oneness.

Apparently, there are Good Samaritan birds too. These Purple Martins, being a colony bird, seem to have a knowing that they are joined together, united, and that aspects of their lives are to be in active service to each other. Rather than sitting and watching a potential accident ready to happen, or a possible problem become a reality, they become pro-active, joining other members in steering one of their own away from danger, toward safety and their greater good.

"The earth shall be full of the knowledge of the Lord, as the waters cover the sea." (Isaiah 11:9) Just as there is water everywhere throughout the sea, God's knowledge and wisdom blankets the earth and is everywhere to be found throughout all its creation. Not all birds are like the Purple Martin, just as not all people find it important to be kind, caring and giving of their time and talent in service to others. But those who do are rewarded.

There is a well-known spiritual principle that says as we give we receive, that we reap according to what we sow. Although not the purpose of giving, there is a return, a receiving, that is the fulfillment of the law. We receive back in kind. It is the law of cause and effect. I have a person on my staff that cannot resist stopping to help any stray dog she may see on the streets. She will pull over in her car, no matter where it is, stop, get out and take the dog with her. If it has a collar, she does all she can to find the owner. If she doesn't, she takes the dog home and cares for it until she finds the owner, puts up signs in the area where she found it, and in some cases makes the dog her own pet. She doesn't have the heart to leave it on the streets or take it to a dog pound. Through the years, I've known her to have as many as eight or nine dogs at her home. Naturally, this giving, caring quality also flows into her human relationships, always helping others; as a result she is dearly loved by all.   When you are alert to the opportunities that may come your way to be kind, helpful and compassionate to others, by your acting on it, you open yourself to a rewarding feeling of being used by God and a beautiful feeling of connection with that person... or animal.

I recall reading about a female Humpback Whale that had become entangled in a spider web of crab traps, nets and lines. She was weighed down by hundreds of pounds and hundreds of yards of Line

Rope wrapped around her body, her tail, her torso, and even had line tugging in her mouth. She struggled to stay afloat. A fisherman spotted her just east of the Farallon Islands, outside the Golden Gate, and radioed for help. Within a few hours, a rescue team arrived and determined the only way to save her was to have divers go in and cut her free. They worked for hours with curved knives and eventually freed her. When she was set free, the divers said she swam for a while in what seemed like joyous circles. Then she came back to each and every diver, one at a time, nudged them with a gentle push as if to be thanking them. Some of the divers said it was the most incredibly beautiful experience of their lives. The diver who cut the rope out of her mouth said her eye was following him the whole time, and he would never be the same. William Shakespeare said, "One touch of nature makes the whole world kin."

Every diver went away from that whale experience having received a gift: a sacred connection between them and another of God's creation. While the whale was the recipient of freedom, the divers' hearts had been opened to the precious relationship that exists with all life. It proves again that One + One is One, no matter what form of life comes into play. Our compassionate acts of caring are what can cut away the knots that bind us, leading to our spiritual freedom. May we all be fortunate enough to be surrounded by people who will help us get free and untangled from the nets of limitation that bind us. And when opportunity presents itself, may you and I be moved to help others get untangled from their nets of negative emotion brought on by the challenges they might be facing.

When you enter another's life and somehow relieve their pain and discomfort or help them in some way, what might have been separateness on some level can melt away. It's as if the two merge into a sacred place where differences disappear. The divers had entered the whale's homeland of the sea. It wasn't the divers' natural environment. But that didn't matter. Though different from themselves, this massive God-creation with large fins and a huge tail was trapped and going to die if it wasn't freed. It was suffering and something could be done to bring relief. It wasn't a question of "if" but "how", and a way was found. In the process, something beautiful happened. All parties involved were changed and pulled into a magical moment where man and beast experienced a truth that has been there all along. It is Oneness. One + One is One in all of life. And when members of creation, across all lines and of all forms enter that sacred vibration, a bit of heaven is brought to earth.

Man has shown cruelty to both man and animal for false and shallow reasons, mostly related to survival. Of course, it need not be, for there exists a higher level of consciousness that has always been available. It's the level at which everyone and everything is your friend and has a right to its life and quality of living. In many ways nature teaches us this truth. May your heart become open and your arms extended to embrace the whole earth and all its forms as one family of the One Life. For it is all God.

The whale modeled for us ever so beautifully an important spiritual value, which is gratitude. It was moved to return to each and every diver to convey its genuine appreciation with a gentle nudge as a touch of kinship. Gratitude is important to learn because it takes us to the heart. It puts us in touch with Source energy. We give praise and thanks to God, not because God needs it, but because we do. It is the energy of oneness. There is a gospel story that tells about an event in Jesus' travels on his way to Jerusalem. While passing between Samaria and Galilee, we are told, he entered a village where he was met by ten lepers who had been waiting for him. They asked for mercy and Jesus told them to go and show themselves to the priests. As they turned and were departing they were cleansed. Yet all of them kept going, except one. He was a Samaritan, who turned back and fell at the feet of Jesus expressing thanks.

Jesus asked, "Weren't there ten that were cleansed? Where are the other nine?" Ten percent isn't very good. If we remember to enter into gratitude just one out of every ten days or for just one out of every ten good things that happen in our lives, then that needs to be improved upon. Jesus acknowledged the one who remembered to return to express gratitude. It wasn't that Jesus needed to receive thanks, but that they needed to learn the meaning and power of gratitude. He was highlighting the importance of this principle. It is essential to your going into higher states of consciousness. The whale in our story was teaching us this same truth by returning to each diver, one by one, giving the nudge of kinship. As the earlier quote from the book of Job states so well, ask the beasts and they will teach you, the birds of the air will tell you, and the fish of the sea will explain to you. As you delve into all of nature, it will testify to God's existence and teach you many of His truths.

One of my favorite Bible stories is the one of Moses and the Burning Bush. I like it for a number of reasons, one of which is that it contains a message that everything in life, including creations in nature, have a message if you are open to listening and seeing. To briefly review the story and some of its key points, Moses at an earlier time in the passage had stated; "I have been a sojourner in a foreign land." It seems he was feeling out of place and wanted to get on with what was next in his life. We're told he is in the wilderness, and he came to Horeb, the mountain of God. There he encountered a bush that was burning but not being consumed. This doesn't necessarily mean it was on fire, but that a bright Light, which God has been described to be in many instances, was emanating from the bush. Moses saw it and said to himself, "I will turn aside and see this great sight..." Then God speaks to him from the bush and he is told to remove his shoes from his feet, for the place he was standing on was holy ground. Then God revealed Himself to Moses, "I am the God of your father, the God of Abraham, of Isaac, and of Jacob." Moses is told that he is to lead the people out of bondage to Egypt and into the promised land of freedom.

First, it is worthy of taking note that the voice of God was communicating a message through a bush, one of nature's forms, seemingly validating that it can happen with other forms as well, be it a tree, mountain or star. Second, it hints that all of God's creation is sacred, for whenever, wherever, and in whatever you find God's Presence, you make of it holy ground, and understanding can come as a result of it.

I find it easy to relate to this story. You may see some aspect of your life played out in it as well. Maybe there are times when you have felt like you were in the wilderness of unhappiness, struggle or negativity of some kind... like being a sojourner in a foreign land. Moses says he will "turn aside and see this great sight..." Perhaps it can mean that when you are open to guidance, willing to turn and look at life in a new way from a new perspective, that the light of understanding begins to speak. Moses was willing to turn aside, to engage with the light and life coming from the bush. He was ready for what was next in his life. He was looking for guidance. Only after displaying an openness to learn and gain insight, did a message come and he was given a new path.

Moses is told to take off his shoes because he was standing on holy ground. The feet are known to be symbolic of understanding. To take off your shoes means to remove all the current forms and outer layers of human understanding and conditioning, so as to gain the light of inner spiritual understanding. After Moses removes his shoes, God reveals he is the God of the Patriarchs. "I am the God of your father, the God of Abraham, of Isaac, and of Jacob." Meaning, I am the God of ALL through all time, not just an exclusive chosen group. God is the God of ALL and All That Is. God then gives Moses guidance and directs him to his calling.

There will be moments in your life when you are willing to turn aside from your sense of separation, be it fear, resentment, unforgiveness or whatever it is, and receive a message of guidance. By being willing to listen to your inner spiritual voice calling you to a new and higher direction… it is then that you find you are standing on holy ground. You will feel a sense of God's Presence steering you to your higher path. You will find that when you listen to the impulse, to the "still small voice within," you will feel the higher thought of the divine calling and guiding you — and also a feeling of holiness. Understand that a feeling of holiness is actually a feeling of spiritual wholeness. Sometimes it is easier to feel that sense of holy wholeness when you are out in nature.

I have been to Paradise several times. That sounds like a lofty claim, doesn't it? Actually, I am referring to the name of a lodge area at about the 8,000-foot level of Mount Rainier in the State of Washington. While in my first ministry in Olympia, and during the time my family lived there, we took a number of day trips to Paradise with our kids.

Several years ago, when Diane and I were back in the area visiting, we went by ourselves on a day outing to Paradise. On one of the roads that lead up the mountain to the lodge, there is a place to stop and take a fairly short hike into the woods to what is called the Grove of the Patriarchs. Somehow we had not noticed it was there when we were on previous trips to Mount Rainier. It is a lovely walk on a wooded trail that eventually comes to a grove of the oldest and largest Fir trees in the whole area. As you enter the trail there is a sign stating that these trees are 200 and 300 years old. The sign also actually states that there is a sort of holiness about the place. We found ourselves to be the only ones there at the time. After a short hike, we arrived in an area where the forest floor was carpeted with clean, rusty-colored pine needles and no other vegetation. It was there that we entered a grove of trees that must have been 35 feet in circumference and towered majestically into the sky. It was like entering a massive cathedral of magnificent beauty and grace. The enormously high ceiling created by the trees' canopy dimmed and softened the light penetrating its branches. The life of these trees seemed to embrace you. It was quiet and peaceful. There was no wind moving there on the forest floor. The stillness and energies were captivating. It was like being in the midst of a group of wise old souls. There truly was something sacred about that place. You could feel it coming from the trees themselves. While looking up at these powerful, proud trees… at their strength and might, I felt one with the Source of it all. The life in them was the life in me. There was a sense of oneness. We must have stayed there for around thirty minutes, meditating part of the time. My wife and I said very little and if we did, it was in almost a whisper. There was a sacred silence that we did not want to break, being caught up in the spiritual vibrations that enfolded us in that grove. What Shakespeare has stated seemed true, "There are tongues in trees…" It felt as if they spoke to us that day.

That experience taught me once again the value of remembering that the One Spirit of life and intelligence is found everywhere and in everything. It wants to commune with you. It wants to be known, felt, heard from, experienced, and entered into relationship with. It wants to extend its gifts. How can you separate anything from the one life that

God is? It is the All That Is, offering its life-giving energies in numerous ways, through many life forms. As you continue to practice the Presence, and make it your intention to consistently feel the vibrations of oneness, it opens you to a richness of life beyond it being simply an exercise in day-to-day survival. One + One is One is a universal principle that exists everywhere and within everything, including nature.

An old Apache storyteller was once quoted as saying, "The plants, rocks, fire, and water are all alive. They watch us and see our needs. They see when we have nothing to protect us, and it is then they reveal themselves and speak to us." Help comes to you in many forms. If you accept that it is all God, then it is to your advantage to be attentive to whatever guidance may come to you in any form. The universe is your friend. At all times, something greater than yourself is present and one with you, even when you are not consciously one with It. The Divine is still there in moments when your awareness of it is seemingly absent. Even when you are distracted by life's challenges, there is constant support, help, guidance, and assistance being offered, sometimes in seemingly mysterious or even miraculous ways. It will find a way to capture your attention and communicate its message.

There was a time, while visiting family back in my hometown in Wisconsin, that I was dealing internally with a difficult matter. I was troubled and heavily caught up in some problem I was facing. I decided to take a drive to an area of my hometown where there was a familiar park. I had been there many times in my youth. It had lots of trees surrounding an open area where a circular covered bandstand stood. Beyond it was an area of the park with walkways and paths that went along a creek and through some wooded areas. It was a very peaceful and pretty area.

It was an autumn afternoon of a dreary, overcast weekday when most of the local community was at work. Getting out of my car, I noticed there was no one in sight. That pleased me, for I wanted to be alone with my thoughts and be reflective. As I walked along I became lost in nostalgic thoughts of my childhood and youth, of all the times and reasons I'd been to that park. There were baseball fields in the distance that I'd played on many times and the lighted outdoor basketball courts where I'd spent hours shooting baskets. And even the high school I had attended was there within sight through the trees. So many memories flooded in. I felt sort of melancholy and sad that those days were past. Life in that current moment, with what I was wrestling, seemed dim and dreary, like the overcast day. My thoughts took me back in time contemplating how life seemed somehow easier back then and had taken on a more serious and demanding tone.

While walking along in the midst of this sort of sad, dark state, my head down, suddenly my attention was taken to the sound of rustling leaves a ways in front of me. I lifted my head to see a flash of movement amidst the trees and brush up ahead. As I kept walking in its direction I got within range of something I had never seen before in my life. I could hardly believe it, but there before me, some yards ahead, was a pure white albino squirrel. I honestly didn't know such a thing existed. I'd never heard or read of anyone seeing one, but there one was, right before my eyes.

My heart started beating a little faster and I felt a bit of excitement. How special was this? The animal was beautiful. I even recall wondering how it was able to appear to be wearing such a clean, unsoiled white coat of fur while living out in nature. I walked slowly toward it, getting closer and closer. I stopped about fifteen yards away, and just stood there very still, watching it with great interest as it hopped through the leaves. Next, it climbed a nearby tree, went out onto one of its branches, and leaped onto the branch of a neighboring tree.

In the next moment, I felt my heart open as I had the thought drop in that the One Source, the Divine was somehow involved in this. I had the realization that God was not only in the albino squirrel, but God was that squirrel. With that, my eyes began to tear up as I asked myself, "What are the chances of seeing an albino squirrel at this moment, while in this particular time of personal struggle?" There are no accidents, only divine appointments. And I was having one. I then asked myself, "What is the message being offered to me in this squirrel?" It struck me that what had come into my presence was a very rare specimen of a squirrel that was the embodiment of "Bright, White, Light!" With that thought came a special feeling accompanied by God-bumps. One might say it was my own burning bush coming to me in the form of a light, bright, albino squirrel. Next, I had the thought, what does a squirrel do but climb to high places. It leaps from branch to branch, tree to tree, without having to touch the ground.

I realized that upon my arrival at the park, my consciousness had been somewhat grounded or at ground zero... and that this unique, eye-catching white squirrel, planted there by the Divine, was delivering a message that I needed to absorb and follow. It was the message that I was to look to that which was deep inside of me that had the properties and energies of "bright, white, light." I was being guided to let the Light of Truth back into my awareness and let it take me higher. It was telling me that I, too, had within me the ability to climb higher, to leap through and beyond whatever the challenge confronting me, without hitting the ground. I knew then that everything would be okay. Things were going to work out for good. And it did.

I stood there, in a profound stillness, looking at the squirrel as these thoughts from somewhere beyond me downloaded into my awareness. I knew, from a place deep inside, this albino squirrel had as its purpose that day, to be there for me, one with me, loving me with its message. In some ways it was not very different from having some person who loved me show up and do the same as a messenger of the Divine. For our help and guidance comes in many forms and packages. I was humbled and thrilled by the experience. My heart took a leap upward that day, trailing the creature of light that had shown the way. This was powerful evidence to me once again that we really are never separate from the One, that we are forever contained in the All, always supported in becoming Whole. One + one IS ONE... in ALL of life.

Even later on, I found myself wondering about this unique meeting with an albino squirrel. Was that squirrel living there in one of those trees? Had others come to that park on other days and seen the albino squirrel? Or did it somehow materialize for me in that few minutes of time, fulfill its purpose, deliver its gift, and move on, somewhat like an angel appearing and disappearing? This is one of the mysteries of life. What was important was that it did happen and with divine timing, conveyed a clear message with a divine purpose. In its unique way, it cast a light on what was a dark time and revealed that I was to get off the ground level of consciousness and go higher. It was reminding me that as a spiritual being it is in my nature to look up, think up, gain a higher perspective and see my way above the problem.

That walk all alone in the park of my hometown was the remedy for what ailed me that day. Maybe you've had times when you've been weighted down with some challenge and just needed to find a quiet place to be alone, reflect on things, and seek guidance. If there is a place nearby that allows you to be in a setting of nature, then you should consider it. It has always had a nurturing effect on me, as it has on millions down through time.

Anne Frank, the German-born diarist and writer, is one who put it rather succinctly when she wrote, "The best remedy for those who are afraid, lonely or unhappy is to go outside, somewhere where they can be quiet, alone with the heavens, nature and God. Because only then does one feel that all is as it should be and that God wishes to see people happy, amidst the simple beauty of nature." Perhaps you've had moments in your life when something in nature appeared with perfect timing to convey a message, or a truth, so as to help you go forward beyond some fear, sadness or difficult situation.

Early in my family's move to Houston, my wife, Diane, and I met a wonderful couple, Bill and Madeline, who immediately embraced us and our young family. We became very close and connected to them and their three boys who had graduated college and were into their young careers.

With both Diane's and my family living in Wisconsin, Bill and Madeline made us feel like one of theirs. We celebrated holidays and birthdays, and even traveled together on several Caribbean and Mediterranean cruises. We were there for each other through many happy times and whatever challenges came along.

One of the most serious and difficult of times was when Bill and Madeline's middle son, Steve, married and father of two children, became ill and over a period of months passed on. There is no way to measure the pain of losing a child, whatever their age. Bill and Madeline were devastated and the sadness of their loss lingered on. They owned a small Texas ranch in the Texas hill country. The small, somewhat modest quarters on the property was leased to a sweet and humble family they had come to know and love. It just so happened that the mother had also recently lost a son.

One day Madeline was guided to make the drive out to the small ranch home and pay the mother, Nettie, a visit. As soon as Madeline was greeted, welcomed, and invited in, her eyes went directly to a picture on the TV of Nettie's son, Victor, who had died suddenly of a ruptured spleen. Coincidently, her son was the same age as Bill and Madeline's. They talked about their loss and cried many tears together during the visit.

When it was time to leave, they moved onto the porch, and in unison reached for each other in a heart-warming embrace, joined by the commonality of having to face the pain of this kind of loss. It had been a sacred meeting for both. They had shared at length fond memories of times spent with their respective sons and it had somehow brought to mind and heart a feeling of their sons' proximity and closeness in spirit.

It was a cloudy day, and as they broke free from their tender hug, they turned to see a ray of light break through the cloud-filled sky and shine onto the sprawling fields before them. It was unique, unusual and beautiful. It split into three rainbow-like beams, the largest beam in the center, accompanied by one on each side that was a tad narrower. All three beams landed on a grove of trees a couple hundred yards away, brightening them into a glorious glow of surreal green. Nettie and Madeline just stood there in silence, captured by the moment. Finally, with both still gazing at the sight, Madeline said in a sort of whisper, "Nettie, what are you thinking?" At first she didn't answer, then turned to Madeline as a tear streamed down from each eye, said, "I think it's our boys, tellin' us... they's okay."

It was obvious to each of these women that through nature a clear message was being sent that the two sun-beams were their two son's beams united with the larger stream of God-Light in the middle. The three shafts of light held their pose for at least a solid minute, but the extent to which love and peace was brought to these two loving mothers could never be measured. In the words of the playwright and novelist Thorton Wilder, "There is a land of the living and a land of the dead and the bridge is love, the only survival, the only meaning."

How thin the veil separating two worlds can be at times when love between souls, a mother and her son, demands a curtain call and magnifies a message made of clouds, sun and sky. Nature has the God-given capacity to create and author a message that can transport one's heart and soul to a place where two worlds touch. Whoever it is among your loved ones that has passed beyond this physical world, you can know they are around you and may offer up their messages of love and guidance through their partnership with God's many forms of nature. It is all alive, intelligent, and speaks in every language via love. Incidents like these, having gone on millions of times, throughout thousands of years, can put you and me in a sacred place of beholding nature. Nature is God and God as nature is always surrounding you. It can deepen your conscious connection to the Divine Presence as you learn to go deeper in your awareness and reverence for field and flower, tree and sky.

One of my true heroes in demonstrating a connection and oneness with the Divine Intelligence of all life is a man named George Washington Carver. I love everything I have come to know and learn about the man. I read about his life around 40 years ago, and was moved then and continue to be impressed by him, his life and what he demonstrated. This man showed that he could communicate with nature in a manner that should be an inspiration to us all. He was an American Botanist and inventor. The exact date of his birth is unknown, but thought to be 1861. He started his life as a slave. His father was a slave on a nearby farm and was killed shortly before Carver was born, while still in his mother's womb. He was just a baby when he was kidnapped by night riders. His mother, brother, and he were held for ransom. Before they could be rescued, his mother died.

A German farmer named Moses Carver traded a $300-dollar race horse for George. He was orphaned and put in the custody of a white guardian from early childhood. He was able to attend a school for Black children some nine miles from the home of his guardian. Every day he walked there with his brother, James. He was in his mid-twenties when he completed and graduated from high school in Kansas. His education continued, graduating from Iowa State College of Agriculture with a Master's Degree in Agriculture in 1896.

He accepted an offer from the African American educator, Booker T. Washington, to teach at Tuskegee Institute in Alabama. He became an expert in the study of fungi and cross-fertilization. Through the years he developed a national and international reputation for his expertise. He had a deep desire to help the southern farmers rebound from the ravages of the Civil War. When he realized that the single crop of the South, cotton, was wearing out the soil, he encouraged farmers to grow crops in rotation. Carver was convinced that the answer was to be found in the planting of peanuts and sweet potatoes.

He was a deeply spiritual man and prayed that God would reveal to him the secrets of the universe. He shared with those close to him that the message coming back to him from prayer times was that although he would not receive the secrets of the universe, he would be shown the secrets of the peanut. His research at the Tuskegee Institute resulted in the creation of more than 300 products from the peanut and more than 150 products from sweet potatoes.

You may wonder along with me; how does a man discover such an enormous amount of use for the products of these plants? Actually, it was a kind of guidance and communication that came from the plants or creations themselves. Carver got up early every morning before dawn to talk with God. He began each day with the intense prayer that God would reveal to him the secrets of the flowers, plants, soils and weeds, so he might help put more food in the bellies of the hungry, more clothing on the backs of the naked, and better shelter over the heads of the homeless. He said, "Anything will give up its secrets if you love it enough. Not only have I found that when I talk to the little flower or to the little peanut, they will give up their secrets, but I found that when I silently commune with people, they give up their secrets also, if you love them enough." Here again we see evidence that in the life of Carver, he had come to know and experience truths from plants and nature that were universal and applicable to the lives of all of us. It appears that he treated his relationships with people and plants in much the same way, with love.

He stated that God would reveal things He never revealed before if we put our hands in His. He always spoke about the beauty of the earth and God's handiwork in all things. He talked about one's spiritual evolution and growth when he wrote, "How far you go in life depends on your being tender with the young, compassionate with the aged, sympathetic with the striving, and tolerant with the weak and strong. Because someday in your life you will have been all of these." That statement, like many of his, contains a wealth of wisdom from which you and I can benefit. You get a feel for the heart of the man and his sensitivities by his emphasis on key virtues like tenderness, compassion, sympathy, and tolerance. All are worthy of incorporating in consciousness because of their connective properties, whether with people, peanuts, sweet potatoes, or any creation.

It is truly astounding what Carver was able to accomplish through his deep communication with God in all its forms. He was able to connect so intimately with them that, as he says, they revealed their secrets. He showed us that it was possible to have and be in relationship with all life. He made it a common exercise to daily commune with nature as if every creation was his friend. He said, "I love to think of nature as an unlimited broadcasting station, through which God speaks to us every hour, if we only will tune in."

Contained in that statement is much of what this chapter is intended to be about and convey to you, the reader. Nature has its own vibratory network that is broadcasting to you in unlimited ways. Divine Intelligence is sending signals to you through the frequencies of nature. It's possible for you to become tuned in consistently to its energies and dialed in to its messages. As a spiritual being, you are not only able, but also are intended to progress in spiritual consciousness toward a Oneness with the All That Is. Becoming attuned to commune at this deeper level is another way of experiencing oneness with God. It requires that you learn to steer your spiritual faculty of will toward a greater willingness to commune more deeply with nature's many forms around you. It also calls for you to go to your heart and extend love to all creations. They are ready and willing to communicate their secrets, and extend help, guidance, love, and truth, that can take you into a powerful unity consciousness. The universal spiritual principle is One + One is One. You + nature, in truth, are One.

Carver stated, "There is literally nothing that I ever wanted to do, that I asked the blessed Creator to help me to do, that I have not been able to accomplish… it's all very simple, if one knows how to talk with the Creator." Do you know how to talk with your Creator? It is the same way you would talk with your best friend. It is with honesty, ease and authenticity. It is not being afraid to address any topic. It is being able to talk to your Creator the same as someone you are extremely close to and could share anything. You are meant to cultivate as deep a bond with your God as any you've had with another person in this life. Make it your intention to be as close and intimate with the Divine Presence as any you have had or felt with another, whether it was with a parent, spouse, child or friend. Have your relationship with God equal or exceed it. It doesn't require some kind of flowery language. The presence of Spirit is not there to judge your delivery or content. God wants you to be real with Him, not contrived or superficial.

Most importantly He wants to converse, commune, and talk to you throughout the day, not just a morning and evening prayer. The Apostle Paul advised us to pray without ceasing. He understood that the presence of Spirit wants you to be engaged with Him continuously in consciousness. In other words, you are asked to talk, talk, talk. The Father knows what you have need of before you ask, but He still wants to be asked. As Jesus has stated, we are to ask, seek and knock. He also said we were to hunger and thirst after a relationship with the Divine. In other words, there is nothing aloof or nonchalant about it. The talking is not in regard to our needs alone. Talk to God through the good times as well. The Psalmist said to enter His gates with praise and thanksgiving. It's not that His gates are closed until he receives our praise. As I've shared earlier, God doesn't need our praise and gratitude, we do. We do because it opens us up and puts us into a heart vibration.

George Washington Carver understood also that there is a time for us to talk and a time to listen. He meditated in the outdoors of nature and had a deep acceptance that it would be a two-way conversation. In quieting his mind, he created a receptivity to listen. He meditated very early in the morning which is a great time if you can do it because most of the world is quiet and the impulses of Spirit and Life can better be felt and heard within.

Early-morning times in the silence are a sacred treasure. Mother Teresa stated, "We need to find God and He cannot be found in noise and restlessness. God is the friend of silence. See how nature – trees, flowers, grass – grows in silence; see the stars, the moon and the sun, how they move in silence... we need silence to be able to touch souls." You and I need times of silence built into the schedule of our lives if we are going to have our souls receive the sacred touches and wisdom whispers of Spirit.

George Washington Carver was a mentor to his students and wrote, "Oh, how I want them to get the fullest measure of happiness and success out of life. I want them to see the great Creator in the smallest and apparently the most insignificant things about them. How I long for each one to walk and talk with the great Creator through the things He has created." You can capture in Carver's words just how deeply he longed for others to walk and talk with the Divine in all of its creation as he had learned to do. He experienced a level of oneness that he sincerely wanted others to have. It's apparent he was convinced that you, too, can learn to cultivate an ability to see the Creator in the smallest and largest of things about you, as well as learn to walk and talk with it all.

For the past forty years, since I first read about the life of this man, he has been a mentor and an inspiration to me. How is it that a man is able to find over 300 uses for a peanut and over 150 uses for the sweet potato through some kind of communication born of a oneness with the peanut and sweet potato themselves? Shakespeare would likely say, "See, there truly are tongues in trees, books in running brooks, and endless products to be found inside peanuts and sweet potatoes, when you develop an ability to communicate with all forms of life that are of God."

What George Washington Carver was able to do is inspiring to me in an immensely powerful way. It substantiates that everything is alive and we can be in relationship with it. Maybe we will never communicate with a peanut or any plant as he did, and yet, one can never know when, where and in what way ideas from on High might be communicated, solutions extended, and guidance forthcoming. Everywhere we turn, the manual on life and living is providing a message of help and inspiration. And everywhere we turn, the principle of One + One is One, is being revealed. There are many stories that provide evidence of animals and birds having displayed a kind of oneness, despite having seemingly glaring differences. Not always do birds of a different feather flock together, but they can sometimes show us a way to interact from which we as humans could learn.

About a decade ago I came across a true story that I made notes on and stuck them in my files. Unfortunately, I didn't write down the source. Nevertheless, it was another example of what nature has to teach us. It's about a woman living on the eastern shores of Maryland around Chesapeake Bay who tells of how she could look out her picture window upon coves and creeks of water where she could see Canada geese, white swans, and ducks. She points out that the geese and swans do not take kindly to each other, and can be indifferent or even unfriendly. The lady arose one cold morning, looked out her picture window and saw that some sleet and light snow had fallen during the cold night. A freeze was occurring on some of the smaller inlets of water.

Then she noticed what appeared to be one lone goose. She grabbed her binoculars for a closer look and realized that the goose was very still, had its wings pinned to its side by a layer of frozen sleet and had its feet frozen in the ice. Then, in the next moment, her eyes went to a flock of swans flying in a single line formation toward the goose. Suddenly they formed a circle and descended onto the ice, encircling the goose.

The woman immediately went into fear for the life of this goose frozen to the ice, assuming the swans were going to use their strong, hard beaks to cruelly peck away its life. But what happened next amazed her. The swans, having formed a circle around the goose, began to hammer the ice surrounding its feet with their beaks. This went on for some time until finally the feet of the goose were free. The swans then took to the air, but hovered for a time as if watching and waiting for the goose to fly away. But it still couldn't because of the layer of ice and sleet that had coated its wings and body. Amazingly, four swans from the hovering flock returned and again, with their beaks, chipped off the ice that pinned the wings and feathers of the goose tight to its body.

The goose slowly spread its wings and shook off the now broken particles of ice. Seeing it spread its wings, the four swans flew to rejoin the group. Once together, the flock of swans resumed its earlier formation and were in the process of leaving the area. The lady was again amazed as she watched the goose, now free, joyously fly into the sky and join the formation of swans. Together they flew as one, until they all disappeared out of sight. The experience brought tears to her eyes and a question to her mind: "If so for birds, why not for man?" A very good question.

This was an actual happening this woman was blessed to observe. It was a magical event that moved her emotionally. For me, the details of the story acted as a zip line to my heart. It caused something in me to want to laugh, cry, dance, and sing, jump and shout, for it is such a beautiful demonstration of what not only is possible but is intended to be commonly accepted behavior for all of us. Two very different breeds of birds overcame their differences in appearance, behavior, character, and even instinct to put on a display of caring oneness. They somehow stepped into a unified field of being and demonstrated the principle of "One + One is One," even for them.

This was an event that would be extremely rare to duplicate in the bird world. Consider how much larger our physical hearts are as humans than theirs and how vastly more capable we are intended to be in opening to a feeling of being connected. If birds can do it, that is, show this kind of response, surely much more of humanity can find its way beyond the reasons and appearances to feel separate and can learn to demonstrate greater unity and cooperation. Even the goose serves as a metaphor for your life and mine. Surely you've had times, as I have, where you are inwardly stuck, frozen in a place of fear, loss, resentment or unforgiveness. Our lives can't seem to get off the ground, can't break inertia. It's not only cold feet that can hold us back, keep us from a decision or from getting off the ground, but it can be a heart turned cold with indifference, cynicism, competitiveness or resentment.

Unfortunately, we can't depend on a flock of white swans to come thaw us out or chip away our resistances. The work of thawing, warming and freeing the heart starts within us. If circumstances have brought a chill to what was a warm heart or one wants to get some lift back in the spirit of life, it starts with a willingness to face one's self, and begin to do the inner work that shifts our attitude, perspective and consciousness.

The songs, sights and sounds of nature are many and all around us. They, too, carry a wisdom of their own that if we look and listen will emit a message that can often teach us some life lesson that furthers us on our way. We are mysteriously all interconnected to the One that stands behind and in it All. Whether it's a bird, a flower, a tree, a mountain, a peanut or potato, it's all alive and on some sacred level we can connect and communicate because we are one. In his series of writings known as *Meditations*, the great Christian mystic, Marcus Aurelius, shared, "All things are linked with one another, and this oneness is sacred; there is nothing that is not interconnected with everything else. For things are interdependent, and they combine to form this universal order. There is only one universe made up of all things, and one Creator who pervades them."

Awakening spiritually into oneness and building a consciousness that lives from the universal principle of One + One is One, is a gradual process. As I've said before, it's a journey, not a destination. As you heighten your awareness that school is wherever you may find yourself, more of God comes into view. In addition to people and circumstances serving as your teachers and opportunities for learning, the potential is there to be a student of oneness through all of God's creations.

Continue to heighten and expand your conscious awareness that it's all God, everything, everywhere. Practice seeing the world around you in a new light. See everything as being alive, teeming with energy, connected to you, related to you, willing to communicate with you. Continually remind yourself to establish and deepen your relationship with all forms of God's creation. All relationships require time and attention. All relationships can be improved upon. God is all around you in all Its creations waiting to be engaged. Allow yourself to enter into conversation with a flower, tree, mountain, or twinkling star. There is nothing weird or odd about it. We talk to our pets and think nothing of it. If others are around, you need not speak out loud, but do it internally in mind and heart. Guidance and messages of inspiration can come to you from anything, anywhere, at any time. Hopefully, that is exciting to you. It makes life all the more sacred and stimulating, moment to moment.

The concept some have of their God as a Being off in the heavens only to be known after you die is both limiting and separating. We are to go beyond that. Enter into the practice of realizing the Presence of God is all around you right now, as the life in all of Its creatures and creations, extending Its love and support. Your consciousness of oneness will heighten. Your life will take on a new richness and depth.

CHAPTER SIX
The World As One

"We are the opening verse of the opening page of the chapter of endless possibilities." Rudyard Kipling

You and I live in a spiritual universe that operates on spiritual laws in which endless possibilities exist. Because this is true, individuals and the world as a whole are always evolving either slowly or in spurts, according to the awareness levels of those who are in the world. In any era of time, humanity has the ability to turn the page, take the next stride forward in consciousness, and begin a new chapter for our world. You and I have a part to play and can be the opening verse in creating this potential new chapter.

The time has come for the world as a whole to have a leap in spiritual growth by creating a kind of renaissance toward living the principle of Oneness, and that is One + One is One. That can only happen when individuals like you and me, as well as leaders in all areas of our world, begin to make it their conscious intention. Everyone is able to contribute to the betterment and healing of this world we all share, through the powers built into the principles of oneness.

The potential for change is always in the air, and it seems that people are ready for greater peace and happiness for all. Perhaps the time has come for a mass movement in which the ideas and ideals around the power of oneness are brought to the forefront in every sector of life. Let it become the topic of our times, the very principle we all want to live. Let it be an emphasis in what we teach our children in our homes and schools. Let there be classes taught on it at all levels of education, including seminars and workshops presented in the work place. Let there be conferences on it for executives of corporations, politicians, and leaders across all lines. Let us rethink everything we are doing in our world from the standpoint of creating an uptick in the awareness of oneness in our societies. Perhaps a tidal wave of energy can be built on the ideas and ideals of oneness so that it reaches the shores of every heart and tugs at the deepest dimensions of our inner beings where we remember this is the very thing for which our souls have all come.

More and more we hear people making the distinction that they are "spiritual" and "not religious" when describing their soul path. I don't see that as a bad thing. Rather than view it as anything anti-religious, we can see it as a hint of spiritual awakening and the role of oneness entering into the people's awareness. It may be an indication that these people are more in favor of inclusivity than exclusivity and more into a cooperative unity than anything that would separate us. People of today are more aware than ever of the dividing elements that are part of our history. There have always been clashes and conflicts brought on by bodies of people who have formed unhealthy attachments to a political or religious doctrine or ideology. It's the kind that promotes the idea that there are those who are exclusively right and correct – and those who are considered to be wrong, incorrect, or outside what has been deemed acceptable as the established letter of the law.

We have seen instances too often in our world where differences in ideologies have been taken to extremes, fostering violence and loss of life. But now, perhaps more people are awakening to a more universal view that sees everyone as a part of the greater whole that honors the life and freedoms of all of humanity. We are all equal in the eyes of our Creator, but that equality sometimes is filtered through the consciousness of a segment of humanity. All forms of separation consciousness eventually show themselves and become problematic in society. Certainly, the religions of the world have an important role to play and have done their share of good. And they are not innocent of some dark times as well. However, religions, much like people, can evolve to where they move out of ego tendencies of superiority, division and separation.

Religion is man-made. It contains human interpretations of a body of teachings that sometimes get misdirected or even distorted, causing people to be set apart when the original intent was to unify through love for all. Spirituality is not man-made, but of the Spirit. It can be found in religion, of course, but in varying degrees. Spirituality in its purest sense contains an all-inclusive universal message that leaves nothing and no one out. It is the movement of a pure, unifying, loving energy that binds all together in and of the One God... the One Spirit in all.

Paramahansa Yogananda, considered by many to have been an enlightened teacher, made a good point when he said, "Worshipers within divisions of religion have not the full realization of those whose lives have inspired true paths.... if Jesus, Krishna, Buddha, and other true emissaries of God came together, they would not quarrel, but would drink from the same one cup of God-communion." All avatars and enlightened masters through the ages have taught love and oneness. Their emphasis was on the teachings, which were universal, rather than on creating an institution around their message.

The Apostle Paul refers to the fact that teachings go beyond written words and the mind. He refers to there being a message of truth that is, "...written not with ink, but with the Spirit of the living God, not in tables of stone, but in fleshy tables of the heart... for the letter killeth, but the spirit giveth life." (2 Cor. 3:3-6 KJV) The ego mind always wants to dissect the letter, draw a line in the sand, establish exclusivity, where the heart goes beyond the letter, sweeps away the line in the sand, and opens its arms in acceptance of all. The great teacher, Jesus, said, "For where your treasure is, there will your heart be also." (Matt. 6:21 KJV). Consistently, Jesus' teachings sought to direct our hearts toward the treasures of love and oneness.

It is interesting to consider that America was essentially founded on principles of spirituality beyond religious dogma. Our founding fathers, in coming up with our Declaration of Independence, attempted to be spiritual rather than religious, to be inclusive and avoid exclusivity. It was men like Thomas Jefferson, John Adams, Benjamin Franklin and others who believed in the principles of freedom. Thomas Jefferson was selected to write the Declaration of Independence. When he completed the document and read it to the others, it distinguished itself for many reasons. Among them was the amazing way it was written, with a spiritual base that was free of the trappings of religion. It was undergirded by a faith in a Supreme Being. You could be any religion or no religion for this God that was seen to be in all of us. If the document were to exclude anyone, then it would not be in alignment with the One True Spirit of freedom, for their God was the God of all. In the eyes of God we are all equal, with God-given rights of life, liberty, and the pursuit of happiness. And these belong to everyone, not just Americans. From my studies of Thomas Jefferson, I found him to be a spiritual man. He had done his own exhaustive study of the teachings of Jesus and even created his own bible of sorts which has been called "The Jefferson Bible."

He and John Adams corresponded a great deal and many of their letters have been preserved for historical purposes. In one of them he wrote to Adams that the teachings of Jesus are quite simple… that there is only one God, that God is perfect, God and man are one, and to love God with all our heart and your neighbor as yourself is the sum of religion. He concluded in his letter, "These are the great points on which I endeavor to reform and live my life." Jefferson kept it simple and I believe that if most of the world did the same, and just practiced living their lives from these basic truths, we would have a world of greater peace and harmony.

From the time of my youth, the idea that we are all one has lived in me, taken me into its arms and not let me go. Although I teach and live the teachings of Jesus to the best of my ability, I have always felt that God's love is total, unconditional, and inclusive of all, as ours should be. This includes Hindus, Buddhists, Muslims Jews and others because I believe that in the heart of God there is no separation nor segregation of Its love.

From where I first heard this analogy I do not recall, but I have used it for decades. It can be helpful to think of the different religions and paths to God as spokes on a wheel. Bring to mind the image of an old-time wagon wheel. Every spoke represents a different path, with the hub at the center being God. Out on the rim is where most of us begin our journey. We move toward the Source, which is God, at the center where total love and oneness resides. On the rim we seem farthest apart in consciousness from all others due to different approaches, conditioning, emphasis, dogma, and so on. But as we evolve and grow spiritually, we move closer and closer toward the All-Knowing Center. As we do, the distance diminishes between each spoke, path, or person. There is less and less that separates us while evolving more and more toward discovering a commonality and increasing oneness. At the Hub is God, Bliss, Nirvana, the glory of the Lord. It is there that we discover, experience, deeply know and live the Universal principle that One + One is One. Humanity has shown that it has a significant way to go to achieve a world of oneness. Yet it is a reality that is growing and speaks to the heart of many.

You have a work to do in this world. It is the work of God, which is about love and oneness, and you must not allow this work in you to become thwarted by what might be happening in the world. You must not become disheartened, even when things appear to be going in reverse. Despite what you may see going on in the world, humanity is evolving. Sometimes the pendulum swings far out of balance before it gets man's attention so as to correct and alter the course. Regardless of what is going on externally, or how dark things may seemingly get, you are to hold fast to remaining positive and doing your inner work; that of being a light.

At the Oneness University that I have attended in India, they have shared that in the realm of cosmic math, the consciousness of one spiritually awakened person can offset and impact 10,000 who are not. It really does matter how many times and in what ways you make an impact toward oneness, whether large or small. You may recall Jesus said, "If I be lifted up, I draw all men unto me." Can it be any different for us? It is the same principle as that shared in India. It is a spiritual principle that is reliable and works for everyone when applied. Therefore, every prayer you pray for peace and oneness in the world is a force for good. Every time you meditate you are opening to the divine energies of light, love and goodness to be poured through you as part of this world. Never under-estimate the role you play in consciously choosing to bring the best of you into each day. You become a blessing to the world. It genuinely feels good inside to know that you have given yourself to the good works of the Infinite. You are helping the light to win in the world.

One of my very favorite movies is "Hoosiers." It is an old movie that I saw years ago when it first came out. I have watched it a number of times since. It is a great movie that spoke to me about love and carried many lessons in it. It is based on a true story that involves a coach who comes to a very small Indiana town to coach the high-school basketball team. He runs up against quite a bit of resistance from the townspeople about his approach to coaching. He didn't inherit a very good team. Although there was lots of room for improvement, he believed in his players. I found it a heart-warming movie that helped me see the many ways in which this coach contributed to the lives of the boys on the team and others around them.

Before the first game, at a rally in the gym, he told the student body, "The boys and I are getting to know each other, seeing who we are, what we can be." Then at the first practice, he told the boys, "Let's be real clear about what we are after here. TEAM, TEAM, TEAM! Five players functioning as one single unit, no one more important than the other." Sounds like the principle of "One + One is One" doesn't it? They lost the first few games. He almost lost his job over it. Then, as the bond grew among the team members, they began to win. They ended up doing well enough in their conference to go to Sectionals. They were underdogs, but won anyway. That sent them on to the Regional tournament. No one expected them to win there. They were up against all the big schools. In their entire school there were only fifty-six boys. Somehow, they won. Every ensuing challenge had a way of always pulling them together as a unit, building a sense of closeness, love, and sense of team.

Now they were in the State Championship. They were in a bigger field house than they had ever been in whether to attend or play a game. There were thousands of people in the stands.

Again the odds were heavily against them because of the big strong team they were facing. In the locker room before coming out onto the floor, the team is sitting quietly together and you hear the final words from the coach before going out to play the game. In the most heart-connected tone, he says, "I love you guys." The game was exciting. They were losing for a time but staged an inspiring comeback and won the state championship with a 25-foot shot in the final seconds by their team leader and best shooter. The jubilation and celebration was something that made you want to jump inside the TV and become part of it. The movie made me feel like I was on that team. It spoke to me. I've felt like an underdog at various times during my life. And I've known what it can be like to push through the doubts and fears and let love live out its best.

As the movie ends, a young boy, maybe eight or nine years of age, is in the gym shooting baskets. It is implied that this youngster must learn some of the principles the coach brought to life and instilled in the players, if he, too, is to have some "wins" in life. Echoing through the gym in a sort of ghostly fashion is the voice of the coach stating some of his most important teachings from earlier days with the team: "We are getting to know each other, see who we are, what we can be. Let's be real clear about what we are after here... Team, Team, Team! Five players functioning as one single unit; no one more important than the other. I love you guys." Wow! Every time I watch that movie, it deeply moves me and takes me right to my heart. Those are universal truths that reflect the spiritual principle that I so believe in, "One + One is One." The messages expressed by the coach to his players should resonate as having value for you, me and the masses. He communicated ideas to those boys, that if incorporated by us, would contribute to a better life and world.

In the world in which we live, we are still getting to know each other, seeing who we are and what we can be together. We are still learning to see who we all are on the inside, that at our core essence, we are all spiritual beings, connected by the one Spirit. With that as a foundation, we can begin to see what we can be together, and build on the energies of love and oneness. Ideally, we want a world where everyone is given a chance to win at life. Maybe it is possible for humanity to become more of a team, with groups of people, bodies of people, nations of people functioning with an intention for unity, no one more important than the other.

Have you noticed that most true advances for the greater good of the individual and humanity, be it a new idea, invention, cure or creation, has contained within it some aspect of the principle of oneness? In other words, it brings the masses together in the use of whatever it is. Everyone sees the value in it. So in a sense, we become one in the use of that product, cure, or invention that serves as a helpful advance to all.

Usually, people who are the most creative and innovative have a sense of selflessness that connects them to the greater whole. They feel part of something larger, united with the part of themselves that is connected to all. Long ago, Plato said, "The essence of humanity is to comprehend a whole." You and I and humanity are all parts of a greater whole. The key is to comprehend that and live from it. This similar idea that we are all part of the greater "whole" was brought out by another of the great minds, Albert Einstein, when he said; "The human being is part of the whole called by us the 'universe,' a part limited in time and space. He experiences himself, his thoughts and feelings, as something from the rest – a kind of optical delusion of consciousness. This delusion is a kind of prison for us, restricting us to our personal desires. Our task must be to free ourselves from this prison by widening our circle of compassion to embrace all living creatures and the whole of nature in its beauty."

There is that word "compassion" again, which is really about love, and leads to oneness, or as he says, "the Whole of nature in its beauty." He suggests that we look at what personal desires we may have that act as a factor to set us apart and put us in the delusionary prison of separation. What thoughts and feelings do we have that seem to distance us from the whole? They are to be released and replaced with thoughts and feelings that unite us to the whole. The dynamic of oneness is seemingly always forward moving. It has progress built into it. The truth of an acorn is that it is a mighty oak. And how is that accomplished? It is by sending its roots deep into the earth, becoming one with it, drawing what is needed to expand and grow into its true design.

The seed ideas for cures, inventions, and other progressive visions were always there waiting for a mind that was open to foster the possibility and bring its applications to the whole. By passionately believing in an idea, you become one with it. You have it and it has you. Add to that the creative energies of a clear vision with the possibilities it has to serve the whole, and God, the universe, will reveal a way. The Wright Brothers found a way for man to fly, Clara Barton founded the American Red Cross, Ben Franklin discovered electricity, Jonas Salk discovered a cure for polio, Rosa Parks was

"The First Lady of Civil Rights." Thomas Edison said, "I never perfected an invention that I did not think about in terms of service it might give to others." Dr. Martin Luther King had a dream for humanity — the list goes on and on.

The principle of oneness is evident in the healing of body, mind and soul, as well as in the healing of relationships, be it that of individuals or nations. All progress and movement toward greater peace, love, joy and freedom begins with the emerging energies of oneness having been put into motion. A consistency of creativity, abundance and generosity will be born from properties of oneness. Spiritual awakening, growth, empowerment, and the opening to an expanded deep bonding with the Divine are founded upon an expansion of oneness of consciousness.

Most all healing hinges on our spiritual awakening and the return to our true purpose on earth, which is love. Stated many times and in many ways, it's been the redundant solution conveyed emphatically by masters, mystics, saints, saviors, and seers down through the ages. The reason is that love has always been recognized as a binding, bonding, unifying energy that connects us to the true nature of that from which we come and therefore that which we are. The fall of humanity is essentially a fall from love, and unfortunately goes on all too often in the hearts of humans. And the fall from love is, of course, a fall from oneness into separation.

I've learned a lot in my life from participating in and observing team sports. Coaches and managers often talk about the importance of team chemistry being created if they are to realize success. This was one of the points brought out in the movie "Hoosiers." Team chemistry is a code for oneness. It means to care about more than just one's self. It is to do all you can to help the team do well, not just yourself. It is to genuinely be in relationship, caring, rooting, helping, and wanting others to succeed as much as yourself. There is unity, bonding, cooperation and celebrating of each other's successes. Nowadays, coaches talk about and hope to establish a love that emerges in their team that brings them together to realize success. Not all teams achieve this, of course, but these are the energies that contribute to the making of champions. The reverse of that would be a selfish self-centered group of individuals, caring only about their own statistics, jealous of teammates' successes, and with no sense of team. In this case the energies are fragmented, lack any cohesiveness and the team becomes vulnerable to conflicts, separateness and mediocrity.

So, what are the teams that make up our lives? For starters, there is the team of "you" and "yourself." How is the chemistry there? Do you love yourself? Certainly, other teams include our families, co-workers, friends, organizations of which we are a part. We can expand this metaphor into our neighborhoods, communities, nations and the world. Spiritually, we are the family of humanity and in every application, love and oneness produces success, while separation, division and selfishness brings problems. The famous NFL football coach of the Green Bay Packers, Vince Lombardi advised: "Build for your team a feeling of oneness, of dependence on one another and of strength to be derived by unity."

A common cause for good, driven by the chemistry of teamwork and a sense of unity, will always be a factor in the advancement of the common good of humanity. This chemistry applies to a family and even a nation. When people team up with the One Source from whom all ideas for good flow, the strength these people have together is multiplied. Love and unity really is the only thing that can ever bring a world together and solve its problems. Now and again we get a small taste of what this can be like.

In the fall of 2010, virtually the whole world was learning about and watching 33 miners trapped in a mine in Chile. For 69 days they were trapped deep inside the earth while an amazing rescue effort went on from the surface to bring them back to freedom. If this situation had taken place some years earlier, the technology would not have been in place to locate the men, provide support, view the proceedings on TV and eventually get them out. The whole experience seemed to capture the compassion of hearts and souls of people around the globe.

I happened to be on a trip to Italy during some of the drama, especially when they were beginning to bring the first men out. As I channel-surfed in my hotel room, it was being shown on every channel. We got to know and become close to a number of the miners over the course of the ordeal. While in the earth, one man had his wife give birth to their child, another made a proposal of marriage. So many around the world were praying and pulling for these men to survive. Our imaginations wondered what it must be like to be trapped this way for so long. These men didn't even know if they would be discovered alive. It was on the 17th day when contact was first made. Then they were told it would take months to get them out. Fortunately, a way was found to free them sooner.

How difficult it must have been and how much faith must have been required for those miners to remain positive. How easily it would have been to lose themselves in fear and hopelessness. But for the most part they did not lose touch with or become separate from the Self that identifies with inner strength. Surely there were lapses, but always a seeming return to inner strength. And what a celebration occurred when they were brought to the surface! Church bells rang all over the country of Chile at the request of their President. One miner named Mario came out shouting and chanting in jubilation. He began handing out rocks from deep below he had brought out as gifts.

We all could ask ourselves how we might have done in that situation, surviving 69 days in all, the first 17 on a spoonful of tuna and a sip of milk per day, not knowing if anyone would discover they were alive. Then, the next 52 days living on hope, faith, and what I believe was oneness. In some ways, for their collective survival, they had to remain united, connected, and pulling for each other. Once on the surface, the men humbly stated that there were 34 trapped in the mine, not 33. There were 33 men, and God. They were a team. I was touched by what I found to be a beautiful coming together of a significant portion of humanity on the planet, pulling for and praying for these men. In some mystical way, those 33 men were us. We wanted them to be saved, to survive, because… they ARE us.

Many people, all over the world, shed heart-felt tears as they watched with heightened emotion as the miners surfaced and drew their first renewed breath of fresh air. These were not perfect men. They had their flaws just like the rest of us. But in our hearts we joined their team, and together felt the joy of their success. Somehow their happiness was also our happiness and their sense of renewed freedom also became our freedom. In the principle of oneness, one + 33 men is one. And 33 men, + a large segment of the world, were also one. Again, the principle of "One + One is One" held true.

It was the great author and scholar Patanjali, who said it so well, "When you are inspired by some great purpose, some extraordinary project, all your thoughts break their bonds, your mind transcends limitations, your consciousness expands in every direction, and you find yourself in a new, great, and wonderful world. Dormant forces, faculties, and talents become alive, and you discover yourself to be a greater person by far than you ever dreamed yourself to be." I believe that greater person lives in all of us. And it can be found when we become saturated with our true purpose for which we have come into this life, which is to be an instrument of love and oneness. Author Jennifer Ott expressed it well: "Separate, the world will crumble; together the world will thrive."

I've found this to be true of our personal worlds and the world at large. Whether we look into history or present times, the evidence is overwhelming that when nations or groups within nations enter into separation consciousness, for whatever reason, conflict unfolds, violence often comes into play, wars get fought, and cities crumble with the lives of those affected. In our own day-to-day lives, to the degree we feel separate from family, friends, co-workers... separate from life, God and even ourselves... peace and joy goes out the window, conflicts emerge and dominate, often causing our lives to crumble and break apart.

As with most everyone, I can look at my own life and see many instances where I created my own great inner divide. As a kid growing up, at times I felt alone, inadequate, stupid, self-conscious, and the many forms of "not good enough." Residues of all these characteristics followed me into adulthood. However, whenever and wherever I let love in, whether for others, for life, for God or for myself, I felt reconnected and at one with elevated feelings of peace, joy, love and oneness. Like most of us, I was and continue to be a work in progress. Even after learning the principles and applications of oneness, it's been a long journey of passing and failing to practice it. I've continued to be challenged to rise above separation, distance myself from any separate self, and embrace as my identity, the Higher Sacred Self.

We all live in a beautiful world that has problems to be solved and issues to be healed. One of them is the illusion and belief that we as human beings are separate. The truth is that we are connected, woven together by the invisible threads of our Divine Seamstress. This is the one world in which we live, and there is the One God that has put us here, for the purpose of learning to love and BE ONE.

I invite you, the reader, to deepen your awareness of oneness, be it through prayer, meditation, practicing the Presence, or just being in the now moment. Be free of past conditionings and fears of future concerns, with an open heart and the conscious intent to contribute to the Whole of which you are a part. Never underestimate that you can make a difference in this world.

An elderly Anglican bishop was quoted as concluding the following toward the end of his long life: "When I was young, I wanted to change the world, but the world did not want to be changed. So, in discouragement, I decided to change my community, but to my disappointment, my community did not want to change. As I grew older, I decided that perhaps at least I could change my family, but alas, I could not. Finally, as a last resort I decided to at least change myself. And then I realized, that had I begun by changing myself, my change might have influenced my family, my family might have influenced my community and my community might have begun to change the world." All change begins with ourselves. All contribution begins with our own inner transformation of consciousness. And that transformation occurs when we move from fear to love, from separation to oneness.

Many have made statements about the power of love to change a life or to transform the world. One of the most admired, revered, and respected souls of the past one hundred years is Albert Einstein. He has tended to be admired for his mind. However, he had a big heart. In the late 1980s, Lieserl, the daughter of the famous genius, donated 1,400 letters, written by Einstein, to the Hebrew University, with orders not to publish their contents until two decades after his death. Now I can share with you one of them, written by Albert to his daughter, Lieserl, on the topic of love.

"Dear Lieserl,

When I proposed the theory of relativity, very few understood me, and what I will reveal now to transmit to mankind will also collide with the misunderstanding and prejudice in the world.

I ask you to guard the letters as long as necessary, years, decades, until society is advanced enough to accept what I will explain below.

There is an extremely powerful force that, so far, science has not found a formal explanation to. It is a force that includes and governs all others, and is even behind any phenomenon operating in the universe and has not yet been identified by us. This universal force is LOVE.

When scientists looked for a unified theory of the universe they forgot the most powerful unseen force. Love is Light that enlightens those who give and receive it. Love is gravity, because it makes some people feel attracted to others. Love is power, because it multiplies the best we have, and allows humanity not to be extinguished in their blind selfishness. Love unfolds and reveals. For love we live and die. Love is God and God is Love.

This force explains everything and gives meaning to life. This is the variable that we have ignored for too long, maybe because we are afraid of love because it is the only energy in the universe that man has not learned to drive at will.

To give visibility to love, I made a simple substitution in my most famous equation. If instead of $E=mc2$, we accept that the energy to heal the world can be obtained through love multiplied by the speed of light squared, we arrive at the conclusion that love is the most powerful force there is, because it has no limits.

After the failure of humanity in the use and control of the other forces of the universe that have turned against us, it is urgent that we nourish ourselves with another kind of energy… If we want our species to survive, if we are to find meaning in life, if we want to save the world and every sentient being that inhabits it, love is the one and only answer.

Perhaps we are not yet ready to make a bomb of love, a device powerful enough to entirely destroy the hate, selfishness and greed that devastate the planet.

However, each individual carries within them a small but powerful generator of love whose energy is waiting to be released. When we learn to give and receive this universal energy, dear Lieserl, we will have affirmed that love conquers all, is able to transcend everything and anything, because love is the quintessence of life.

I deeply regret not having been able to express what is in my heart, which has quietly beaten for you all my life. Maybe it's too late to apologize, but as time is relative, I need to tell you that I love you and thanks to you I have reached the ultimate answer!

Your father,
Albert Einstein"

The idea of oneness becoming a growing reality and possibility for the world has not eluded the hearts and minds of other creative souls. The topic of universal oneness has found its way into some very powerful songs. One of the most inspiring songs, with lyrics that have captured the heart of masses of people, is "Imagine" by the great John Lennon. In it he asks that we imagine a world different from today's. Everything new and good had its beginnings first in the visible field of possibilities called our imagination. It shows how you change, transform, and make your individual life better, too. And because we are all connected, woven together in one great tapestry of humanity, we want to embrace a vision of what could be possible for the whole, the All.

John Lennon asks us to "Imagine all the people, living for today." It means to be in the moment, free of the past, free of issues that have previously separated us. He invites us to "Imagine there's no countries... nothing to kill or die for, and no religion, too... Imagine all the people, living life in peace." I can only assume John Lennon is singing an epiphany that has risen up from deep within his soul. It is truly a great piece of inspiration. It seems to carry a message that there is nothing the mind can use to separate us. No boundary lines between countries, no religions driven by minds of separation, but a spirit that comes from the heart and promotes "A brotherhood of man." Instead of greed and hunger, the inspired lyrics call us to "Imagine all the people, sharing all the world."

I know it is not easy for everyone to imagine such a world, especially when we have thrown in our faces the nightly news of various forms of negativity and separation. It's very difficult for a person dealing with lack to imagine abundance, for a person dealing with illness to imagine healing, for a person engulfed by problems to imagine a solution. However, that has always been one of the powerful ways we become co-creators and transform our lives and the reality we live in. The misdirected mind must be re-directed to the higher way, a greater good, married to the passion of the heart, conscious of being a co-creating partner with the One Presence. "Let this mind be in you that was in Christ Jesus." "Be transformed by the renewing of your mind." People have done it in their individual lives. And when a critical mass of people grasp a vision of what is possible on a larger scale, the same laws and principles produce the promised results.

You may think I'm a dreamer, as the song goes. But the song also says, "I'm not the only one." And that last line is not to be missed, for I join the voice of Mr. Lennon in extending to anyone reading this page the powerful words of invitation he so beautifully put to music: "I hope someday you'll join us, and the world will be as one." I've watched large bodies of people weep through the singing of that song. That should tell us something – that at the core many believe such a world exists, long for it, or believe this is how it should be.

It seems to me that John Lennon and Thomas Jefferson were in the same creative zone where the Divine forces of oneness were moving through them. Jefferson, with his document, was about the business of creating a country where freedom, equality and oneness could live. In many ways it has, and yet at times and in other ways it hasn't. The song "Imagine" strikes a chord at the heart of humanity, for those who inherently have an overriding sense of what is possible. It is a reality that already exists in the absolute mind of God. And although we may appear to be a good distance from the finish line, there are those who can see it and believe in it. There are many who are praying for it. Let us not allow a day to go by without joining in the prayers of others for peace on earth and a world that works for everyone.

We change the world by changing ourselves. Every one of us is an instrument of energy that feeds into the collective energies of all. Let us rise above any attachment to what is going on in the external world that seems to oppose oneness, and get busy in our own awakening to oneness within our own consciousness. All change in our world, small and large, begins with our self. All sense of contribution to the world at large begins with our own transformation of consciousness.

I know there is great power in prayer. It's predicated on a conscious awareness of one's partnership with the One True Source of energy for good that fills the universe. I know prayer works because it has worked in my own life and I have witnessed powerful results in the lives of others. It feels right and good inside our hearts to bless the world and everyone in it... to know that despite appearances to the contrary, a vast amount of good is happening. To realize that beyond "evidence" of division and separation there is a higher reality that exists waiting to be realized. We live in a universe founded on spiritual laws and principles that in their application allow for amazing, miraculous results.

As Desmond Tutu stated so well, "The God who existed before any religion counts on you to make oneness of the human family known and celebrated." ONE + ONE is ONE! BE ONE!

CHAPTER SEVEN
Ideas To Integrate

It's been obvious to you that the continuing theme of this book has been oneness. The concept of oneness is surely nothing new. Unfortunately, for too long and for too many people, it has been just that... a concept, not an experience. Oneness is what you and I have come into the world to learn as a way of life. It must become more than a flowery ideal or a word on a page. Your soul assignment in this life is to learn and live oneness. It must become an inner spiritual hunger. "Like a page that aches for a word that speaks on a theme that is timeless" is a line from the lyrics of a song by Neil Diamond. We must become that page that aches for the theme of the timeless truth known as oneness.

Your soul's evolutionary path is to advance further and deeper into the consistent realization that God is everywhere and in everything. Whatever you are facing or dealing with at this time, large or small, realize that you are an eternal spiritual being, living and learning that not everything is about life and death. Instead, everything we face and deal with is actually about Life and DEPTH. There are sacred moments to be had in this life that are of divine depth. We are being called to go deeper in awareness and higher in consciousness. The spiritual truth is... humanity is a family. I am you and you are me. We can do so much more to help each other, by becoming united rather than divided. An Ethiopian proverb says, "When spider webs unite, they can halt a lion." When the world learns to unite, and bridge its many divides, a web of power will have been created to halt its existing challenges and bring with it a taste of heaven.

Through the pages and chapters of this book we have covered many ideas, concepts, and teachings, some of which may be new to you and others familiar. The stories, examples, analogies and metaphors I have shared all reflect the theme of oneness and support the spiritual principle that One + One is One. It may be helpful to review and highlight some of the important points addressed from each chapter.

In CHAPTER ONE, aside from introducing you to aspects of the course my life has taken in relation to oneness, I also introduced you to some initial thoughts on the main theme. They include:

Life is a precious gift. It is to be honored and treasured as an opportunity to bring into expression that which you came here to be: love and oneness.

You and I are in a continual process of learning to live life, finding what works, and committing to it. Along the way we will err, adjust, and choose again, but higher.

This school called life has consistently sought to provide evidence designed to teach you and me that we live in a unified field ruled by the universal spiritual principle of One + One is One. When we fail to cultivate this field within our consciousness, there is suffering.

We are in the daily classroom of living, being given opportunities to pass seeming tests in which we get to choose whether oneness wins over separation, and whether love prevails over fear.

The spiritual journey of every soul is one of letting love cast out all fear.

The mind cannot be trusted with its worldly conditionings and attachments to the past. Instead, we must learn to follow our heart, for it knows the way. It draws on a deeper knowing of the truths of Spirit.

An experience of oneness with our Source, God, can occur anywhere and anytime, and is not limited to being inside a temple, church, or religious structure.

No path or dogma calling itself spiritual should in any way contribute to the creation of division and separation. The letter divides and the Spirit unites.

God is not a punishing God. We punish ourselves and each other by being out of harmony with universal spiritual laws and principles.

Ego is the voice of separation, and lives in any religion where a sense of superiority exists.

There are many paths, but One God.

Jesus was a master teacher and Son of God. He did not see himself as the great exception, but the Great Example, of love and oneness.

To paraphrase Paul's statement in Colossians 1:27, Christ is in you, as your hope of glory. If we want to move toward a world that works, we need to progress toward taming the energies of division and separation while opening to and expanding the energies of united cooperation.

The quality, character and frequency of every person's life energy becomes a tributary that flows with good or ill into the collective ocean of all.

Awakening into oneness involves a neurobiological shift in the brain. By changing mental focus patterns, we begin to create new neural pathways.

In God's great house of eternal life there exists other rooms and realms beyond the veil of this three-dimensional, physical world in which we currently live.

CHAPTER TWO focuses on our most important relationship, which is with God. All others branch off from it. Its points include:

God is found and experienced in the heart, not the head. You can't feel or experience anything with the mind. You must transcend the intellect and be in your heart to fully feel and know God.

To approach, connect with, and bond with the Divine, make God your Supreme Friend.

Unconditional love cannot be achieved with the mind, only with the heart.

Oneness is like a stream of Divine current and every soul is in the process of moving into its flow, bit by bit.

The true experience of oneness is a feeling beyond words. When in it, trying to put words around it takes you out of the experience and into mind.

An amazing life is waiting for you once you take the steps to expand your perspective.

Life is a dance, but you have to be open to hearing the music, and be willing to be led.

Courage is a choice, to go on, hold to ideals, affirm life, and continue to strive to make a difference.

In the energies of oneness with the Divine Presence, you can ask of it most anything in the way of help and guidance — and get it.

We are one with the Source of all life at all times whether we are in a body or after we have passed beyond it.

Oneness involves a partnership that carries the feeling you are being accompanied by the most powerful force for good in the universe, and it is assisting you in the fulfillment of your desires.

It truly is possible for us to live the life we have imagined, to pass an invisible boundary, to live with the license of a higher order of being.

In CHAPTER THREE, the focus is on our oneness with the Higher Self, the God part of us. Its points include:

Your Higher Sacred Self opens the door where you begin to throw the switch that turns on the Divine circuitry of your being, allowing the energies of love, peace, wisdom, and joy to flow.

There is so much more to us than meets the eye or even enters our awareness.

The world in which you live can cause you to lose yourself for a time, and your inner work then becomes at all times to "Know Thy Self," God in you.

The egoic mind argues for separation, sends us into fear, edges God out, and looks outside one's self for validation.

The Truth is, God created you and put Its Spirit of wholeness, light and divinity with you. It is the "what" you are that has permanency, regardless of where you are in your journey as a soul.

Whenever your energies feel contracted, own the feeling, and realize there is, obviously, a higher and better choice to be made.

Be in the world, but do not tie your identity to it. Instead, realize the inner world is what rules and will keep you whole and happy.

We become conditioned to what is most familiar from the time of our birth and particularly through what we are exposed to in our childhood. Our fears have been conditioned into us, and the good news is they can be conditioned out. Self-awareness is the key to breaking free.

Happiness is a factor of inner freedom. Fear is only a thought. You are not your thoughts, and not your mind. Learn to observe the mind before identifying with its thoughts.

Our feelings are like gurus that communicate to the body whether what is being passed on from the mind is truth or error. You eventually realize you are not your feelings. They are temporal.

Death is just another illusion we have bought into because we are conditioned to the appearances of a three-dimensional material world. The spirit and soul of you never dies.

We have a mind, but we are not our mind. We must learn to use it or it will use us. Whatever idea you accept with your mind, you accept with your body. When the mind accepts health and wholeness, the body follows.

The Divine has sent forth Its Spirit into your heart and therefore you are a child of God, and if a child, then an heir of all the good God has to offer.

The focus of CHAPTER FOUR is to heighten our awareness of our oneness with all others. Jesus said to love our neighbor as ourselves. Its points include:

Humanity is truly one family. In the grand scheme of things, we are all brothers and sisters in the family of God.

If you accept that it's All God, then nothing is outside the Circle of God-life.

Inside the principle of One + One is One, life is no longer just about "me," but becomes a "we." I am you and you are me.

To match negative energies of another, and give back the same, in no way helps the world move forward, nor does it help us.

The earth, humanity, other species and all life essentially make up one living organism. We are interconnected. We need each other.

We are to learn unconditional, causeless love. It is a love that need not be earned or have reason or cause. It is the kind of love that loves, no matter what the circumstances.

In life you are going to make some mistakes. But you are not your mistakes. Learn from them and go beyond them.

We punish ourselves and each other. Punishment doesn't come from God. Forgiveness frees the spirit to keep loving. Learn to forgive yourself and others so as to remain free.

We live in a world in which the imperfect are being perfected. Choose not to meet low with low, but instead choose the way of the Higher Self.

We slow ourselves down in our spiritual progress when we are unable to rise above the pain others may seemingly have brought to us.

If you think in terms of "I am you and you are me," you will be led to do what is best in most situations.

When faced with an annoying or difficult person, we must stop to ask ourselves what it is that may have caused this person to be the way they are.

What the mind and five senses focus on consistently contributes to the molding and making of a person's personality, make-up and level of consciousness.

Anything unhealed from our childhood or past will surface in current situations and relationships so as to be healed.

Relationships are for gaining self-awareness, clearing the way for love, and healing our past.

Being in loving service and kindness to others puts in motion a dynamic that opens us to opportunities by which life loves us back.

Communication is creation. The power of the spoken word can be a factor in manifesting health, wealth and happiness.

See with the "single eye" of truth, love and oneness.

CHAPTER FIVE addresses our relationship of oneness with God in nature. Its points include:

Growth of oneness can come by developing a deeper bond with the spirit and energies of earth, sea, and sky, and all that is in them.

The earth itself is a living being. Everything in it is alive with God and provides numerous channels of wisdom, assistance and truth.

Nature seemingly has a language of its own that speaks to your heart and soul.

Nature is your friend and when you become fully present and give yourself over to it, it will gift you with tremendous beauty, inspiration and insight.

God's many forms of nature are an example of beingness, essence, and authenticity.

Everything has energy, and as you expand your awareness of and sensitivity to whatever there is of nature around you, it extends to you the gift of its energy.

Humanity has shown its cruelty to all forms of creation. It need not be. There exists a higher level at which everyone and everything is your friend.

As you genuinely build a relationship with the many forms of nature, it will testify to God's existence and teach you many of God's truths.

The One Spirit of all life is everywhere and in everything, wanting to commune, to be known, felt, heard from, experienced, and entered into relationship with.

At all times, something greater than yourself is present and one with you.

It is possible to have moments in your life when something in nature appears with perfect timing to convey a message, a truth, or an insight to help you go forward beyond some obstacle or situation.

Nature is God and God as nature is always surrounding you. It will share its secrets as you learn to love it enough.

You need times of silence built into the schedule of your life if you are to receive the help God is offering through all of creation.

CHAPTER SIX takes a look at the movement of consciousness toward oneness in the world. Its points include:

Everyone is able to contribute to the betterment and healing of this world through the principles of oneness.

Let us all rethink everything we are doing in our world.

In its purest sense, spirituality contains an all-inclusive universal message that leaves nothing and no one out.

In the eyes of God, we are all equal, loved, and one.

Regardless of what is going on externally in the world, you must not become disheartened, but remain positive and do your inner work.

Never underestimate the role you play by consciously choosing to bring the best of you into each day.

In the world in which we live, we are still in the process of getting to know each other, seeing who we truly are, and what we can be and do together.

We want a world where everyone is given a chance to win at life.

The dynamic of oneness is always forward moving and has progress built into it.

By passionately believing in an idea, you become one with it, whereby God and the universe will reveal a way.

Creativity, prosperity, and wholeness are a few of the properties of oneness.

A common cause for good, driven by the chemistry of unity, will always be a factor in the advancement of the common good of humanity.

There is greatness in you, and it can be found when you become saturated with your true purpose, which includes being an instrument of love and oneness.

All change begins with yourself.

Never underestimate that you can make a difference in this world.

My hope is that you will continue on the path of oneness and make the spiritual principle of One + One is One something that you build into all sectors of your life and consciousness.

As for me, I know that my life will be devoted to furthering this message and helping all others see their way to attaining and living higher states of oneness. The ideal of oneness has been in my veins all my life and my commitment to promote it grows. I am willing to be used by Spirit to further the message of oneness in all the ways I am guided. That will likely mean any or all of the following: teaching classes, seminars, workshops, speaking, consulting, coaching, presenting, writing, and traveling so as to help people awaken spiritually into oneness and the universal principle that One + One is One.

You are on this earth as a sort of container for God, and that container is expandable. Happiness is about becoming a larger container for love and oneness. Happiness is about learning not to get lost in the valleys of lowly thinking, and not to get lost in limiting views and perceptions. It is about not becoming self-absorbed with circumstances and allowing them to make you small. Stay large in your faith and expansive in your perspective on life, God and yourself.

I have one final story to share. It is about an aging Hindu master who had an apprentice who had a pattern of complaining, being rather negative and unhappy. So one morning the master sent him for some salt. When he returned, the master instructed the unhappy young apprentice to put a handful of salt in a glass of water and take a drink. The master asked him how it tasted. The apprentice said it was bitter and spit it out. The master chuckled and asked the young man to take another handful of salt, in the same amount, and put it in the lake a short walk away. They walked to the lake where the monk put his hand in the water and shook all the salt out. He was then told by the master to take a drink from the lake. The master asked him how it tasted. As the water dripped down his chin, he said it tasted fresh. The master asked if he could taste any salt. The young man said no. The master then sat down beside the young man, lovingly took the monk's hands in his, looked him in the eyes and said, "The amount of pain in life remains the same. But the amount of bitterness we taste depends on the container we put the pain in. So when you are in pain, the only thing you can do is to enlarge your sense of things. Stop being a glass. Become a lake."

This is a question we all might ask ourselves. Are we willing to stop being a glass and become a lake? Are you willing to enlarge the view you have of the role you are meant to play in life and the world? The universal spiritual principle of One + One is One, is the lake you and I are being invited to become. As the Course In Miracles states, "Your littleness deceives you, but your magnitude is of Him who dwells in you, and in whom you dwell. Give up every plan you have accepted for finding magnitude in littleness. It is not there. Magnitude is found in the Holy Instant, beyond past and future..."

"You will be content only in Magnitude, which is your home."

As you continue to review, ponder and integrate the highlights and teachings of each chapter, magnitude will assert itself over littleness and Oneness will win out over separation.

CHAPTER EIGHT
Spiritual Practices

There are two main reasons for building into your consciousness the awareness and energies of oneness. One is for you alone to grow, evolve, move beyond any disconnect, and to become a happier, freer, more loving, fulfilled person. The second has to do with going beyond your own personal needs and asking yourself what you are doing to bring this oneness into the world. There are spiritual practices to be integrated into your life so as to build your consciousness of oneness. Here are some suggestions and ways you can put some of the contents of this book and its ideas into application.

MEDITATION

If you don't already meditate, learn to do so and devote at least fifteen minutes per day. Eventually, work up to thirty minutes or more of quiet time. If you are new to meditation, you can begin by focusing on your "in and out" breath. The idea of meditation is to slow the mind down, so all the chatter that typically goes on and acts as a block to inspiration can have holes punched in it, allowing the vibrations of Spirit to flow through.

Although I don't like the labeling contained in the title, a good book for learning meditation is "Meditation For Dummies" by Stephan Bodian. There are several meditations related to oneness that I suggest. In all of these, you will want to take preliminary steps to become relaxed, take some deep breaths and then move into whichever one you choose.

CLEARING MEDITATION

Imagine you are taking a shower; however, instead of water, it is droplets of golden light. Imagine God is showering you with pure healing light. It penetrates through the inside of your entire body from the top of your head and out through the bottoms of your feet, taking with it all impurities; physical, mental and emotional. It is a clearing and cleansing of the physical body, leaving a sense of wholeness. It washes away and frees you of negative thoughts and emotions, leaving you with a totally fresh, free, and invigorating feeling. Upon completing this exercise you embrace and take with you the thought and feeling that what is left of you after this shower is pure Being, and an awareness that God is alive in you on every level. You have been filled with the Light of God. You and God are one. Do this meditation for five minutes at least once every day for thirty days and as often as you like after that.

SEVEN-MINUTE ONENESS MEDITATION
The number seven is a very spiritual number that carries creative power. There were seven days of creation recorded in the Bible. In this practice, you are taking the words of a spiritual truth deep into your awareness and feeling nature. The words are:

"I AM one with God and All That Is."

Speak it out loud to yourself for approximately two minutes. Whisper it to yourself for approximately another two minutes. Next, internally affirm it for approximately three minutes. Do your best to have it add up to seven minutes total. You may want to set a timer for the seven minutes. Do this meditation as often as once a day.

GLOBAL MEDITATION
This is a meditation that we did at the Oneness University I attended in India. Become aware of your breath for a few moments. Bring your awareness to your heart. Visualize a golden dot at the center of your heart. Inhale into the golden dot and exhale out of the golden dot. As you inhale, visualize the golden dot expanding. As you exhale, visualize the golden dot radiating Golden Light. Visualize it expanding and radiating with each breath, eventually engulfing your whole body, ever increasing in wider circles to cover the room you are in, the building, the state, and then the world. Once you have it covering the whole world, just continue to see, feel and experience it all as One, in the Golden Light. Do this meditation for seven minutes as often as once a day or a minimum of once a week.

DAILY PRAYERS

In oneness, prayer is less about praying "to" God as if off somewhere separate and apart from you, and more about praying "from" the awareness that there is nothing that separates you from Spirit. God is right there, all around and within you. Pray daily that the awareness of oneness grows and expands in you. Pray that all sense of separation in your consciousness be healed and released. Pray that the feeling of oneness with the All That Is, all forms of life, all people, continues to be experienced in your heart. Pray that the energies of oneness take hold in all humanity and the whole world.

A book that I recommend on prayer is "The Universe Is Calling" by Eric Butterworth.

PRAYER NOTEBOOK

Get yourself a notebook and in it create a column on the far left of the page for the date, then an area to write the content of your prayer, and at the far right side, a column for putting the date upon which your prayer was answered. It only takes a couple of each day to keep this notebook current. Some prayers are answered before the day is out while others may take longer for an answer. This expands your prayer awareness and gives you a kind of record of your prayer life. You get to see all the many answered prayers that have taken place.

TAKE A STAND – AFFIRMATIVE PRAYER

Affirmative prayer is to take a stand for spiritual truth. It can be taken with us throughout the day and continue to be affirmed. It changes the energies of how we show up in the world, and affects the world around us for good. Take one of the prayer affirmations below with you each day, or create one of your own that touches your heart.

"I Am one with God."
"I Am a loving being."
"I Am a Light in the world."
"I Am a magnet for God's good."
"I Am one with the peace of God." (Or strength, goodness, love)
"I Am determined to see things differently."

"I see God in everyone and everything."

"Today, I walk in love." (Or peace, joy, oneness, forgiveness)

GRATITUDE

Taking time to reflect on all that you can be grateful for is a good daily practice. Gratitude is a sure remedy for moving from head to heart. It is one of the best ways to feel connected to our Source, and feel the energies of oneness. Once a week make a gratitude list of what has gone on during those past seven days. If you choose not to write them down, go alone to a quiet place and reflect on those things for which you can express thanks to God.

BEING IN THE MOMENT

Each day, set the intention to practice being as fully in the present moment as you can throughout the entire day. So often we tend to be off somewhere else in our minds rather than being focused on where we are.

When taking your morning shower, practice being there, experiencing it fully, rather than allowing your mind to take you somewhere else. When drinking a glass of water, be with it. When eating, experience fully your food. Learn to be present and fully listening to others rather than allowing your mind to jump ahead or away with separate thoughts. When emotions and feelings come up in you, be with them, rather than being dismissive. Oneness is learning to be fully present to experience what is there before you or happening within you.

PRACTICING THE PRESENCE

Establish a day or days where you have the strong intention to practice the presence of God all day long. You invite the feeling to overtake you and stay with you. Two things can help build this into your awareness. One is to think of the best friend you have, or the best relationship you have ever had or could ever imagine. Totally loving, accepting, nurturing and empowering. Now God is at your side the entire day as that Supreme Friend. Secondly, understand that God wants to converse with you. You don't have to be inside a church, synagogue or place of worship. You don't have to be on your knees or prostrate to connect with God. None of that is required by Spirit. Talk, talk, talk with God all day. The Divine will come alive all the more through consistency of communication.

HIGHER SELF

Choose a day, at least once a week, to be consciously in your Higher Sacred Self. Carry with you the awareness that the highest and best of God that is in you will express itself and experience all aspects of the day. All interactions with people and life will be from a sense of what would the God in me do, and how would it be in this situation... from the person who cuts in front of you on the drive to work, to the aloof clerk in the store, to the co-worker who rubs you the wrong way. You will look for the good in everyone and everything, remain positive regardless of the situation, listen with your heart, and see everyone as a child of God.

JOURNALING

Begin to journal at least once each week. Focus on what seems to be most dominating your attention and focus... good or bad, positively or negatively. If you are absorbed by some negative feeling, issue or emotional charge, do the deep inquiry and questioning that is contained in Chapter Three and the reference that your feelings are being your gurus. Write honestly and authentically about what you are thinking and feeling, and invite Spirit to flow through you and onto the page with solutions, answers and insights.

CREATE A ONENESS CHEST

Create a container or folder for all the materials you might gather related to the theme of oneness. It's a place to put any prayer booklet, spiritual articles, poems, photographs, quotes, journaling, CDs of music or a speaker, DVDs of a movie or beautiful scenery. Whatever touches your heart and bolsters a feeling of oneness should be in it. This is the container you open each day and spend a few minutes reviewing some part of it before entering into your meditation time.

Additional Ways To Foster Oneness

TALK IT OUT

Whenever you have something that has you in an ongoing feeling of disconnect, seek out that best friend who you can talk to about anything, or meet with a therapist. By expressing your thoughts and feelings about what you may be dealing with, it breaks up the contracted energies, and helps you release, let go, and create anew.

SUNRISE, SUNSET

These are some of the most beautiful scenes of nature and times of the day. Watching a sunrise as a day begins or a sunset as a day closes can bring deep feelings of sacred oneness with the Source. Occasionally get up to greet the dawn or make an appointment with yourself and God to watch one of Its sunsets.

STAR GAZE

On a clear night with the stars shining, spend some time alone looking into the night sky. It has moved souls to awe and wonder throughout the centuries.

WALK IN THE PARK

Take a walk in a park or some favorite nearby setting in nature, preferably by yourself. Be open to all that is around you and the subtle messages that may be sent your way.

ACTS OF KINDNESS

It can really feel good to do something kind for another and take the focus away from ourselves. Think of someone you can surprise with some unexpected act of kindness. It might be a co-worker, neighbor, or friend to whom you take some, mow their lawn because they've been out of town, or send a note of acknowledgment. Perhaps you decide to pay for the order of the vehicle behind you while you are in line at Starbucks to get a coffee. A feeling of oneness and satisfaction accompanies these actions of the heart.

PLANT A FRIEND

Some people already love to garden and do so regularly. Others don't take the time or it's just not their thing. Nevertheless, you might consider getting one or several potted plants for inside or outside. By taking an interest in and caring for another of God's life forms, you are opening yourself a bit more to a sense of connectedness to it all.

GET A PET

Many people have had their lives enhanced by purchasing a pet puppy or kitten. In some cases, it has brought healing or even extended their lives. A pet can open a person's heart, activate feelings once gone numb, and connect their energies to something positive.

Oneness Steps

Here are a series of steps which are my version of what some might refer to as master mind steps. You can use whatever word you are most comfortable with for God, be it Spirit, Presence, Divine, or the Infinite. Ideally, these steps are to be affirmed daily so as to build them into your consciousness. They can also be used with a prayer partner or in a small prayer group.

I SURRENDER. God is the only power in my life. With God, I can do anything. I accept help and guidance. With Christ as my inspiration, I am open to infinite possibilities.

I BELIEVE. I now believe that God is the only real Presence and Power in my life. God and I change my life.

I AM WILLING TO CHANGE. Because I realize that erroneous, self-defeating thoughts cause problems, unhappiness, fears and failures, I willingly change my beliefs and attitudes so that my life is transformed.

I AM CHANGED. I (your name), now accept Divine help. I consciously release control of my will, my mind, my emotions, my body, my relationships, and my entire life to Spirit. I AM one with the wisdom of God which is my assurance of being guided in right ways. I express the wisdom of Spirit in all that I do.

I AWAKEN TO WHO AND WHAT I AM. I now own the Truth of my real identity. I AM now, and always have been a Divine being, one with God.

I AM a magnificent expression of all God is – love, power, wisdom and life energy.

I AM WILLING TO FORGIVE. I now completely forgive myself and others, for all imperfect acts.

I AM committed to demonstrating that forgiveness is complete by having my life reflect wholeness, abundance, and oneness with God.

I LOVE MYSELF. I joyfully receive the gifts from my creations by loving every part of myself. I practice loving everything I see in me, the people in my life and in the world I see. I also gladly receive all the love God gives me through others.

I ASK. I now share my specific vision, and prayerful requests with God (and/or) my prayer partner/s. I know that God and I manifest this vision or something better.

I GIVE THANKS. I thank God for responding to my request and I assume the same feeling I would have were my vision already manifest. I thank God for guiding me to my vision or something even better. Thank you, God in me.

MY ENTIRE LIFE IS A PRAYER. Since my most powerful prayers are my everyday actions, I now rededicate myself to making every action in my life be a joyful prayer of gratitude to God and an affirmation of the abundance of God. With Divine wisdom and insight, I create a life of purpose and meaning, and my entire life is a prayer.

I GO FORTH with enthusiasm, excitement, gratitude and expectancy.

I AM at peace.

ABOUT THE AUTHOR

Howard Caesar has been speaking, teaching and inspiring audiences with his transformational spiritual messages since his twenties. Recognized as a leader in his field, he has served and built two large ministries, the most recent being Houston, Texas where he served for 30 plus years. His positive, practical, progressive approach to spirituality has empowered thousands of people to live happier, more prosperous and fulfilling lives.

He has traveled the world, led pilgrimages to other lands, presenting uplifting messages to tens of thousands via radio, TV, and the internet, always communicating inclusivity, diversity, love and oneness.

Howard and his wife, Diane, have three grown children, three grandchildren and reside in Sugar Land, Texas.

www.howardcaesar.com

ABOUT THE BOOK

With heartfelt sensitivity and humor Howard Caesar, in ONE + ONE IS ONE, offers up powerful life changing universal principles woven into stories and examples from day to day life that all can relate to. In a very personal way he will inspire you, make you laugh and perhaps shed a tear as he takes you deep into the heart of life as it is meant to be lived.

This book focuses on the spiritual principle of oneness, arguably the answer to every human problem. No matter where you are on the spiritual path, this book offers teachings and insights meant to shine light into the soul of you the individual, and the world as a whole. ONE + ONE IS ONE has the capacity to bring clarity that is essential to one's spiritual purpose and meaning in this life. It is the kind of book one can read again and again. The world is aching for the message contained within its pages. Reading it will help make for a better you and a better world.